Praise for

After the Miracle

"I just finished reading Art Shamsky's new book about those '69 Miracle Mets and their upset victory over the vaunted Baltimore Orioles. I was a sophomore in high school and this book brought back all those vivid memories of that series. A great and insightful read."

—Keith Hernandez

"Not since Halberstam's *The Teammates: Portrait of a Friendship,* have I read a more heartfelt and inspiring book about what it means to be linked forever. I personally know the kindness of the author, Art Shamsky. Only he could pull off this hilarious and melancholy look at getting old but remaining forever young because of their shared 'miracle' in 1969."

—Ron Darling

"*After the Miracle* is touching and beautiful—a magical book about a magical team."

—Jonathan Eig, author of
Luckiest Man, Opening Day, and *Ali: A Life*

"Charming. . . . a touching rendering of loving comrades reuniting to share memories of past glory. Messrs. Seaver and Harrelson are also astonishingly open about their ailments. I can only express my gratitude, as someone who grew up adoring these two great athletes from afar, for the glimpse this book affords into their elegance and bravery in the face of hard times."

—Alva Noë, *The Wall Street Journal*

"A highly intimate portrait of the men whose half-century ago miracle continues to enchant us. A must for anyone who witnessed their greatness, or wishes they had."

—Gary Cohen, SNY play-by-play announcer

"Wasn't that a time? When the last became first and anything seemed possible, in baseball and in life? *After the Miracle* recalls those thrilling days for now-old boys like me, and shows a new generation of fans that losing serves only to sweeten victory. Warmly and wistfully, Art Shamsky and Erik Sherman reunite the boys of summer, fifty years later."

—John Thorn, Official Historian of Major League Baseball and author of
Baseball in the Garden of Eden

"The Miracle Mets were my team growing up as a kid in Brooklyn. I love how Art gives you all the locker room banter and how the guys kidded with each other. I thought I knew all there was about the 1969 Mets, but this book proves there is so much more to learn about the team that captivated the city and the country."

—John Franco

"Terrific. . . . A testament to how a motley crew of baseball players inadvertently bridged the political and social divides that were so commonplace in 1969, even if it was only for a few days in October 1969."

—R. Zachary Sanzone, *Spitball*

"Teams win championships every year; the '69 Mets transcended victory. They defined an era and changed lives. Mine is one of them. Their story and their obvious bond are eternal."

—Howie Rose, broadcaster, New York Mets

"50 years later, the '69 Mets remain one of the most iconic teams in baseball history. . . . Symbolizing the sheer faith and determination [that] can turn despair and misery into triumph and euphoria."

—Bob Nightengale, *USA Today*

"This heartfelt, nostalgic memoir will delight baseball fans of all ages and allegiances."

—*Publishers Weekly*

"A fond remembrance of a legendary baseball team. . . . An enjoyable tale of a storybook season."

—*Kirkus Reviews*

"Shamsky's account of the 1969 season is exceptional, as is his handling of the team's disparate personalities, the national context in which the Mets staged their Miracle (it was a year for miracles—the first manned moon landing took place less than three months before the World Series), and the coverage of the racial amity on the team."

—*Booklist*

"Shamsky builds his book around what became a pilgrimage for him and former teammates. . . . They set out on a sentimental journey in May 2017 to visit Hall of Fame teammate Tom Seaver, the epitome of what it was like to be young and a Met. It is a revealing look at The Franchise."

—Steven Marcus, *Newsday*

ALSO BY ART SHAMSKY

The Magnificent Seasons: How the Jets, Mets, and Knicks Made Sports History and Uplifted a City and the Country

ALSO BY ERIK SHERMAN

Davey Johnson: My Wild Ride in Baseball and Beyond (with Davey Johnson)

Kings of Queens: Life Beyond Baseball with the '86 Mets

Mookie: Life, Baseball, and the '86 Mets (with Mookie Wilson)

Steve Blass: A Pirate for Life (with Steve Blass)

Out at Home: The Glenn Burke Story (with Glenn Burke)

AFTER THE MIRACLE

THE LASTING BROTHERHOOD
OF THE '69 METS

ART SHAMSKY

and ERIK SHERMAN

Simon & Schuster Paperbacks

NEW YORK   LONDON   TORONTO   SYDNEY   NEW DELHI

Simon & Schuster Paperbacks
An Imprint of Simon & Schuster, Inc.
1230 Avenue of the Americas
New York, NY 10020

First Simon & Schuster trade paperback edition March 2020

SIMON & SCHUSTER PAPERBACKS and colophon are registered trademarks
of Simon & Schuster, Inc.

For information about special discounts for bulk purchases,
please contact Simon & Schuster Special Sales at 1-866-506-1949
or business@simonandschuster.com.

The Simon & Schuster Speakers Bureau can bring authors to your
live event. For more information or to book an event, contact the
Simon & Schuster Speakers Bureau at 1-866-248-3049
or visit our website at www.simonspeakers.com.

Interior design by Paul Dippolito

Manufactured in the United States of America

1   3   5   7   9   10   8   6   4   2

The Library of Congress has cataloged the hardcover edition as follows:

Names: Shamsky, Art, author. | Sherman, Erik, author.
Title: After the miracle : the lasting brotherhood of the '69 Mets / by Art Shamsky with Erik Sherman.
Description: First Simon & Schuster hardcover edition. |
New York : Simon & Schuster, 2019. | Includes index.
Identifiers: LCCN 2018021020| ISBN 9781501176517 | ISBN 150117651X |
ISBN 9781501176524 (ebook)
Subjects: LCSH: New York Mets (Baseball team)—History. | World Series (Baseball) (1969) |
Baseball players—New York (State)—New York—Biography. | LCGFT: Biographies.
Classification: LCC GV875.N45 S47 2019 | DDC 796.357/64097471—dc23
LC record available at https://lccn.loc.gov_2018021020

ISBN 978-1-5011-7651-7
ISBN 978-1-5011-7653-1 (pbk)
ISBN 978-1-5011-7652-4 (ebook)

For Toni and Terri. No father could be prouder.
—A.S.

For my mother, JoAnn, who always believed in me.
—E.S.

CONTENTS

AFTER THE
MIRACLE

CHAPTER 1

THE IDEA

– December 16, 2016 –

MY OLD FRIEND AND MIRACLE METS TEAMMATE TOM SEAVER was ailing.

The greatest Met of all time, the heart and soul of our '69 championship team, and the Hall of Famer who had a baseball career marked by brilliance and a burning desire for perfection, was now practically homebound.

The long-term manifestations of Lyme disease, which include extreme fatigue and memory loss, have induced the Franchise to no longer travel outside of his beloved Napa Valley in Northern California. For the onetime fearless power pitcher, a true warrior out on the mound, and one of the most intelligent ballplayers I've ever been associated with, his limitations are now practically unfathomable.

Another Mets teammate of mine from our halcyon days and one of Tom's closest confidants, Buddy Harrelson, was a maestro in the infield who possessed great range and a strong arm in making the most difficult plays look easy. Once a vibrant and fiery All-Star shortstop in a slender 145-pound frame, Buddy was also now greatly slowed—in his case, by the harsh early stages of Alzheimer's disease.

It's a cruel twist of fate what time has done to two men synonymous with everything great about the game of baseball—and the history of the New York Mets.

Buddy and I have remained especially close since our playing days ended, with geography being the main driver. I have lived in Manhattan for decades, following up my playing career with jobs in sports media, partnering in a successful downtown restaurant, making special appearances, and even writing a book entitled *The Magnificent Seasons.*

Harrelson, a baseball lifer who always loved the game, would rise through the coaching ranks of the Mets organization before eventually being promoted to manage the club for a two-year stint beginning in 1990. He's now co-owner of the Long Island Ducks, an independent minor-league team, and, despite his ailment, actually still throws batting practice to the players before games.

So like me, Buddy never left New York, and we see each other fairly often.

I keep tabs with as many teammates from our 1969 championship team as possible, as well as manager Gil Hodges's widow, Joan, whom I try to call as much as I can to let her know the guys still think about her. She was, after all, a significant part of our whole wonderful experience when we went from finishing in ninth place— a half game from last place—my first year with the club in 1968 to world champions the following season.

From my perspective, there was something, well, amazing, about that feat. And to have played a role in our miracle, it's always made me want to stay in touch with the guys. There's no ulterior motive other than to say hello and reminisce a little bit.

There were now just twenty of us still around from our World Series roster—coaches included. And there is a unique, personal sadness I feel when we lose one of our guys.

The most shocking, of course, was Gil dying of a heart attack two days shy of his forty-eighth birthday on the eve of the 1972 baseball season. The words of our bullpen coach, Joe Pignatano, who was with Gil at the time of his death, still haunt me.

"We had just played a round of golf—Gil and his coaches," Piggy told me. "After we grabbed a beer, Gil bought some oranges and arranged to have them sent home. Then, just as we got back to the hotel and were about to part ways—Gil and I on one side of a path, and Eddie Yost and Yogi Berra on the other—Hodges says, 'Don't forget: dinner at seven o'clock.' But then his heart just stopped, and he fell backward. I'll never forget the sound it made. It was over. The doctors at the hospital tried to bring him back for two or three hours, but nothing worked."

Aside from Gil, there were others who passed on relatively young, like Tug McGraw, Cal Koonce, Tommie Agee, and Donn Clendenon.

I think my feelings of sorrow all fall back to how we were all a part of this very important thing that happened early in our lives, and when one of us dies, so does a part of the youthful invincibility we once shared.

When another member of that team, Don Cardwell, passed away, I wrote a piece in the *New York Times* about how not only was he a terrific pitcher and a great teammate, but also that baseball was always going to remember him because he pitched for the '69 Mets. And history has proven that to be true.

I've traveled around the country and run into people all the time who can rattle off the players from our club. The '69 Mets are like folklore now. The legend has taken on a life of its own.

So when we lose somebody from that team, or if I hear that one of them is not well, it truly affects me in a powerful way.

It's a hard reality for me to accept that it's been almost a half century since our club shocked the baseball world. And with time ticking away toward that milestone, I began to wonder how the Mets organization would commemorate it. Considering what the team meant to the franchise, to baseball, to New York City, and even to our country,

I thought we merited the biggest anniversary celebration ever given a Mets team.

I've met Vietnam veterans who were in the worst place in the world tell me that when we were winning, it helped get them through that awful time in their lives. But they're just one example of how the team collectively helped a lot of folks forget—if only for three hours a day—some of the most turbulent times in the history of our nation.

But something dawned on me while having lunch with baseball historian and author Erik Sherman one late December afternoon. If a celebration for the '69 Mets was to take place, an individual who had as much to do with our winning the World Series as anyone, Tom Seaver, would be unable to attend.

"So bring the celebration to *him!*" Sherman exclaimed. "And we could write a book about the reunion so Mets fans could be a part of it, too."

I *loved* the idea.

That's because countless fans have come up to me over the years to share their memories, tell me what the '69 season meant to them, or to shake my hand and simply say 'Thank you.' They tell me how they were at Shea Stadium for Seaver's near-perfect game, or when the black cat came out near the Chicago Cubs' on-deck circle, or when Jerry Koosman plunked Ron Santo with a retaliatory pitch to show we weren't going to be pushed around by veteran teams anymore. And if they weren't actually there in person, they were there through osmosis. And that's okay because whatever it is that's in their mind, the final result *really* happened: we overcame the greatest of odds to bring a world championship to our fans. And as long as I'm around and am able to talk and write about it, it will always be the most special part of my professional career.

So I believed that, in some small way, if this story could bring the fans back to reliving that season—even the ones who weren't born yet but learned all about it from their parents and grandparents—and include them in our inner circle a half century later, it would be a gift.

And to do it right, I wanted Erik to come along with me to get a feel for the camaraderie and special bond we had on that '69 team firsthand. I also thought it would be valuable to have an "outsider"—a nonplayer—to add a little more objectivity to the story. And because Sherman was a talented author of a number of well-received baseball books, including three Mets-related ones, I knew the guys wouldn't have an issue with him joining us.

But, still, a flood of questions raced through my head.

Who should I invite?

How many should I invite?

How will the logistics of flying guys in from around the country with different schedules work?

Will Tom be up for it?

Will it overwhelm him?

I left the lunch with Erik feeling that the next logical step would be to contact Tom and his wife, Nancy, to get their feelings about such a reunion with some of the guys. Physically, I knew he might not be up for some things. But for just a few of his closest friends from that team to spend some time with him and reminisce a little bit, I thought it would do him a world of good.

As I walked back to my apartment, I began to think about who to invite should the trip be a go.

I instantly thought that Buddy, if physically and mentally able, would be a natural. There was a closeness he and Tom have always shared with each other. They were best friends while Mets, both were Californians, and they were roommates on the road for more than eight years. You could really see a camaraderie there.

And now, sadly, they both had something else in common: memory loss. And because of that, I thought it was especially important for Buddy to make the trip. I believed it would do him as much good as it would Tom.

Koosman also seemed like a no-brainer. For so many years, he and Tom formed one of the greatest pitching rotation duos—one from the right side, the other from the left side—in Major League Baseball. I can barely recall any instances when either was hit really hard. We always felt like we had an excellent chance to win when either of those guys was on the mound.

And in '69, particularly through the last two months of the season and the postseason, no two hurlers were better. You could argue that Mike Cuellar and Dave McNally in Baltimore, Juan Marichal and Gaylord Perry in San Francisco, Fergie Jenkins and Bill Hands in Chicago, and Bob Gibson and Steve Carlton in St. Louis were comparable that year, though having seen them all like I did, I thought the greatness of Seaver and the toughness of Koosman stood above the rest.

With both of them, even in '68, when we were still kind of just feeling our way through, everybody knew they were special. Their mannerisms, their special arms, and their command gave us a swagger that wasn't on the club before.

Obviously, we don't win in '69 without either one of them. But for all the attention that Seaver gets, on any given day, Jerry was as good as any pitcher in baseball. Seaver may have been the Cy Young Award winner that year, but Kooz pitched in so many important games that, had we not won, we probably don't win the division, the pennant, or the World Series.

When you look back at the great pitchers of that era—Marichal, Jenkins, and Gibson—Seaver was, of course, right there with them.

Koosman?

You can argue all you want that he wasn't quite at their level. But I do know one thing for sure: nobody was a better big-game pitcher than he was. Just look at the '69 Series. If we don't win the second game that Kooz pitched, who knows what happens? We go down 0–2 to the Baltimore Orioles, and we're liable to lose four in a row. And then, of course, he goes the distance to win the game five clincher.

To be perfectly frank, if someone asked me back in 1969 or 1970, *You need one guy, one game to be won, who would you pick: Seaver or Koosman?* well, I'd really have a hard time answering that. And it wouldn't be because Tom wasn't a great pitcher, but because Kooz was such a superb competitor. Kooz really should have had far more consideration than he did in the Hall of Fame voting, but his win total was hurt by pitching for some really lousy Mets teams in the late seventies.

As a person, he's one of the most gregarious characters I've ever known. And what a great joke teller! He's got amusing stories galore, starting with his experiences as a kid growing up in Minnesota, right through his long, illustrious baseball career. So I knew it would be fun and entertaining to have Kooz out there with us.

My third choice was Ron Swoboda. Rocky was a guy I was particularly close with because we platooned quite a bit in right field. Even though we played the same position and each of us clearly wanted more playing time, there was absolutely no jealousy or problems between us. We both had a lot of respect for Gil Hodges and his decision to split our time out there. And who were we to complain? The platoon worked brilliantly. Our combined output in '69 was 24 home runs and 99 runs batted in. Gil had successfully *fused* us into becoming an All-Star right fielder. Besides, Rocky was a guy you *had* to root for: *nobody* worked harder at improving his game than he did.

On a personal level, we always got along great. Not only does he have a great sense of humor, but he also has a serious and contemplative side as well. One of the things I like about Swoboda still today is how he always says what's on his mind. He's one of the most outspoken people I've ever met in the game. He's liable to say anything, at any time, anywhere. He'll sit there and argue with you all day if he believes what he's saying is right. And while I may not always agree with him, I have always respected his point of view.

Rocky's career went all the way back to some of the earliest days in Mets history. He signed his first major-league contract with the organization in 1963 and made his big-league debut two years later when the manager was the legendary Casey Stengel.

Often, Swoboda's baseball career mirrored his personality.

One of my favorite Rocky stories occurred in a game at Crosley Field while I was with the Cincinnati Reds. After he hit what should have been ruled a grand slam over the concrete center field wall, the ball bounced off the wood behind it—making a big *thud* sound—and came straight down on the warning track. Shockingly, one of the umpires called it in play. So Ronnie ran hard, as he should have, but overran the runner at first base. The other umpires, despite seeing that the ball did, indeed, go over the wall, called it—by rule—a mere single because Swoboda passed his teammate on the bases.

Not surprisingly, there was a huge controversy on the field over it. Casey ran out to argue, but it was first base coach Yogi Berra who shouted at the umpire who'd ruled it in play with the classic line "You must be blind if you didn't *hear* it!"

But knowing Rocky like I got to know him so well later, I've often thought, *Who else would that happen to but Ron Swoboda?*

I also thought Ronnie would be a great choice to invite to Seaver's because of how their relationship and mutual admiration grew during their years with the Mets and how it continues to grow to this day. The pre-Seaver Mets that Rocky started out with were the so-called *lovable losers*, a team for which winning only fifty or so games a year was accepted because National League fans in New York were just so grateful they had a club again after losing both the Brooklyn Dodgers and the New York Giants to California following the 1957 season. In many ways, Tom felt those early Mets teams—of which Swoboda was a part—weren't taking the games seriously enough. Thus, when Seaver arrived in 1967 as a rookie, he believed the losing attitude of the old guard was unacceptable.

So it was more than ironic when Swoboda, after working so diligently at his defense, helped preserve Seaver's *only* World Series victory of his storied career in game four of the '69 Series with one of the greatest catches in baseball history. In a way, Seaver's appreciation for the kind of player Swoboda was came full circle on that autumn afternoon. He was now a lovable *winner.*

As for Rocky, his esteem for Seaver as an all-time great pitcher was always there, but his admiration for Tom the man continued well after their baseball careers were over. While both men excelled in the broadcast booth, Ronnie has long been enamored with Tom picking up and leaving his high-profile announcing gig with the Mets and home in tony Greenwich, Connecticut, to follow his dream of owning a vineyard in the Napa Valley. In fact, Swoboda has kept close watch of how Seaver's wines have been judged and awarded by various industry magazines over the years.

So, in my mind, if Buddy, Kooz, and Rocky could join Erik and me in seeing Seaver, it would be as formidable a group as any from our '69 team. And I thought having this collection of *four* of Tom's teammates visit him was a good, manageable number. The last thing I wanted to do was overwhelm him.

But the reality was that I could have tried to put together an entirely different cast of characters from our club—like Cleon Jones,

Eddie Kranepool, and Ken Boswell, for example—and it would have been just as wonderful. Part of the reason for that is that everybody got along on our club and contributed significantly to our miracle season.

Still, there was bonus, if you will, in having Kooz and Rocky on this trip. I knew that the dynamic of having the diametrically opposed viewpoints of the politically conservative Koosman and the liberal-minded Swoboda would make for some lively and entertaining banter during the inevitable traffic jams we would encounter in Northern California as well as at mealtime. So between all the reminiscing and baseball talk—our common denominator—I planned to stir the pot and agitate them both a little bit by bringing up various geopolitical topics. It would be unbelievably interesting and all in good fun—just like the old days.

Now I just had to hope those three old teammates of mine could make it.

Once back at my apartment, I gave Seaver a call, and he picked up on the second ring.

"Hey, Tom, it's Sham," I said.

As always, Tom was eager to hear how everybody from our club was doing.

"Have you talked to Buddy?" he asked.

Then later on: "Who else have you seen lately?"

While Tom is somewhat secluded from them out in the hills of Calistoga, it's a different story for me living in New York. Until he passed away in 2018, Ed Charles lived in Queens, and Buddy and Ed Kranepool are out on Long Island. And I see others like Rocky and Cleon from time to time at various events.

So while I gave updates to Tom, I didn't bring up the latest medical news on Krane, who had just had his left big toe amputated after an effort to treat an infection related to diabetes had failed. Thinking that Seaver had his own problems to deal with, I didn't think the time was right to give him that kind of bad news over the phone. I was a bit torn, so I just kind of danced around it. Instead, I got down to the primary reason of my call.

"I'm writing a book on our team, and I'd like to come out with some of the guys to see you in May," I said. "At this point, I'm going to try to get Buddy, Kooz, and Rocky to come along. We'll sit around, laugh a little bit, reminisce, and tell the same old lies—the balls that we barely hit over the fence that are now five-hundred-foot blasts— those kinds of lies."

Seaver chuckled and said, "Ahh, but those are *good* lies."

After a brief pause, Tom said, "Look, Art, I'm not going anywhere. I don't travel anymore. So let me know what you guys plan. I would love to see you all again. It would mean a lot to me."

"I'll do the best I can," I told him.

I hung up with Tom feeling invigorated. There was no doubt in my mind that this would be great therapy for him. And Buddy, too. The reunion would be exactly what the doctor ordered for them both—especially if guys like Koosman and Swoboda, whom neither had seen in a long while, would be able to make it.

My first call was to Swoboda.

"Hey, Rock, it's Sham," I said. "I spoke to Tom, and I think it would be great for some of the guys to go out there and see him. I'm going to try to get Buddy and Kooz to come along. It would be a fun two or three days if we can pull it off. And if you could make it, it would be really great. We could all sit around and do some reminiscing about '69. I think it would be helpful for Tom. As you may recall, he is really struggling from the effects of Lyme disease."

"Yes, it's really sad," Swoboda said. "I've heard about it."

"I'm also planning on bringing a writer out with me, a good guy, to do some interviews for a book on our team. Would you be interested in coming along?"

"I would love to go, Sham," Rocky said. "But I don't know if I can to make it. Cecilia hasn't been well." Ron and the former Cecilia Hanna have been married since 1965. "She recently had a very serious surgery to remove a malignant tumor. I would have to see how she's doing at the time. But maybe if she's doing better, I could ask her sister to come stay with her. When do you plan on going?"

"We're hoping for some time in May," I said.

"Well, I'm also doing games, so that might be difficult for me."

Swoboda was working as a color analyst for the New Orleans Baby Cakes, the Triple-A minor-league affiliate of the Miami Marlins.

"Well, how about this," I said. "We're going to look for a couple of days when you're not working, and hopefully Cecilia will be feeling better. But obviously, if you can't make it, you can't make it. But let's try because everybody would love to see you."

A couple of days later, I got hold of Koosman on the phone. As I mentioned, Kooz is a staunch conservative and often sends me emails supporting right-wing politics and denouncing the Left. So after about ten minutes of politics, I told him about my idea of visiting Seaver. Kooz, who grew up in Minnesota, is kind of a good old Midwestern guy who cut right to the chase.

"When are you going?" he asked in his low, raspy baritone, sounding receptive to the idea.

"Well, we're going to try for early May, but it may have to be later in the summer—perhaps in August."

"That sounds good. If I'm free when everybody else is able to g
you can count me in."

As far as I knew, Kooz was now completely retired after spending much of his postcareer years piloting his own plane and spending afternoons out on the greens as a scratch golfer. But he still had
various commitments, like autograph signings and other personal
events. And he was thinking about putting a landing strip on his
property and possibly resuming his flying. Still, after talking to him, I
was optimistic we could work around his schedule.

So that left Buddy. I had left him a couple of voice mails but
hadn't heard anything back. Then finally, my third attempt was the
charm, as I was able to reach him live—but he said he had to call me
right back. After several days, I was still waiting for that return call.
In my mind, the prospects of Buddy joining us weren't good at all.

By April, the time had come to coordinate the trip and check on
plane schedules. While Erik and I finalized the reservations on his
laptop, I sighed and looked over at him.

"Well, what do you think?" I asked. "One more call to Buddy?"

Buddy was Tom's best friend, and we both knew how important it
would be to Seaver to have him come along.

"Absolutely," Erik told me. "You should give it one more try."

Buddy's phone rang, and, to my surprise, he picked up. The voice
on the other end of the phone was soft and measured. I thought I
should get right to the point and asked if he would like to join our
group to see Seaver.

"I'd love to," Harrelson responded quietly, yet sincerely, without
adding another word.

After a short pause in which I thought he might say something
else, I started talking again.

"Well, that's great, Buddy. You can fly out with me and an author who is helping me write a book on our '69 team. We would fly out of JFK Airport on Friday, May 12. I checked the Ducks' schedule, and they're away that weekend."

"That sounds great," he said. "Thank you."

I gathered all of his information from him, including his first name, which hardly anybody knows: Derrel.

"We'll reserve your ticket, print out a copy, and mail it to you," I said.

"Okay, that would be fine," he said slowly.

"I'll call you in a few days," I said. "Be well, Buddy."

After adding Buddy to our flight, Erik printed out his reservation and dropped it in the mail to him. Harrelson was, at last, on board. Our group was now complete!

A few days later, Erik received a call from Buddy's ex-wife, Kim, who has remained close with Harrelson—often stopping by his house on Long Island, where he lives with their adult son. After finding the plane reservation printout on a table, she contacted Erik, whom she initially mistook for a baseball card show promoter.

"Buddy no longer does autograph signings," she told Sherman.

But after Erik quickly explained who he was and what was planned, she thought it would be a wonderful thing for Buddy.

"Take lots of pictures for him," she requested. "It will help him remember the occasion."

Kim also offered to drive Buddy curbside at JFK on the day of our trip, as well as arrange to have him picked up after arriving back in New York. Even though they were divorced, it was clear that Buddy and Kim still loved and cared for each other.

"I think this is going to be great therapy for him," she added. "And it's going to be great for Tom and you guys, too. I just hope he's feeling well enough to make the trip."

I swear, as someone with experience in this department, Buddy and Kim should write a book on how to divorce amicably.

I called Tom to let him know that, barring any unforeseen circumstances, Buddy, Kooz, Rocky, Erik, and I were all confirmed to fly into San Francisco on May 12, a Friday afternoon, and we would come by either that evening or the next morning.

"Hey, Sham, let me put Nancy on the phone so you two can get it on our calendar," he said.

High school sweethearts, Nancy and Tom have been married for more than fifty years—a reality almost unheard-of in the baseball life. During the '69 season, more than any of the other Mets players' wives, she was often caught on camera rooting on her man while wearing her trademark assortment of stylish hats. She was the Mets' very own fashion icon—and a wonderful lady.

I told Nancy about our plans to go out there, and, while she was excited by the news and said they would be home the weekend we planned to come out, she was cautionary as well.

"Well, Art, to be perfectly honest, we just don't know how he's going to feel—he gets foggy sometimes," she said. "I think it's a wonderful idea and will really be great for Tom—*and Buddy, too*—but just understand that some days are good and some days are not too good. Every day is different. It's really a roll of the dice."

Still, I wanted to forge ahead. I knew how very special it would be to bring the guys out there to see him.

"Well, let's hope for the best," I said. "We get in about one o'clock on that Friday. By the time we would get up to Calistoga, I guess it would probably be around three thirty or four."

"Oh, I don't think it's a good idea to come over then," Nancy said. "Tom gets tired in the afternoon and a little forgetful. Why don't you come over the next morning about nine o'clock? Hopefully, he'll be doing well. I'm sure he will want to take you out to the vineyards."

"That would be wonderful," I said, giving off an air of optimism.

But at the same time, I had come to the realization that our sole chance to see him was limited to just one day: that Saturday. Sunday would be out, as we had to make it all the way back to San Francisco in the early afternoon to make our flights home.

"And then afterward," Nancy continued, "he'll want to take you out to lunch and make you some coffee back here. It's not going to be very good coffee, but pretend that it is—tell him it's good anyway!"

In the final days leading up to the big trip, I was restless.

I called Koosman, Harrelson, and Swoboda at least twice at the beginning of the week to make sure they were still okay. And I phoned Nancy on Wednesday and then again on Thursday—the day before we were to leave—to check on Tom.

"He's doing well, Art," she told me in her usual friendly voice. "He told me how much he's really looking forward to it."

I was thrilled to hear that and just as glad that he remembered.

Still, it was a tense and nerve-racking time for me. The night before the flight out of JFK with Buddy and Erik, I couldn't sleep. In fact, I never even bothered going to bed. I simply couldn't relax. So I watched a little TV and played some Solitaire on my computer while all sorts of scenarios went through my mind.

Rocky's issues. Buddy's issues. Tom's issues.

But maybe I was the one with the *most* issues!

•　　•　　•

Both Erik and I arrived at the Delta Air Lines terminal at JFK exceptionally early the next morning to ensure we would be there when Kim dropped Buddy off curbside.

When Kim and Buddy arrived, I thanked her for everything she had done before walking with Buddy toward the doors.

Buddy, wearing a light Mets jacket, was in great spirits. His Alzheimer's was readily detectable by his slower speaking pattern and how he sometimes had difficulty verbalizing his thoughts, but he seemed genuinely excited about the trip.

We reached our gate well before take-off, so I treated our threesome to breakfast in the Delta Lounge, where I am a member. While we ate, Buddy was especially interested in talking to Erik about a book he had written on the 1986 Mets, entitled *Kings of Queens*, as Harrelson was the third base coach on that club—the only other squad in franchise history to win the World Series.

For the next half hour, Buddy regaled us with stories about the Mets teams of the mid- to late eighties, on which he served as a coach under manager Davey Johnson. Those Mets wrote the next auspicious chapter in club history. The foundation of the 1969 world champion Mets stayed largely intact through 1976. But then came the doldrums: seven consecutive losing seasons. With Johnson's arrival, though, the Mets immediately reversed course, reeling off seven straight winning seasons, including two division championships, a pennant, and a second World Series ring for Buddy in 1986. He would replace Johnson as manager two months into the 1990 season and guide the team to a strong second-place finish, just four games behind the Pittsburgh Pirates. Buddy's memory was surprisingly sharp and his take engrossing. It really passed the time while creating a bond between him and Erik, which I was glad to see, considering we would all be spending the weekend together.

As we boarded the plane, and I got comfortable in my seat, a sudden calm came over me. The plan that Erik and I had hatched up better than four months before was becoming a reality.

I admit it: I'm still a kid at heart. I get around Seaver and Koosman, and I'm still in awe of how well they pitched. With Buddy, even though we've been together countless times, I've never lost sight of the fact that he's a true Mets icon. And with Rocky, I can still vividly recall that incredible catch he made in the World Series.

My admiration has always been there for those guys—and the rest of the team as well. We were a part of something so special in 1969. The common thinking then was, *If the Mets can win the World Series, then* anything *is possible.*

So although I was thoroughly exhausted by this point, the anticipation of getting the guys together again gave me a rush of adrenaline. And as the plane took off, the memories of those glorious days came flooding back.

CHAPTER 2

THE LOVABLE LOSERS

– November 8, 1967 –

I WAS IN COMPLETE SHOCK. IT WAS THE FIRST TIME I HAD been traded, and my immediate thoughts revolved around all the relationships I had built throughout my years in the Cincinnati Reds organization. We were a very strong team, always competing for the pennant. In my first year in the majors, we had some truly great players, like Frank Robinson, Pete Rose, Tony Perez, and Vada Pinson. And in subsequent seasons, we added Johnny Bench and Lee May in a prelude to what would be known as the Big Red Machine that would muscle its way into the World Series in the early to midseventies. The thought of leaving the Reds was bad enough. But I was doubly shocked and dismayed to hear I was going to the perennially awful Mets, affectionately referred to by their fans as the lovable losers. They were so bad that if a team took only two out of three games from them in a series, that was not considered a successful series.

At the time, I also wasn't crazy about the city of New York, which I had always found overwhelming. Even though I came from a good-sized city, St. Louis, and played in Cincinnati, New York was just another animal altogether. Plus, the people kind of talked funny there. When they yelled out my name, it didn't sound like my name at all:

"Hey, *Aw-tee*, can we get yaw autograph?"

The interesting thing about the trade was that when I got the call from Bob Howsam, the general manager of the Reds, I had just come out of the hospital after undergoing lower back surgery. So it was reasonable for me to think he was simply checking up on me to see how I was feeling. Before he could say anything, I said, "Mr. Howsam, I'm glad you called. I just wanna let you know I'm gonna be ready to go for spring training. I'm looking forward to next year."

"Well, that's good," Howsam said, "because we just traded you to the New York Mets. Bing Devine, the GM of the Mets, is going to give you a call."

After the jolt of that news settled in, there was some solace that Devine would be contacting me. I had known Bing since I was a fifteen-year-old kid playing on the sandlots in St. Louis, and he was the general manager of the Cardinals. As I developed my baseball skills, Devine had the Cards scout me. So when he did call a couple of hours after my conversation with Howsam, I was really happy to hear from him.

"We need some left-handed power," he told me. "We've been trying to make a trade for you for some time. And you're going to enjoy playing with us. We have some great young players ready to shine."

Devine really made that initial shock go away. But only temporarily. A strange occurrence took place just two days later while I was recovering at home in St. Louis. I picked up a paper and read where Devine had left the Mets and was returning to his old general manager's post with the Cardinals. So after telling me how great the up-and-coming Mets were going to be, he just left the club and moved back to St. Louis. Now I didn't know what to think, and my initial uneasiness over the trade returned. Of course, I had no way of knowing it at the time, but in the long run, the transaction turned out to be the best thing that ever happened to me in my career.

"We're *not* going to be the same old Mets anymore," Gil Hodges, the new Mets manager and former US Marine, said sternly as he gathered his troops in front of him on the first day of spring training in 1968. You could tell he had been through some lean years with the Mets as a player during the franchise's first two seasons, in 1962 and 1963, and knew the perception of the team was that of a loser, but also that the kind of poor play that had defined the organization would no longer be tolerated. This was a man with a significant baseball pedigree: an eight-time All-Star first baseman and a member of seven pennant-winning Dodgers teams. If anyone could transform a losing team into winners, it was Hodges. Having never met him before, my first reaction to the way he carried himself was, *Be careful. This is someone who's very serious.* I realized on that very first day of spring training that this no-nonsense guy had set the tone for everything that would go on with the ball club from that point forward. We might not win as much as people would like, but things were going to be very different. The Mets had found themselves a true leader of men.

But while his words that day pointed toward a new beginning for the Mets, there were a bunch of veteran guys like myself where the natural instinct, after coming from winning organizations, was to feel less than optimistic about playing for the worst team in baseball. In their first six seasons, the Mets finished a distant last five times, escaping the cellar only once, in 1966, when they climbed up to ninth place out of ten teams in the National League. The Mets had acquired three players that off-season from the Chicago White Sox—catcher J. C. Martin, infielder Al Weis, and outfielder Tommie Agee—who were used to playing for a contender. The White Sox may not have won any pennants in the sixties, but they were consistently solid, averaging ninety wins per season from 1960 through 1967.

"I thought it was a disaster, to tell you the truth," Martin told me, "because '67 was a wonderful year for the White Sox. We battled for the pennant right up until the last four or five games of the season. It was a great time to be in Chicago. Then I learned I had been traded to the Mets—a last-place team. It was devastating." He'd spent all nine of his seasons in the big leagues with the White Sox.

Weis, who came over in the trade with Agee, felt much the same way.

"It was like the kiss of death," he said. "All the years I was with the White Sox, we contended. In 1964 we lost out to the Yankees by one game; in '67 we lost to Boston by a couple of games. The trade was a very disheartening thing to have happen. And back in those days, you had no recourse: either you went in the trade or you didn't play. Years later, Joe Pignatano told me that Gil would not have made the trade for Agee unless I was included in it. He needed me to fill in for infielders like Buddy Harrelson and Kenny Boswell because they had military commitments. That made me feel really good."

But most important, having the three veterans from the same club come over to the Mets helped soften the blow for them.

"Not only did it help with the transition," Martin said, "but I knew those guys could play and were going to help make the Mets better. It was a welcome thing to have them come alongside of me, because I had seen them play for four or five years with the White Sox."

Other veterans who came over via trades the season before were Don Cardwell, who pitched several years with a strong Pittsburgh Pirates team that was usually in the mix, and reliever Ron Taylor, who played a major role in the St. Louis Cardinals winning a World Series over the Yankees in 1964.

There were so many good teams and great players during that era. But up until that point in their history, the Mets were usually buried in last place for good by Mother's Day.

Aside from the few, aforementioned veterans we had, we were a very young ball club—especially in the pitching department—composed primarily of rookies and sophomores. It was a far different dynamic from the Reds club I came from that had thirtysomethings such as Joe Nuxhall, Bob Purkey, Frank Robinson, Joey Jay, and Gordy Coleman—all players with experience and a history of having some good years. By contrast, this Mets club had very little in the way of veteran leadership.

But it certainly wasn't all doom and gloom for me personally. I did see coming to New York as an opportunity to bounce back after having an injury-riddled off-year in Cincinnati. I had gone from belting 21 home runs (including 4 in a row over the course of two games) in just 234 at bats in 1966—the best ratio in that department in the majors—to hitting just 3 in '67. And there was some reason to heed Hodges's higher expectations for the club. I could see right away the Mets were basing their future on pitching, and you couldn't miss all the great young arms we had in camp in '68. It was impossible to know then how terrific the staff would become, but with Tom Seaver, Jerry Koosman, Nolan Ryan, Jim McAndrew, and Gary Gentry, the potential was certainly there.

"I had an instructional league team in '67," recalled Whitey Herzog, our superb director of player development at the time and a future Hall of Fame manager. "I had fourteen pitchers, and eleven of them would go on to make the major leagues. You could just see they were all going to blossom."

Sometimes, as they say, it's more important to be lucky than good. The Mets' three elite starters—Seaver, Koosman, and Gentry—all easily could have ended up with other teams.

"We were lucky to get Seaver in '66," Herzog told me. "The Braves had signed him illegally for forty thousand dollars in the first round, so the names of the teams willing to pay him forty thousand went into a hat. I had a helluva a time getting the Mets to commit to the money. I argued with Devine and Joe McDonald"—director of the club's farm system—"about getting the money from Mr. [George]

Weiss, the team's president, but we finally got it right before the drawing. When our name was drawn from the hat, Seaver was ours.

"With Koosman, an usher at Shea Stadium told McDonald about a left-hander he had heard about in the army. So we sent one of our scouts, Red Murff, to see him pitch. I think he offered Koosman fourteen hundred dollars that October, but he didn't take it. So he went back in November and offered him twelve hundred, and he didn't take that. Then he went back in December. I don't know if Koosman needed to buy Christmas presents or what, but when Murff offered him a thousand, he took it. Maybe Koosman thought, *Hell, I better be careful, or I won't get nothing!*"

Whitey went on to explain how they nearly lost Kooz before he ever pitched a big-league game for the Mets.

"The spring training after signing Koosman, I met with some of the minor-league managers and pitching coaches in Hollywood, Florida, to discuss player personnel. We got to talking about Koosman, and everybody in that room said, *'Release! Release! Release!'* Well, afterward, McDonald goes to Kooz's minor-league manager, Clyde McCullough, and says, 'Look, I loaned Koosman fifty dollars, and if I don't get that fifty dollars back on the first paycheck, I might get fired. George Weiss is liable to fire me!' And McCullough said, 'Well, I'll take him with me.' So McCullough took Koosman with him on his 'A' league team, and Kooz pitched two shutouts by the first payday. Otherwise he would have been released! By the time I got Koosman in the instructional league, he was throwing in the midnineties with an easy, fluid delivery. A goddamn year later, he's in the big leagues. In '69 he and Seaver never lost back-to-back games. Incredible."

And then there was the unlikely, fortuitous pickup of Gary Gentry.

"Gentry was pitching in the College World Series in the spring of '67," Herzog said. "Bobby Winkles was his coach at Arizona State.

Winkles told our scout Dee Fondy that Gentry couldn't come back to school—that he had flunked out. No other team knew that he couldn't go back to school and that he was eligible in the supplemental draft except us. We actually waited until the third round and picked him sixtieth! That's a helluva story right there!"

So when you think about how the Mets got Seaver out of a hat, picked up Koosman in part due to a tip from an usher and retained him because of a $50 debt, and then took Gentry in the third round because the rest of baseball thought he was ineligible, it's hard to fathom that this trio would be our top starting pitchers in the '69 World Series.

The other thing I noticed that first spring was how strong defensively we were going to be up the middle. With Jerry Grote behind the plate, Buddy Harrelson at short, Weis and Kenny Boswell at second, and Tommie Agee in center field to complement good pitching, I didn't think we were going to get blown out of many games. And we wouldn't, despite debilitating injuries: first to Agee and then, later, to Boswell. With Agee, the American League rookie of the year in 1966, it sort of set a negative tone for the season.

"In the first spring training game we had in '68, we were playing the St. Louis Cardinals," recalled Mets third baseman Ed Charles. "Bob Gibson was pitching that day and Agee, having been in the American League up until then, was facing him for the first time. Well, Gibson liked to 'introduce' himself to new players to the National League. So Tommy got into the batter's box, and about the time he got through doing all his little gyrations—*Bam!*—a fastball hits him in the head and sends him down to the ground. He had to leave the game. Tommy didn't hit that whole year like I had seen him do in the American League when I was with the Kansas City A's. He was still feeling the effects of getting beaned by Gibson."

The trade bringing Agee to the Mets reunited him with our

young left fielder, Cleon Jones. Both from the Mobile, Alabama, area, they had known each other for a long time, and, as close, old friends sometimes do, they would argue over absolutely everything—even the mundane, like what the temperature was outside.

"Tommie was a very special guy," Cleon once told me following Agee's death in 2001. "He lived in Whistler, which was about three miles from where I lived, in Plateau. We played together in high school—baseball and football. We even played Sunday baseball against one another. And then we had the good fortune to come up to the major leagues together."

As for myself, I played the outfield corners as well as getting some time at first base, where Ed Kranepool was the regular first baseman. Krane is a Mets icon because he was their first big signing, at age seventeen, in 1962, lasted eighteen years with the organization, and still holds some team records. He would ultimately see the good, the bad, and the ugly with the Mets, and, up to that point, it was mostly pretty awful.

"It wasn't fun as a player," Krane told me. "I think every time you sign a contract or you're playing in a game, you want to win. And I was always accustomed to winning as a Little Leaguer and in sandlot baseball. So when you sign a contract, you have high expectations of leading a losing ball club like the early Mets out of the wilderness and making them a contender. But one player doesn't make an organization. You have to surround yourself with good players. So it was very difficult and very frustrating."

Before coming over to the Mets, I had never met Eddie. I played against him in the minor leagues a little bit, but that was about the extent of what I knew about him. So during a winter publicity event prior to the '68 season, I was sitting next to Kranepool, and he said to me, "I'm gonna tell you something that's going to be very valuable to you in your days in New York."

Very intrigued, I said, "Really? What can that be?"

"Well, if you're gonna be invited to a lot of events like this—dinners, breakfasts, and other things the Mets are gonna want you to do—just remember one thing: When you come to these things, always find a seat by an exit," he said profoundly. "This way you can always duck out sometimes." And, of course, he was right. But to know Eddie was to understand he had this wit about him. He was a New Yorker through and through—born and raised in the Bronx—and had this kind of sarcastic answer for a lot of really funny stuff.

If there was one person in the Mets organization who never received enough credit for our transformation from lovable losers to a championship-caliber team, it was Whitey Herzog. Most people know him as the outstanding manager of the Kansas City Royals and St. Louis Cardinals, but the footprint he left as one of the architects of the '69 Mets is largely underappreciated. His eye for assessing young talent was as good as any in the history of the game. And his work ethic was unmatched.

"Jim McAndrew first got to know Whitey while pitching for the organization's Double-A minor-league club in Williamsport, Pennsylvania, in 1967. Our manager, Roy Sievers, had a death in his family, and Herzog came in and managed the team for ten days," Jim McAndrew told me. "He had the same type of personality as the rest of us. He was younger, he'd catch BP, he'd spend time with you, he'd go out in the field instead of sitting in the dugout or in the clubhouse. He would interact with the guys all the time and kind of get to know you between the ears as well. He had a gift of telling you who was going to be in the big leagues in two or three years and then, a few years later, you'd realize he was right and just go 'Holy cow!'

"He also had credibility in that if he told you you're doing something wrong, he gave you a direction to go in if you wanted to improve. But if a guy wanted to be bullheaded and not listen to him, he'd basically tell him, 'Yeah, you'll be home next year. You'll be carrying a lunch bucket!' He was just a real great guy who helped you both physically and mentally. He was good for guys like myself that were low on self-esteem."

"I didn't play much," said Herzog, who was an outfielder for four big-league clubs over an eight-year span. "I was never what you would call a 'regular.' And I remember guys asking me how the hell I knew so much about baseball at such a young age. I'd tell them it's from sitting and watching while they've been playing, for Christ's sake. When I finally retired from baseball in '63, I took a scouting job for Cleveland. I signed twelve ballplayers for $125,000, and seven of them made the big-league roster within two years. I think that kind of told people, 'Hey, maybe he knows what the hell he's looking at.'"

For the '69 Mets, Whitey discovered stalwarts like Seaver, Koosman, Ryan, McAndrew, Boswell, McGraw, and Wayne Garrett, among others.

What's interesting to me is how the one move that Herzog and the Mets front office long received the most criticism for—choosing catcher Steve Chilcott over Reggie Jackson as the number one pick in the 1966 major-league baseball draft—probably opened the door for the trade that brought me, a left-handed-hitting outfielder with some power, to the club. But even the decision not to draft Reggie had reasonable justification: the selection of Chilcott, a seventeen-year-old multisport star at Antelope Valley High School in Lancaster, California, was based on need at the time.

"Jackson was an outfielder, and we already had Cleon and Swoboda, so we took a catcher," Herzog explained. "And I remember Bing saying to me, 'Well, let's see who had Chilcott at number one. Let's see if we were the only one.' So after I checked with the other clubs following the draft, nine of them had Chilcott first, and ten of them had Jackson at number one. And up until Chilcott injured his shoulder, he was having a good year at Winter Haven. Then he had to go into the service and never really could swing the bat again. But he was a good-looking young player." Chilcott would never play in the majors.

After Gil Hodges's death in 1972, Herzog would have been the logical choice to manage the Mets. However, a strained relationship with board chairman M. Donald Grant led to the club hiring the popular Yogi Berra instead. Whitey left the Mets the following year to manage the Texas Rangers before starting his Hall of Fame–worthy runs with the Royals and Cardinals.

Berra, of course, was one of baseball's most colorful guys, and a part of Hodges's staff as first base coach. Yogi, a lifetime .285 hitter with power and a three-time MVP, was also technically our hitting coach—or so I was told. But in all my years there, never once did he talk to me about hitting. One time I said to him, "Yogi, I'm struggling. What should I do?" And his response was, "See it. Hit it." That was the only thing he ever said to me about hitting. Another time, while he was lobbing the ball pitching batting practice, I said, "Yogi, come on, you've gotta throw it a little harder." He said, "Well, why don't you go complain to a coach?" And I said, "You *are* a coach!"

His Yogi-isms were legendary. And it seems like everybody from our club has a humorous one that they recall, perhaps the best coming from Joe Pignatano, our bullpen coach.

"So one day his wife comes by and goes, 'Yogi, I went to see *Doctor Zhivago* today.' And he goes, 'What the hell is wrong with you now?' So I told him, 'Hey, Yogi, *Doctor Zhivago* is a *movie!*'"

Pignatano, or "Piggy," as we called him, basically had one duty: to keep control of the pitchers out in the bullpen who were out of control; particularly guys like Tug and Kooz. They all played practical jokes on him, but he made sure they got their work in when needed. It's not the kind of job you need a degree in, but still, Piggy was perfect for the role. Some, however, thought he had another important duty.

"Piggy was Hodges's spy," Kooz insisted. "He was the guy that would tell on you if you did something wrong. Rube Walker, by contrast, was like your father."

Walker, a former catcher, was a terrific pitching coach. He was a forerunner to the many catchers that have become really good ones. Hodges, naturally, has gotten so much credit for leading the Mets to the '69 championship, and deservedly so, but I think Rube was one of the unsung heroes on the coaching staff and was overshadowed by the greatness of Gil. Rube had a way about him that really made everybody around him feel comfortable—and he was a conduit to Hodges, who wasn't the easiest to talk to. We could laugh with Rube, something we could never do with Gil. Hodges was a stoic figure on the bench, looking straight ahead at the field—always analyzing and anticipating. As players, most of us avoided him as much as possible. But with Rube, you could vent or say anything to him without fear of repercussions.

"He was very laid back," Gentry told me. "You never saw him lose his temper or get excited. He just went about his job and left you alone, for the most part. He was a very underrated pitching coach. I think Gil considered him his right-hand man."

"He was very easy to talk to," Kooz said. "He'd make you think he was keeping a secret, but I know he'd talk to Gil."

McAndrew's sentiments expanded on Kooz's feelings about Walker.

"He was a good, kind man—period. You could trust him. Half the time you were afraid to talk with Gil or the coaches, but never with Rube."

Jack DiLauro recalled mostly Walker's warm open-door policy even with guys like him that didn't pitch very often.

"If you had a question for Rube, it didn't matter who you were, he'd always sit down and talk with you about it," said DiLauro. "I remember one time, he was sitting with Seaver and Ryan in a lounge on a day off. I walked in, and he said something like, 'Hey, Jack, sit down. We're talking about so-and-so.' So it was really pretty neat to have somebody like that on the coaching staff."

Sometimes when I wasn't playing, I would run with the pitchers and really got to know Rube pretty well. I saw how he interacted with his young hurlers, and it was clear they had a deep respect for him. McAndrew once told me he wasn't teaching them things like how to throw a curveball but rather how to be pitchers.

Rounding out Gil's staff was third base coach Eddie Yost, a wonderful, intelligent baseball man. I used to tease him all the time by saying, "Eddie, you really *look* like a ballplayer. You look like you could still play!" Which he had, from 1944 to 1962. He had the right build, his uniform fit perfectly—we used to laugh about that all the time. Yogi was a different story. I once said jokingly with him, "Hey, Yogi, you don't look like a hitting coach. And you don't look like a first base coach, either!" And he didn't. He was just so short and squatty. But he was also once the great Yankees catcher with ten World Series rings and soon to have a plaque in Cooperstown, so, needless to say, his physique worked out pretty well for him.

Our offense in '68 left a lot to be desired. Even though it was the so-called Year of the Pitcher, a season so dominated by pitching that, in response, the following year Major League Baseball lowered the pitcher's mound from fifteen inches to ten inches to give more of an advantage to hitters, we were nowhere close to the top hitting teams in baseball. We didn't score many runs and hit only 81 home runs as a team. Ed Charles led the club with just 15 dingers, and I was third with 11. Somewhat in our defense was the fact that Gil was platooning at almost every position, making it a challenge for our hitters to put up big numbers.

"At times, the platooning was a little frustrating," said Kranepool. "I was used to playing every day before Hodges got to the ball club. We had our differences over it in the beginning. But I learned to respect him because you had to develop and mature. I thought I knew everything, but obviously I didn't. He was the leader of the team, and you had to follow his rules. If you didn't, he didn't care who you were—you wouldn't get the chance to play. He was tough but fair."

Others, like Ron Taylor, took it a big step further than that.

"Gil Hodges was, without a doubt, the best *man* I've met in my life," he told me. "He knew the players, knew what they could do, and just did a terrific job with each of us. With Gil, I knew I was no different than any other player—he treated us all the same."

"Hodges made sure that there were no 'stars,'" Kooz said. "If you were late for a flight, he didn't care who you were, you were going to be left behind. And once he had Seaver thinking that way, all of us fell in line. There was no one that rated above another guy."

As for me, I respected the heck out of him because he was so honest with everybody, and you knew your place on the team. You might not agree with some of the things Gil did, but you were never blindsided.

Still, the lack of an offensive attack was an issue. And no pitcher at the start of his career received less run support than McAndrew did in '68. A quiet guy, lost in the shadows of Seaver, Koosman, and Gentry, Jim had good stuff—sinkers and sliders—and was always around the plate. He was typical of the good, young pitchers the Mets were developing, but was a victim of our anemic offense.

"I was too naïve to know better," McAndrew told me. "I was a young guy low on self-esteem. Why? I had a 1.80 ERA, but started out with a record of just 1–7. I still have the major-league record of getting shut out my first four starts."

It didn't help that two of our best hitters, Agee and Boswell, saw their numbers decline following their respective injuries that season. Agee, of course, had a tough year right out of the gate following the Gibson beaning in spring training, and hit just .217 with 5 home runs. As for Boswell, he was enjoying a terrific rookie season, batting well over .300, when he broke his ring finger trying to break up a double play that June. Boz would miss the next two months of the season.

One of the few bright spots in our lineup was Cleon's chase for .300 that went right down to the wire. And he and his buddy Tommie had some fun with it.

"The last day of the season, I had a chance to hit .300, against the Phillies," Cleon told me back in 2004. "I needed to go two-for-three to hit .300. But I ended up going one-for-five and just missed it. Anyway, the night before, Tommie asked me if I wanted to go out. But when Angela came home with the kids, I told him I was staying in. I said, 'I'm going to get a good night's sleep because I'm going to hit .300 tomorrow.' To which Tommie replied, 'Well, I'm hitting .200, and I'm going out!' We all laughed about it. So after the final game, he comes over to me and asks, 'I'll bet you wished you had gone out with me now, right?' Maybe I should have joined him. Maybe I would have been looser and wouldn't have been thinking about hitting .300 so much. It may have helped."

We finished the season in ninth place in the National League, just one game ahead of the last-place Houston Astros. But I don't know if our lack of overall hitting was the reason we ended near the bottom. We were still a very young and inexperienced club that didn't win a lot of close games.

"Those sons of guns were trying their best to win with no experience," J. C. Martin said. "It's really difficult for young players to be in the frying pan at such tender ages. But Gil Hodges had the formula. He knew how to handle young players as well as the few older guys like me, and he had a team that was starting to gel. With the young guys, he instilled confidence. With the older guys, he knew how to press them to make them produce more."

I have long believed it was Hodges's indoctrination of how to play the game and how to deal with certain aspects of it that really helped us as players. But the '68 season wasn't just a learning process for us but also for him. Gil was finding out a lot about his players that year. Unlike a lot of managers today who bury themselves in sabermetrics, Hodges's two greatest assets were his feel for the game and how to deal with players. He knew what he expected out of us, and while his players didn't always produce for him, he used what he saw in '68 to his advantage in preparing for 1969. Gil was laying the groundwork, and near the end of the '68 season, we were starting to believe in his determination and ability as a manager. And one thing was for sure: we knew that better days were ahead for us.

"We started believing in ourselves," Harrelson said. "Guys were starting to look and act like professionals—not like a bunch of little kids anymore. There were still things to work on, but looking ahead, some of us were like, *We can do this.* It was no longer a case of thinking, *Someday we may win.* Our growth was coming a lot faster than we imagined. There were times when I looked at some of the talent and was like, *God, look at what we have here now.*"

It was that kind of conviction that gave us a great deal of optimism as we looked toward the '69 season. For the first time in Mets history, there was reason to believe. No more would we be lovable losers.

CHAPTER 3

OPENING DAY

– April 8, 1969 –

"LOSING'S NOT FUNNY, IT'S A SICKNESS," HODGES TOLD US at a team meeting at the start of spring training in March '69. "You lost a lot of one-run games last year. You made a lot of mistakes. We're going to cut that stuff out and change everything around. You're better than you think you are."

Gil's speech was a real shot in the arm to us all.

"We all looked around at each other while he spoke," Cleon Jones recalled. "Hodges was making us think differently about ourselves. We hadn't finished so well the year before, and none of us was thinking we would be that great, much less a championship team. We knew that we were major-league ballplayers and that we were an improved ball club, but on paper we weren't as good as St. Louis or Chicago. He made us feel like we were a better team and were better players than we thought and that each of us had an important role on the ball club. Gil reminded us what we had in place: good defense with a potentially great pitching staff. Now we just needed to put together all the other things."

If Gil was serious the previous spring, he was now a little more intense—with a more determined demeanor and greater expectations for the team. We may still have been a young club, but we were also now a year older and a year more experienced with Hodges as the manager.

"Gil was teaching us the fundamentals of the game, the proper way to play it, how to win, and how to *think* like a winner," Kranepool observed. "But despite all of us improving at the same time, and our rapid development as a team, nobody expected us to win a pennant. In fact, even Gil wanted to get us to .500 first."

"I did hear comments from some of the veterans saying we could play .500 or maybe even a little better," said our rookie catcher Duffy Dyer. "I think some of them were saying that because we now had divisional play, making everything a lot different with less teams to compete against."

The new four-division structure, plus the addition of four new expansion teams—Montreal and San Diego in the National League, and the Kansas City Royals and the Seattle Pilots in the American League—were the centerpiece changes of baseball's centennial year. There was also a new commissioner in Bowie Kuhn.

Las Vegas had us at 100-to-1 odds to win the pennant that spring. It might as well have been 500-to-1. Realistically, where else would you place that Mets team? We finished in ninth place, a game from last place the previous year. And even though we were now in a six-team division, you still had the two-time defending National League champion Cardinals, the hard-hitting Pittsburgh Lumber Company Pirates of Willie Stargell and Roberto Clemente, and a very good veteran Cubs team to compete with in the NL East.

We did add some new pieces in the form of some more young, inexperienced—if talented—players into the fold like pitcher Gary Gentry, third baseman Wayne Garrett, outfielders Amos Otis and Rod Gaspar, infielder Bobby Pfeil, and Dyer. And because of the environment that Gil had created on the ball club, the rookies fit in perfectly.

Up until the late 1960s, not only were rookies generally razzed and punked by the established players, but young players were expected to know their place and to not even make conversation with star veterans. But that wasn't the case on our team.

"You hear all these stories about how rookies are treated," Gentry said, "but I walked into the Mets clubhouse for the first time, and they just accepted me as a member of the family—it was such a great experience. Seaver and I would sometimes do crossword puzzles together. It seemed like everybody was happy all the time—always up and ready to play the game. And everybody was on each other's side. I never saw any animosity in there. The overall feeling was that we were all in this together, and we'll take care of business. It was a wonderful place to go and be a part of."

Garrett, who was just twenty-one but looked even younger, experienced much the same.

"It helped that we were such a young team," he reflected. "We had a few veterans, but the average age was around twenty-five years old, so we all had a lot in common. When I came to spring training, I had no idea who most of these players were. The only one I had seen play was Agee because he was with the White Sox, and they trained in Sarasota, Florida, where I lived. Because the Mets were always in last place, you never got to see them on TV. They were never on the *Game of the Week*."

Aside from all the new faces on the ball club, Hodges made a move that would have a major impact on the Mets for years to come: he anointed Tug McGraw—who had spent all of 1968 at Triple-A Jacksonville and was used primarily as a starter up to that point in his career—as his left-handed closer out of the bullpen.

"Gil just walked up to Tug, looked him square in the eye, and said, 'You're my man. You're going to be my left-hander out of the bull- pen,' recalled McAndrew. "I spent a lot of time with Tug the previous year at Triple-A, and despite his outward persona, he was actually pretty insecure. So in doing this, Gil was his rock and stood right behind him. And there were some nerve-racking moments that Tug would put everybody through when he broke in as a reliever, but Gil was there for him, and he knew it. When Tug struggled, he went to Hodges and Walker, and the next thing you knew, he was getting his rhythm back, feeling confident again. Tug may have been out of the game shortly if it hadn't been for Gil changing his role. I give Gil all the credit for Tug's great career, I really do."

From the time I met Tug, I knew he was a character who at any time would say or do anything to make you laugh. One story that is just so telling of how gregarious he could be involved a spring training "B" game at Miller Huggins Field, the old training site for the New York Yankees for many years, and where we practiced before taking cabs over to Al Lang Stadium, also in Saint Petersburg, to play the main games. B games were organized just so players could get in a little work. Tug was the starting pitcher, and I was playing first base. It turned out that McGraw was ambidextrous. Tug, a left-hander, gets on the mound and sees a right-handed hitter coming up. So he decides to turn his glove around and throw right-handed. The batter, a switch-hitter, changes to his left-handed stance. So the two of them go back and forth like this until Walker comes out to the mound and says, "Tug, what do you wanna be today? Right-handed or left-handed?" And Tug goes innocently, "What do you want me to be?" It was just such a typical "Tug thing." He never did it in a real game, but he could really throw with both arms. McGraw was a wonderful teammate, a remarkable individual, and a terrific pitcher who always kept you loose.

The rest of spring training turned out to be a real downer for me. I had started off swinging the bat pretty well, hitting 2 home runs in the first three games. But I needed work at first base, a new position

Gil wanted me to start playing. So I went over to my roommate, Boz, during a practice at Miller Huggins Field and said, "Hey, come throw some balls in the dirt for me." I went down to get one of his throws and felt something snap. So I went to see our head trainer, Gus Mauch, and said, "Gus, I think it's something in my back." And he asked, "Are you scheduled to play today? How do you feel?" And I said, "I think I'll be okay. Just give me some Tylenol." That was a mistake. I went to take infield practice prior to that night's game at Al Lang Stadium, and on the very first ground ball I went to field, I bent over, and it felt like somebody shot me in the left leg. I went down on one knee and didn't play another game for the rest of spring training. The team put me in the hotel bed for the rest of the month. They didn't even bother to have me come to the ballpark for any treatment.

When we broke camp, Gaspar took my place on the roster.

"When Art couldn't go the night he got injured, Gil starts me in his place," Gaspar recalled. "I proceeded to go on a fourteen-game hitting streak. Here I was, this rookie, coming out of nowhere and making the club out of spring training. They didn't know what else to do with me. So it was because of my buddy, Art Shamsky, that I made the club. What a great feeling that was!"

But it certainly wasn't great for me. I started the season on the twenty-one-day disabled list. I was so discouraged and disheartened by the isolation away from the team. And the pain was so bad that I honestly wondered if I was ever going to play again. Back in those days, they didn't treat you like they do now. All I was prescribed by the team doctor and the trainer were muscle relaxers and Percocet. To make matters worse, I would get hooked on Percocet, an opioid analgesic, relying on the pills when I started playing again and taking sleeping pills at night to sleep.

Subsequent to that, over the years I've been to so many different doctors, chiropractors, and osteopaths for my back pain. I once saw a doctor who stuck cotton swabs of cocaine up my nose to deaden my nerves.

Another time, I flew to Boston to see a doctor nicknamed Dr. Feelgood who supposedly had treated John F. Kennedy for his bad back. He injected me with some muscle relaxants. All I remember was walking wobbly as I tried to get on the plane home.

I don't know if I was supposed to be seeing these doctors, but I desperately wanted to keep playing ball, to contribute to this exciting young team, and to feel the exhilaration of winning.

In May, after essentially being away from the club for seven weeks, I was called into Gil's office to discuss my predicament with him and our general manager, Johnny Murphy. Getting right to the point, Hodges asked, "So, how do you feel?" I said, "You know what? Thank God, I feel great. I'm ready to play." But Gil wasn't so sure, saying, "Well, you know you missed all of spring training and then went on the disabled list. We think you might have to just get some practice in." Thinking I would stay with the big-league club, I said, "Okay, I'll come out early tomorrow and take some extra batting practice."

But Gil had other ideas: "Well, we're thinking maybe we'll send you to Tidewater and see how you feel."

"Tidewater?!" I blurted out. The Tidewater Tides were the parent club's new Triple-A affiliate. "I don't need spring training to play on *this* team!"

As soon as I said that, I regretted it. I wanted to just turn around and walk out of the room. I didn't mean it as a dig against the Mets. I meant that I just felt like I was ready to play.

Gil gave me an icy glare, paused for what seemed like an eternity but was probably two seconds, and said, "Well, you still need to see if you can play."

I left his office depressed. I had missed most of spring training and the first three weeks of the season and now they were sending me to Tidewater, Virginia. I thought, *I've got years in the big leagues, and I'm going down to the minor leagues.* I was told to call Herzog, and the first thing I did was complain, saying, "Whitey, why do I need to go to Tidewater?" Herzog said simply, "Look, Art, just go join the Tidewater Tides, swing the bat like you can, and everything will work out. You'll be back up to the Mets in no time." Whitey was so great to me. And it turned out he was right. I joined the Tides in Syracuse, New York, hit a grand slam the first day, and was back in Flushing ten days later. The experience taught me humility, because if I didn't come back from that injury or played poorly at Tidewater, who knows what would have happened to my career. It could have all ended right there.

It killed me to miss Opening Day. There isn't a player in baseball that doesn't have a little extra nervous energy and excitement on the first day of the season. Instead, I was at my Manhattan apartment, depressed, nursing my back injury and watching the game on television. After starting spring training filled with so much promise, I now felt completely lost in the shuffle.

The Mets were at home playing the Montreal Expos in the very first game of the expansion team's history at Shea Stadium. For a new team in the league, the Expos had some good players, like Maury Wills, Rusty Staub, and their starting pitcher that day, Mudcat Grant. But even though the Mets were notoriously bad on opening days to that point in their history, we had to feel pretty good with Tom Seaver on the mound for us. And while Tom may not have had his best stuff that day, he left after five innings with a 6–4 lead.

However, our middle relievers Cal Koonce and Al Jackson had

trouble finding the plate, and when they did, got lit up to the tune of six earned runs over just two-plus innings. The Expos would take an 11–6 lead into our bottom half of the ninth. With past Mets teams, they would have folded like a cheap suit. But this was clearly the best team the Mets had ever put on the field, so I wasn't surprised when we battled back. Just prior to a Grote two-out single that cut the lead to 11–7, the bullpen phone rang, summoning our rookie third-string catcher, twenty-three-year-old Duffy Dyer.

"When they called Piggy, and he turned to me and said, 'Gil wants you in the dugout—you're going to pinch hit for Ron Taylor,' my knees started shaking," Dyer told me. "On my way through the tunnel, my heart was beating so fast. When I walked into the dugout, Gil said, 'You're on deck.' And when it was my turn to bat, I was literally shaking. It was just a few days before when Gil told me I was going north with the team. It was such a shock that I almost said to him, 'Are you sure?!' But now I was coming to the plate for the first time at Shea Stadium. Thankfully, I was facing a pitcher I knew a little bit about—Don Shaw—whom I played with at Triple-A the year before. Thankfully, I got a sinker that was a little bit up and hit it out of the ballpark for a three-run homer. Since it was my first day at Shea, I didn't know how well the ball carried there, so I started sprinting toward first. As the ball cleared the fence as I rounded first, I thought to myself, *My God, I just hit a home run in the major leagues!* That's when it really hit me. I slowed down a bit because that was one of my fastest trips around the bases. I was just so excited; I slapped everyone's hand. I was ten feet off the ground when I finally realized what I had done. It was one of my greatest personal thrills that I will never forget."

Amos Otis followed with a single and Agee walked to put the tying and winning runs on base, but Gaspar struck out to end the game.

"I had to keep my excitement inside," Dyer said. "I couldn't get too excited in the clubhouse because we had lost, but I was walking on clouds, for sure."

I'm sure a lot of people probably said after the game, "Well, same old Mets. It's going to be another bad year." After all, we had just lost to an expansion team, and fan reaction was likely very cynical. But we'd scored ten runs, never gave up, and showed a lot of character by the fight we displayed in that ninth inning. These were anything but the same old Mets.

CHAPTER 4

THE STREAK

— May 28–June 10, 1969 —

ONE OF THE QUESTIONS I GET ASKED MOST OFTEN ABOUT 1969 is at what point did I think to myself, *You know, we may actually have a chance to win a championship.* For most of us on the club, we began to "believe" during an eleven-game winning streak about a third of the way through the season.

It began innocently enough on May 28. Up until that point, it was a typical Mets season. We had a losing record of 18–23 and found ourselves in fourth place, already nine games behind the surging first-place Cubs. In a game against the San Diego Padres at Shea Stadium that Wednesday night before a paltry crowd of fewer than twelve thousand fans, Kooz pitched an absolute gem, striking out fifteen batters over ten shutout innings. Buddy would drive in the winning run in the eleventh to secure a very typical pitching-strong, offense-weak 1–0 Mets victory. Little did we realize that it was the start of something special.

"We started off the season so-so," recalled Kooz. "Grote had sciatic nerve problems. Different guys had other injury-related problems early. But then they got well, and we won eleven in a row. We beat San Diego, we swept Frisco, we swept LA, and then we beat up on the Padres some more on the West Coast, sweeping them, too. When we returned home, we had feathers in our caps. That streak made us believe that we could go out and beat anybody. We were no longer second-guessing ourselves on whether we could beat a good club. We went out there and started kicking ass. We knew we could win or at least have a good shot at it."

If there was one game during the streak that served as a microcosm for the bizarre victories that defined our miracle season, it occurred on June 4 against the Dodgers at Shea. It served as exhibit A of how every player on our roster contributed to the success of the '69 Mets. A rookie pitcher named Jack DiLauro, just brought up from the minors in mid-May to pitch primarily middle-inning relief, got a spot start that evening and would forever be a part of Mets lore. DiLauro wasn't the typical hard thrower that most of the other Mets pitchers were and wasn't exactly on anybody's radar as a big-time prospect. He was, after all, a twenty-six-year-old career minor leaguer. But there were attributes that Herzog saw in him on the farm that he really liked.

"I put a good report in on him," Herzog told me. "He was one of the top three pitchers I scouted in the Northern League that year. I really liked him and told the Mets to bring him up. He was a left-hander that could use both sides of the plate, had good movement, and didn't try to overthrow. Left-handers that can do that today, Christ, they make millions!"

DiLauro's first taste of big-league life came on the night of a particularly sloppy effort by the club against the Atlanta Braves at Shea on May 15. Following the game, Gil came storming into the clubhouse and started balling us out.

"We're all getting undressed; nobody had even showered yet," DiLauro recalled. "Gil comes in from his office. Some of the guys had taken their jockstraps and underwear off and threw them into a plastic laundry bucket in the middle of the floor. Hodges makes this speech—and it didn't end on a positive note. He shouted something like, *'I don't ever want to see that kind of negative effort again!'* He then turns around and kicks the damn bucket up in the air; underwear and jock straps went flying everywhere! One of the jockstraps went ten feet across the room and landed right on Yogi's head. Yogi just dropped his head down. I glanced over at Gil, and he had a smirk on his face as he turned to walk back to his office. Everybody just busted up laughing. It *really* loosened us up. From then on, I'm telling you, it was like a different world."

DiLauro had waited more than six years for that first big-league start against the Dodgers and was determined to make the most of the opportunity.

"I had pitched against some of those guys in the minor leagues, so I was pretty confident," Jack told me. "But, still, I was nervous as heck. But you know what was nice? On my way out to the mound, the home plate umpire that night, Tom Gorman, walked out to give me the ball and said, 'Jack, just throw strikes.' Believe it or not, that helped. Bill Russell doubled in the first and Ted Sizemore doubled in the second, but that was it—no more hits. I got in a rhythm and had major-league guys behind me playing great defense in the infield and outfield, so it was pretty relaxing."

"Jack had great stuff that night," recalled Duffy Dyer, who admired DiLauro's performance from the bench. "He could throw anything over for a strike and had great command. That was the best I had ever seen him throw. He particularly had a great breaking ball. He wasn't going to get you out with just his fastball—that's for sure. But he amazed me at times with the stuff he had and how he could make it look so easy. He was a great competitor. You had to beat him; he very seldom beat himself."

As DiLauro walked out to the mound to pitch the ninth inning, the better than thirty-one thousand fans in attendance rose and cheered. Somehow he kept his emotions in check—at least for three more outs.

"I never looked in the stands," Jack said. "People talk about being in the zone and not hearing anything. Well, it's true, unless you let it get to you."

After DiLauro retired the Dodgers in order, his night now over, he allowed himself to take in the roar of the crowd.

"For nine innings, I didn't hear anything—not until I was done and started walking off the mound toward the dugout," DiLauro said. "That's when I felt the vibrations from the fans. The ones behind the dugout were standing and screaming my name. That's when I saw everybody and became very emotional. I cried after that inning was over."

The only downer for Jack was that he would not qualify for his first big-league victory, as the Dodgers' Bill Singer matched his effort—also pitching two-hit shutout ball to our still offensively challenged club through nine. DiLauro would have to watch as our bullpen walked a tightrope for the next six innings, giving up six hits, two walks, and two wild pitches—but no runs!

"Our relief pitching that night reminded me of the minor leagues, to be honest," Jack said. "When you're younger and in the minors, pitching can be a struggle. But this was the big leagues, and I thought, *What the hell's going on here?* But you have those games. My problem was thinking, *Is this game ever going to end? And if so, God, I hope we win! I'd hate to have my name attached to a game like this and lose it!* But it was still pretty cool."

DiLauro had faith in the bullpen. After all, as a reliever himself, these were the guys he was closest with on the team. The first to come in was McGraw, a fellow southpaw who lived down the block from Jack and kept the rookie loose with all of his shenanigans in the bullpen during games.

"Tug kind of ran that bullpen—with his mouth, with his antics, and with his positive nature," DiLauro began. "The bullpen is so far away from the action, but Tug would be yelling out to whoever was playing right field. Then he would start talking to the fans seated above us. Sometimes, for fun, we would beg for money, and they would throw us some change that we would try to catch in our hat. I started juggling baseballs, and they would throw down more change. It was so relaxing and fun. Tug was very positive all the time—just so upbeat."

McGraw pitched four shutout innings before Ron Taylor entered the game to start the fourteenth. Taylor had been flawless from the end of May through late June, not giving up a single run over that monthlong stretch.

"I knew I was playing a factor in our success," said the always-reserved Taylor, who would lead the team in saves that year with thirteen. "I knew I fit in with the crowd—with Seaver and Koosman. Around midseason, everybody just came together, and there was never any friction at all. It was just a team that was starting to feel like it was going to win—and we did. I was enjoying it all. I felt no pressure at all."

After Taylor retired the Dodgers relatively easily in the four-teenth, he ran into some trouble in the fifteenth when Jim Lefebvre led off with a double to left and a walk to Ron Fairly followed. Russell then moved Lefebvre to third by hitting into a force-out at second. So with first and third and one out, the always dangerous Willie Davis came to the plate.

"We had a conference at the mound," Al Weis recalled. "Gil told us that if the ball was hit to either me or Buddy or any infield posi-tion, we would try to get the runner at home. Davis hit a shot off of Taylor's glove that changed directions and was going toward second base. I went to my right, backhanded it, completely spun around, and threw a ball to Grote in the dirt, which he made a great catch on and tagged out Lefebvre."

Gil later told reporters it was the greatest infield play he had ever seen. It served as just another example of one of our unsung heroes from that season—in this case, Weis—making a miraculous play to save a game.

We would, *at last*, win that marathon game in the bottom of the inning when Wayne Garrett's single up the middle went under Davis's glove all the way to the center field fence to bring Agee around the bases from first with the winning run. It was another of those instances that year when you just scratched your head and wondered, *How in the world did we win that game?*

"I saw a bunch of guys that weren't gonna give up," said DiLauro, who would go on to post a remarkable 2.40 ERA over 62⅔ innings that season. "We had some pretty smart players, and the talent was there. It was just a matter of if it would all come together."

Four days later, on June 8, Seaver continued to establish a dominance he would enjoy for years over the Padres, striking out fourteen in seven innings of work en route to a 3–2 victory.

Earlier that day, the new president, Richard Nixon, met with South Vietnamese president Nguyen Van Thieu at Midway Island in the Pacific. Nixon announced that 25,000 of the more than 540,000 US troops would be withdrawn from Vietnam by the end of the summer. The soldiers would be replaced by South Vietnamese forces. In addition, Nixon discussed a new policy that came to be known as the Vietnamization of the war: steps to increase the military might of the Republic of Vietnam's armed forces so that they would eventually take over full responsibility of the war and allow for a complete withdrawal of US troops. As history would show, that would never happen, and the fighting would continue another four years.

That summer, New York was the epicenter of the anti–Vietnam

War movement. Although I didn't march in any antiwar protests, I was opposed to the war. At the time, I thought, *Who would want a war in Vietnam?* I didn't even know where Vietnam was—just that it was in the Far East somewhere. And I was a ballplayer, just trying to get better at my game. For me, the world changed forever when JFK was assassinated in 1963. I knew then that things would never be like they were as a kid growing up. I realized there was a lot of evil in the world, and the Vietnam War was no exception. I couldn't imagine anybody being in favor of it. There were so many young people getting killed over there or coming back here as paraplegics. The shame of the war was how these veterans were forgotten about, shunned, ostracized, or not taken care of because it was an unpopular war that nobody wanted. Imagine fighting for your country, and nobody wants you to come home? It was one of the darkest and bleakest times in our country's history.

We players didn't talk with one another about it too much, aside from somebody saying something like, "Hey, did you see in the paper what happened over there?" We all knew about a lot of the problems going on in Vietnam, but we were just so isolated because we were going to the ballpark, then back home, then to the ballpark, and then on the road.

"We didn't talk politics," said Kranepool, whose father died in World War II shortly before he was born. "Nowadays guys are into a lot more things than playing the game. But then, no; we weren't politicians, we were baseball players."

Still, the war affected us all in different and profound ways. We had players going back and forth to perform military service throughout that season. I was married at the time and got a deferment. And then after two operations on my left hand, I got reclassified because of my medical condition. I guess I lucked out. Some guys might say getting deferred wasn't the right thing to do, but I couldn't imagine going to Vietnam.

None of our guys went to fight there, although Kooz came the closest.

"When I went into the service, I had volunteered for the draft," he told me. "At the time, you could pick what you wanted to do. So I wanted to go to flight school and fly helicopters. But I didn't get to do that. Hell, they sent me into missiles! Well, had I gone to chopper school in Texas as I'd wanted, I later learned I would have been killed. Most chopper pilots over there were shot down. It was one of the highest death rates there was in Vietnam. I got out of the service in October '64 when they were only sending 'advisors.' But had I gone to chopper school, I would have had to enlist as a warrant officer, where you had to stay for three or four years. That would have extended me well into the time when they were sending troops over there and the war really started to explode."

Others, like Gentry, were ready to go if called.

"I just remember saying that if it's my turn to go, I'll go," Gary said. "But I never got drafted, so I guess I was lucky on that part. Although I stayed away from protests and didn't take one side or the other, I didn't agree with our being there. I didn't agree that we had rules of engagement and the other side didn't. I don't think it was a fair war. I was kind of frustrated around that time because there was no question in my mind that we could have won. I was a little disappointed when Barry Goldwater didn't win the '64 election, because I think he would have gotten the military to say we either win this thing or we're out. He would have been very aggressive and not as passive as everybody else with the rules that were preventing us from going ahead and winning that thing. I don't think he would have let it go on like it did. I had some friends who went over there, and a couple of them were killed. So I was very frustrated with the way the war was handled."

Some, like Rocky, were opposed to the war but supported the troops as much as anyone on the club.

"I went on goodwill tours following both the '68 and '69 seasons," Swoboda said. "Guys were drafted into that war largely as conscripts. They didn't go there because they wanted to be there. So I felt like if they had to go there and I was able to dodge that bullet because I was married and my wife was pregnant, then I should at least pay some attention, go there, and see if I could let them know that somebody was interested in where they were, who they were, and what was going on. I didn't go to support the war. I went to support *them*. Because back here, they all became 'baby killers,' and people turned on them. I felt like from the get-go there was something wrong with that war. That's a long way to go from home to protect America."

Swoboda passed on an opportunity to earn $10,000 to join some of us following the World Series to do a two-week Las Vegas act because he had already made a commitment to visit the troops.

"That was a fair piece of change back then," Rocky said. "I think I was making around five thousand a month as a player. When I came back, I went on *The Tonight Show* with guest host Joe Garagiola. I said some things about supporting Nixon's efforts to Vietnamize the war and draw down American troops, which was happening. I ended up getting invited to the White House. Nixon had been briefed on the fact that I had gone on the USO tour instead of going to Las Vegas and brought it up. He told me I did the right thing and that I would make up the money somewhere else along the way. But, you know, even though he wanted to Vietnamize the war and draw down troops, Nixon sort of tricked us a little bit. He was trying to win the negotiations in the war, so he escalated the bombing and invaded Cambodia. So 'Dick' tricked us a little bit."

But out of all of us, nobody's direction in life changed more because of the Vietnam War than Ron Taylor's did. Ron visited military hospitals there and saw the horrors of war firsthand. He took phone numbers from soldiers and called their families after he returned stateside to let them know their sons were okay. So moved by the experience, instead of sitting on the sidelines, he wanted to do his part. So he decided to help the sick and wounded by becoming a doctor.

"The turning point for me," Taylor said, "was going on those Vietnam trips and seeing what was going on over there. So many people were getting killed or badly injured—just a *terrible* situation. I wasn't necessarily opposed to the war. I was opposed to people *dying*. It turned my life around because, at that time, I knew I wasn't going to be able to play baseball forever. That's when I decided to go to medical school."

It was a very ambitious decision for Ron to make because of two factors: his age, thirty-four when he retired in 1972, and the fact that he already had a degree in engineering. He would be starting over again in a completely different field.

"I met with the dean at the University of Toronto and said, 'I think I'd like to go back to school and get a medical degree.' He asked, 'What have you been doing?' I said, 'Well, I've been playing baseball.' He said, 'What's that?' I thought, *Oh boy, this isn't going well.* He then asked how old I was. I said simply, 'Well, I'm old.' He said, 'We very rarely take anybody over a certain age. But let me look over your transcript.' He looked it over, saw that I had straight As in engineering, and said, 'Well, these are very good. Why don't you take a year and see how you do with some courses in the sciences. If you do well, we'll support you.'

"And that's what I did," said Ron, who was born and raised in Toronto. "It was very difficult because I had gone from being an easygoing baseball player to studying day and night. Engineering was really quite easy for me, but in medicine, a lot of it is memory work. That was something I wasn't used to, but I managed to get through it. I ended up getting straight As and became the oldest person at their medical school."

After graduation, Ron trained and practiced medicine in Toronto before returning to baseball as the team physician for the Blue Jays for well over thirty years.

Here at home, the war changed the way people lived and how they looked at leadership and authority. We had political upheaval, social unrest, and a lot of hate. The country was in rapid decline. To paraphrase Bob Dylan's song—the times were a-changin'.

"In '69 I went to a basketball game at the University of Iowa," McAndrew, a native of the state, recalled. "I hadn't been back there since '66, when it still had a pre—Vietnam War environment—still fairly conservative and easygoing. But just three years later, I thought I was in a different world. It was like I didn't know where I was. The culture had changed so much that it was 180 degrees different. It really shocked me, I guess, because I was in my own little world and not aware of everything that was going on around me until that point in time. It was, as you say, the best of times and the worst of times. Of course, one of the beautiful things that happened in '69 was our miracle season."

Nothing could be more true. We were a blue-collar team that no one expected to win. When we started to play well during our eleven-game winning streak, we made New Yorkers, baseball fans around the country, and even our soldiers over in Vietnam feel like there was potentially hope in anything they did. We started making people feel better about a bad time—whether it was the war, the economy, the racial unrest, or anything else negatively affecting their lives. People saw the lovable losers starting to win, and it did more than just make them happy, it gave them reason to believe that there was some light at the end of the tunnel for all the problems of the time. Anything was now possible.

When I worked on my book *The Magnificent Seasons*, I tracked down Vietnam veterans and found some who followed sports while stationed overseas. When I heard from them how we made them feel better about being in one of the worst places in the world at the time, it actually gave me chills. I have always felt that if a person can do something to make someone else's life a little better, then you've really accomplished something.

"The United States needed something to believe in," Donn Clendenon told me back in 2004. "We helped relieve some of the agony of losing so many of our young American people in the jungles of Vietnam."

And perhaps even more than that, we created thousands of new baseball fans that year.

"When we started winning, we turned people's heads and hearts where they became baseball fans for the first time," J. C. Martin said. "They thought about miracles that had never taken place in their lives. They felt like they were a piece and a part of the New York Mets. They saw this miracle happening and thought how this could happen in their own life and in our country. It made a great statement of what can happen when people get together for one effort. It really picked up the whole country. Even foreign people started paying attention to what the Mets were doing."

In essence, we were becoming an escape from reality for so many and began drawing huge crowds every game. It was a crazy world outside the stadium, and for a couple of hours a day, fans could get caught up in what we were accomplishing. Nobody was thinking World Series at that point, but now in second place and six games above .500 following our eleventh consecutive victory on June 8—a come-from-behind 3–2 squeaker over the Padres, saved by Taylor—we dared people to think of what was possible. Up until this point in team history, the Mets had never before been over .500 one-third of the way through a season. Shea Stadium was becoming a field of dreams.

CHAPTER 5

THE CLUBHOUSE LAWYER

– June 15, 1969 –

FOLLOWING THE STREAK, WE COOLED OFF AND LOST THREE of our next four games. Our offense was as anemic as it had been all season, scoring a total of just seven runs in those contests. Of course, it didn't help that we faced three future Hall of Fame pitchers over that span—Gaylord Perry, of the Giants, and the Dodgers' Don Sutton and Don Drysdale—but the fact remained that we needed more juice in our lineup. And in a trading deadline deal on June 15, we accomplished just that, acquiring six-foot-four-inch slugger Donn Clendenon from the Montreal Expos in a trade that would have a profound effect both in the clubhouse and on the field.

I remembered Donn best as one of the big, strong bats in the middle of those great-hitting Pittsburgh Pirates teams of the sixties that also featured Willie Stargell and Roberto Clemente. He was often overshadowed by the greatness of those two Hall of Famers, but I was hopeful that he was going to use the hot spotlight of New York as a platform to put his underappreciated talents on display.

"All those years with the Pirates, I thought we would eventually win a World Series because we had great hitting," Clendenon told me in 2004, a year before he died of leukemia. "But we lacked good pitching. So when Johnny Murphy asked if I would report to the

Mets, I was thrilled because I knew they had a wealth of pitching and were strong up the middle. I just felt they needed a little better timely hitting. So I was glad to get over there."

Similar to the way we acquired Seaver, Koosman, and Gentry, the thirty-three-year-old Clendenon also came to the Mets under highly unusual circumstances. "Clink," as he was nicknamed following a box score abbreviation that once appeared in a Philadelphia newspaper, was selected by the Montreal Expos in the 1969 expansion draft. The Expos then traded him to the Houston Astros. But there was just one issue: Clink refused to report to the Astros because he didn't want to play for their manager, the cantankerous Harry Walker. Clink, who went on to practice law, knew his rights, so he remained with the Expos until the club worked out a deal with the Mets for Steve Renko, Kevin Collins, and three minor leaguers. The deal paid dividends immediately, as we would win eight of our next ten games with Clink, and all his swagger, now on the ball club.

"When Clendenon came on board," McAndrew said, "you got the feeling that if the pitchers kept a ball game close, he would help us win it with his bat. Up until then, if we gave up a run, it was like, 'Uh-oh.' We were blessed to pick up Donn because he was one of those guys that could carry a club for a couple of weeks when he got hot. He might start hitting long balls, and all of a sudden, instead of losing 1–0 or 2–1, you start winning those games 3–2. At the end of the year, you win a hundred games because you win twenty or thirty more one-run games than you lose. It's such a fine line."

As a club, we were universally enamored with what Clink could bring us—even Krane, who knew he would lose significant playing time at first base to the right-handed-hitting Clendenon as a part of Gil's platoon system.

"Obviously, that part of it was frustrating," Eddie told me. "I just wanted to play. We didn't get to the major leagues by not playing in the minors. There's no platooning there; you play every day. And if you can hit, you can hit. Period. Give me enough opportunities, and I see that curveball start to look fatter and fatter. But Gil just had a theory about platooning. You either had to respect him for it and accept your role, or he would get rid of you. But to his credit, he never fooled around with the lineup. There were never any surprises. We didn't come to the ballpark not knowing who was going to play, so you could really prepare yourself for the game. If the other team was throwing a right-hander, I was at first. If they threw a left-hander, Donn was there. Life around Gil was very easy. To him, there was just one way to play each game: with the intention of winning it. We would have won many more pennants if Gil did not pass on. He was our inspirational leader. Other managers filled in afterward, but they were not the leader that Hodges was, and that's why we all respected him. Even though I had my discrepancies with him when he first joined the club, at the end of his time he was my biggest rooter because he saw me develop. And I respected him for having disagreements with me, not playing me, and forcing me to play my way back into the lineup. He made me a better player.

"So I was now forced to play some outfield and pinch-hit more," Krane continued. "But Donn was a great guy and came from a Pirates organization built around hitting, so it was a good balance for the Mets, who previously were only concerned about the pitching staff. With Donn, we got a little more offensive minded."

Aside from what Clink provided us on the field, his outspoken nature and never-ending needling also contributed to a clubhouse dynamic already filled with a diverse and larger-than-life cast of characters.

"How many teams had a clubhouse lawyer like Clendenon, who was actually studying to be a lawyer and was good at it?" Rocky once asked me rhetorically. "And he was a black guy in the sixties that had what a lot of us didn't have: a winter job. Most of us just farted around and did appearances in the off-season to stay afloat but didn't have a real job. He did. But 'Clen' was a motormouth, and sometimes you wanted to go, '*Shut the f—k up!*' I mean, he got on *everybody*, top to bottom. I don't know what the hell you would get on Seaver about, but he would. He wasn't above sitting there holding court. It was funny the way it happened—nothing was assigned—he just assumed that role. He could say shit because of his stature, the fact he was a good, veteran player, and had a college education. Most people took it in the right way. But he was special because I think his razzing kept the clubhouse kind of loose."

"He was loud, but he was a *positive* loud," DiLauro said. "And he backed up what he had to say on the playing field."

"His locker was next to mine," recalled Bobby Pfeil, who subbed at third base, second, and even put in some time in the outfield. "I didn't have to *talk* to him. I *heard* everything!"

The funny thing about my first encounter with Clink after he arrived in New York was how he started getting all over me about the four home runs in consecutive at bats I hit against his Pittsburgh team when I was with Cincinnati in 1966. He said, "We shoulda hit you after the first one! We shoulda knocked you right down! How in the world could *you* hit four home runs in a row?!" And he never let up on it. When we were both out of the game—even when he was sick!—he would tell me, "You know what? We should have knocked you down!" He never got over it. The guy had an unbelievable memory.

It turned out that was just a prelude of things to come. Clink simply wasn't afraid to try to embarrass you. He was particularly relentless with Boswell and me. One time we went out with him for a few drinks, and the next day, in front of the entire clubhouse, he yells out at Kenny, "Bozzie, you cheap bastard! We had three drinks, and you left the bartender *one dollar*! You *cheap bastard*!"

Another time, he got on Boz and me, yelling across the room how horrible we looked in our uniforms, that they were too baggy, and we were embarrassing him and the Mets. So Kenny and I took them off and threw them on the floor. When our clubhouse guy, Nick Torman, started screaming at us for throwing clean uniforms on the floor, I told him, "Clendenon said they looked baggy." So he started screaming at Clink.

"That son-of-a-gun Clendenon," Joe Pignatano said. "He had a Doberman pinscher—a real big one—and he says to Gil, 'I gotta bring my dog to the vet; he's gotta get a shot. Can I bring him to the ballpark and keep him there?' Gil said he could. So the next day, Clendenon brings the dog into the clubhouse and makes a motion for him to go to my locker and to sit right in front of me. So I go to Donn, 'How long is he gonna sit there?' And every time I tried to get out of the goddamn locker, the Doberman wouldn't let me pass. Gil comes by and says, 'Hey! It's time for you go to the field!' And I said to Hodges, 'Yeah! You're probably a part of this, aren't you?' And he just smiled—he and Clendenon were having some fun at my expense. Donn was actually a good guy who really helped our ball club."

It was like a sitcom, with all the craziness he brought to that locker room. But truth be told, Clink may have been an agitator, but he was never a distraction—at least not for me. In fact, he could take it as well as he could dish it out. To get back at him, Kenny and I would get on him in the batting cage, telling him how bad he looked. Things like, "You're not gonna take that swing in your game tonight, are ya?" Or, when he started practicing law, I'd say, "I wouldn't let you handle a speeding ticket for me!" You just had to know how to deal with him.

To his credit, he wouldn't have acted the way he did if, in any way, it hurt the chemistry we had in the clubhouse. In fact, sometimes he went the other way and actually defended some guys.

"Clendenon was actually my biggest supporter," McAndrew once told me. "I was easily the brunt of jokes in the locker room. Clink was the first one to defend me. I guess he knew that I was a wimp or whatever you want to call it from a personality standpoint, and I was never confrontational. Well, Clink *loved* being confrontational, so he stepped up for me all the time!"

"I wanted to keep everybody loose," Clink once explained to me. "Guys knew I was joking—that was the key to it."

J. C. Martin agreed, noting, "You can unwind a spring in the clubhouse or you can tighten that son of a gun until it breaks. That was the good thing we had in our clubhouse: we all enjoyed the ribbing. It was not only a great time but a successful time."

And that's the thing I miss most since I retired from the game in 1972: the locker room banter. Of course, I wish I made the kind of money they're making now, but it's the friendships, the camaraderie, the characters, the freedom to say anything you wanted, and the ability to deal with adversity in whatever way worked best for you where I feel the greatest void. There was something special on that Mets team: the closeness. We had practically no genuine friction at all. This, despite all of the different characters we had that made up that clubhouse. You had the low-key, sarcastic, and self-degrading Ronnie Taylor, who wore little horn-rimmed, John Lennon–like glasses and sat on the clubhouse floor reading Socrates or some medical journal. And then there was the always-grumpy Jerry Grote, about whom we could never figure out what or who he liked. We had the gregarious Tug McGraw regularly doing outrageous things. You had Tommie and Cleon always arguing over something, as debates raged between the ultraconservative Cardwell and the "flower child" Swoboda at completely opposite ends of the social spectrum. You had Clink screaming something across the locker room at somebody, while Ed Charles was reading, writing, and reciting poetry. And then, of course, there was Kooz, who, when he would bait you, it was hilarious—unlike Clink, whose barbs tended to sting a little more.

"Koosman was always getting on me," recalled Ed Charles. "One game, I was sitting on the bench with the rest of the guys, and here comes Kooz walking down the dugout. When he gets close to me, he hollers out in a loud voice, 'Hey, Glider, you better get your rest because you got to *watch* two tomorrow!' And everybody started laughing. But I came back at him and said, 'You're pretty funny. You better be glad you don't have to pitch to me because I would light your butt up!' That was the kind of stuff that kept us loose. Oh boy, we had a lot of fun on that team!"

"Jerry was our comedian," Wayne Garrett said. "Clendenon was funny at times, too, but Kooz was the best. He was such an even-keeled person that you could never tell by looking at him if he was winning or losing a game because he never showed his emotions. But God, what a great guy. And if we had to attribute our success to one player the most that year, Koosman was number one."

If there was one guy who I would proclaim as the "anti-Clendenon" on the club, it was the Glider, the oldest player on the team at age thirty-six. He had such a calming influence and was able to get through to us on a personal level. In many ways, he was like a player-coach, and served the greatest benefit to our rookies as they adjusted to the big leagues.

"Eddie really helped me a lot," said Garrett, who, at twenty-one, was the youngest player on the team and alternated with Glider at third base. "Gosh, if I had to give credit to anybody for having an opportunity to stay in the majors being so young like I was, it would be Ed. I was always hard on myself, and if I didn't do good, Eddie would always come by, put his arm around me, and say things like,

'It's okay, it's okay, there's plenty of games to play. Don't worry about it—you'll get another chance.' He calmed me down and I appreciated that while I built up my confidence, which Eddie was always there to reinforce. I owe a lot to Eddie."

What a lot of people forget was that Eddie was a terrific player. Unfortunately, in part because of Jim Crow, it took him a long time to get to the big leagues: he was about to turn twenty-nine when he finally broke in with the Kansas City A's in 1962, after almost a decade stranded in the minors. But Eddie could play third base with the best of them. It's long surprised me how the Mets phased him out following the season, because Eddie clearly could still play the field and hit. And his locker room presence and influence were so important to us. To me, he was an icon not necessarily for his stats but for his stature and everything he'd had to overcome in life. When I look back at my career and all the guys I played with, I am most honored to have played with Eddie Charles. So why wouldn't you want a guy like that back on your team? It remains a mystery to me.

For as different as the Glider was from Clink, the Mets paired them up as roommates on the road, and everything worked out just fine. But unquestionably, Eddie had a slightly different perspective of Clendenon than most of the rest of us.

"He gave me my space and knew my temperament," Charles told me. "There was a mutual respect. And I was glad we got him—he really solidified our lineup. But the other thing he did was loosen things up. Some of the guys worried too much or were too tight. He'd come into the locker room with a little humor and banter and get guys to laugh a little bit."

The idea that it was a foregone conclusion in 1969 that once Clendenon joined the club, he would automatically room with another black player in Charles is an issue that's long been troublesome

to me. And to add to that, in our clubhouse, our only four black players had their lockers in the same corner. I'm not saying there was
any form of racism on the Mets, but it brings to mind an inaction on
my part from my earliest days in baseball that still bothers me today.
When I played minor-league ball in 1962 in Macon, Georgia, we
traveled in station wagons, and we would have to drop off the black
players and dark-skinned Latin players at different hotels and restaurants from where the white players stayed and dined. When I look
back at that part of my life, even though I was only nineteen, I regret
that I wasn't adamantly opposed to the blatant segregation that some
of my teammates had to endure. At the time, I was just trying to get
to the next level. Instead, I should have been more vocal over my first
real look at segregation at its worst. I don't know if taking a stand
would have made any difference, but I wish I had tried.

Anyway, the Clendenon trade would go down as one of the very
best in Mets history. Not only did he put up good numbers—.252, 12
HR, 37 RBIs in 72 games—but he also impacted those around him,
making them better players.

"When we saw what Clendenon was capable of doing," said
McAndrew, "we thought, *Well, if he can do it, we can all do it.* So
Donn's play kind of rubbed off on the rest of us."

"We had already begun to play good ball," Boswell recalled, "but
you can't minimize the deal for Clendenon because of the attitude
he brought to us that we may have been missing. And not only did
he drive in some big runs and get some big hits, but he really made
Cleon and Tommie and the rest of us better and more confident
players."

But for me, Rod Gaspar nailed what Clink was all about:

"He could really stir the pot. He might have been the rowdiest
person I ever met in my life. After we were out of baseball, I stayed
in touch with Donn and reached out to him once while he battled

leukemia. He told me the story of how he was sleeping in a hospital bed, and his family thought he was going to die. When he woke up, he looked at them all and asked, 'What the hell are you all doing here?!' He was just too *stubborn* to die at that time. He was something else—*a great talent*—but just crazy!"

CHAPTER 6

A RIVALRY IS BORN

– July 8, 1969 –

BY THE SECOND WEEK OF JULY, WE HAD CUT DOWN THE Cubs' lead to just five and a half games, as we rode a five-game winning streak into a showdown series with them at Shea Stadium. By contrast, Chicago was reeling, having just dropped three straight to the Cardinals. Still, the Cubs were a star-studded team that boasted five future Hall of Famers: players Ernie Banks, Billy Williams, Ron Santo, and Ferguson Jenkins and their abrasive and highly despised manager, Leo Durocher.

"Leo was the kind of guy you disliked just watching him," Kooz recalled. "You disliked the way he managed, the way he argued with the umps, and the way he just looked like an ass chewer."

"Durocher thought he invented the game," said Swoboda. "He was one of those managers you enjoyed beating because, like with Gene Mauch and Billy Martin, you just knew it made him boil inside. It made it so much fun to beat guys like Leo."

"There are certain managers that alienate the opposing team by the little things they do," Krane noted. "His teams were very aggressive, and he managed aggressive. But sometimes when you do that, you wake up the other ball club. You steal a base when you've got a big lead, or you have guys take somebody out with a hard slide—stuff like that. Now you get the other club's emotions going. Sometimes it's better in baseball to let dying dogs die. Just let them lay there until you leave town—then you can talk about them all you want. You need motivation on losing ball clubs. Why wake them up? Why motivate them? So you always looked forward to beating certain managers like Durocher."

Pignatano cut right to the chase, saying simply, "Durocher was a piece of shit."

But while their starting lineup was as good as any in baseball, the Cubs didn't have the pitching depth or bullpen that we did. And they also lacked something else we had heading into that pivotal series: momentum.

"We had come from nine games down and had a lot of confidence that we could beat them," Cleon Jones recalled. "I would actually get on my homeboy, Billy Williams—who was from the Mobile area and went to my high school—and Ernie Banks, telling them during that series, 'Look out, we're gaining on you! We're the best team!' At the time, I was just having fun with them, but I also realized we were now a pretty good team that really got along with one another. Even our wives were doing things together. We really cared for each other, and it started to show around then."

The first of the three-game set was critical for us: the difference between moving to within four and a half games of Chicago or dropping back to six and a half. We all knew the importance of winning the opener.

"After winning all those road games in a row going into that series," Krane said, "it was important that we were taking on the Cubs. But if you don't win the first one, you're not going to make up a lot of ground. Also, they're not going to feel any pressure, and they probably go on to win the pennant. But if you win, you're right behind them, and they know somebody's trailing them."

For a Tuesday afternoon in July, the electricity in the ballpark made it feel more like serious October baseball, with more than fifty-five thousand fans in attendance. Over that last month, it seemed like we were regularly playing before big crowds at Shea. When I would go out to right field before the start of a game, I remember looking out at the subway platform beyond the bullpen, watching people rush to get into the ballpark. They didn't want to miss that first pitch. And now on the opening night of this series, you could hear the crowd start to rev up with excitement and anticipation even before the national anthem was over. I recall looking up at that awesome stadium packed with people. It was a rush like nothing I had experienced before.

It would be a classic pitchers' duel between Kooz and Jenkins. Fergie, on his way to a third straight twenty-win season (with another three still to come), was a terrific pitcher who we referred to as the Surgeon for the way he could pitch to any kind of hitter. He put up remarkable numbers for Chicago despite pitching his home games in compact Wrigley Field, in the daytime, and with the wind blowing out many afternoons. And his effort that night at Shea would be a vintage Jenkins outing. Through eight innings, Fergie was superb, giving up nothing more than a fifth-inning home run to Krane.

So when Jenkins took the mound to start the bottom of the ninth with a one-hitter and a 3–1 lead, the old Mets would have shriveled up and gone home. But that wouldn't be the case with the competitive ball club we had now.

Boswell, my roommate on the road and dear friend to this day, pinch-hit for Kooz to start our frame. Kenny and I were total opposites, coming from completely different backgrounds. Boz was a good old boy from Texas who, whenever he could, wore his ten-gallon cowboy hat, a big belt buckle, and jeans with so much starch they felt like cardboard. Yet I loved him to death. It's hard to explain how two very different people ended up liking each other the way we did. I guess part of it stemmed from the fact we were both thrown into this New York baseball world neither of us knew much about. We were also both left-handed hitters and were in the same boat as far as Gil's platoon system went, with Boz getting spelled at second mostly by Al Weis. And on the road, we usually went out to eat and have a few drinks after games, often joined by Agee, Jones, Swoboda, Kooz, and a few others. Kenny and I basically went out for one of three reasons: The first was to celebrate if at least one of us had a good game. The second was to go out to forget about a bad game. But the worst scenario of the three came when we were frustrated over not playing—the drinking helped relieve some of the tension. And drink we would; no doubt about that. But we were always under control; we just needed an outlet. When you share glorious moments as well as bad games like I did with Boz—and are able to talk about them together—it makes the relationship that much stronger. So that off-the-field camaraderie with him was very special to us both.

Kenny came through against Jenkins, starting things off with a double to center field. After Agee popped out to first, Gil once again went to his bench and brought up Clink to pinch-hit for Bobby Pfeil. Donn promptly ripped a double to left field to give us runners on second and third and just one out. That would bring up Cleon in a position to tie the game with just a hit.

Jones was having a huge year—batting .352 at the time. But working even more to his favor than his hitting prowess was his familiarity with Jenkins.

"I had the pleasure of playing in Puerto Rico with Fergie for two years in winter ball," Cleon explained to me. "We were actually roommates and running partners. I got to watch him a great deal as a teammate, so I knew what his pitches were, and I knew how he tried to get different guys out. He was a situational pitcher. So if he got into a situation where he knew a guy was a good fastball hitter like me, he was going to try to get him out with a curveball. And that's just what he tried to do against me in that at bat."

Jones crushed yet another double to left to score Boz and Clink and tie the game at 3–3.

"He *hung* that curveball," Jones remembered. "Had it been a good curveball, I might have been dragging my bat back to the bench. Thankfully, it was a hanger, and I was able to get a hit."

With the crowd on its feet and a deafening roar reverberating around Shea, I approached the plate with the winning run on second. I was swinging a hot bat of late, and my average had climbed to .330. But before I had the chance to become a hero, Cubs catcher Randy Hundley put up four fingers to signal an intentional walk. It was a move by Leo to set up the potential for a double-play ball to stop the bleeding and send the game to extra innings.

Fergie induced a ground ball off the bat of Garrett, but it was hit in the hole between first and second, so second baseman Glenn Beckert had to throw the ball to first for the second out. In doing so, Cleon and I each moved up a base to second and third.

That would bring up Krane, who had taken Jenkins deep earlier in the game and was seeing the ball well against him. Eddie came through again, blooping one into left center field in front of Don Young to score Cleon with the winning run and give us a big-time 4–3 walk-off victory.

"Our comeback in the ninth inning put us on a plateau," remarked Krane. "Now we've got the Cubs really looking over their shoulders. We were putting a little pressure on Chicago."

"Everything was going our way on what we were concentrating on: winning games," Jones said. "We weren't looking ahead at a possible championship. We were still just looking to get better and improve ourselves because we were a young team. But none of what we were accomplishing surprised me. I actually went to spring training that year thinking that I could hit .300 or better, and when I looked at all the pieces around me, I could see other guys who could do better than the previous season as well. Learning how to win and learning how not to beat yourself—those two things came together for us in the first half of that year because Gil wasn't allowing us to beat ourselves. And that was turning us into a championship-caliber team because if you don't beat yourself, it's difficult for the other folks to beat you. We were beginning to see what Gil saw in spring training when he uttered those words that we were better than we thought we were."

What we were doing was starting to figure out how to win close games no matter what team we played or who we were facing—even someone as great as Ferguson Jenkins. That was the biggest difference with the '69 team compared with the one the year before. We basically had the same pitching and, with the notable exception of Clendenon, pretty much the same hitters. But collectively, we went from a club that always seemed to find ways of losing games to winning them. Part of that was teaching. Part of that was experience. And part of it was just learning how to play better baseball.

While this comeback win against the Cubs can easily be forgotten among all the momentous games of 1969, I would put it right up there as one of the biggest of the year. It really set the tone for the rest of the season. Many of us from that club believe it was our coming-of-age game, as well as the dawning of a fierce rivalry with the Cubs. For the players and our fans, it a game none of us will ever forget.

CHAPTER 7

THE IMPERFECT GAME

– July 9, 1969 –

OUR CLUB WAS ON A TREMENDOUS HIGH FOLLOWING THE previous night's incredible comeback win over the Cubs and their ace, Fergie Jenkins. The Mets, now 46-34, for a .575 win-loss percentage, were absolutely the talk of New York, and we couldn't wait to get to the ballpark.

"We were the hottest commodity in baseball," Jones said. "We now knew that we could beat anybody. No longer were we a young team trying to find its way. Instead, we were now a mature team that had confidence in themselves and in its leadership to go out and win. We came out to the park knowing that there would be fifty thousand people in the stands every game now."

On this night, with Tom Seaver taking the hill and the Cubs' lead down to four and a half games, Cleon's numbers would be way off. The announced crowd may have been 50,709, but the number easily exceeded 60,000, if you included standing room only and the spectators watching from the subway ramp. Our fans were extremely loyal back then and fell in love with all the young stars we had coming up from the farm system. And none was bigger than Seaver.

Many fans were probably wondering how the drama of last night's win could possibly be surpassed. But we all knew that if there was one person capable of doing just that, it was Seaver. Tommy was the kind of pitcher who when he took the mound, you knew he was capable of throwing a no-hitter, a perfect game, or striking out nineteen at any time. He was as good a pitcher as anyone in baseball that year. Playing behind him, you always had to be on your toes, because he was consistently throwing strikes at a quick pace. He regularly threw nine-inning shutouts in less than two hours. You knew you could make plans for after a game he pitched. I'd tell friends I would see them three hours after first pitch—two hours for the game, then a quick shower, and then the time it took to get where I would meet them. It was like clockwork with Seaver.

Never one who lacked in the confidence department, Tommy once told me that when he was on the mound, "You better not leave your seat, or you'd miss two innings."

We were all in awe of him, with some even having a case of Seaver envy.

"He was a child-god to me," said McAndrew. "We all admired and respected him, while at the same time were jealous of him too. You're thinking, *Gee, I wish I could do what he does.* It's kind of like taking an exam, and there's a kid that always gets As, and you get Bs. You wish you got As, but God doesn't make us all the same. But I think Seaver was the main reason that so many of the guys got that much better because they knew he was so good, and you were striving to do your best to achieve the greatness that he was in the midst of. We wanted to emulate his behavior and have it rub off on us. He was just such a tenacious competitor—the ultimate performer—who had dominating stuff. Plus, he had that great, young body with a thirty-five-year-old baseball head on his shoulders. It was mind-boggling how mature and disciplined he was at such a young age." Seaver, in his third season, and the dean of the staff, was still just twenty-four years old.

"He was smart enough to know when he was off his game," Harrelson, his road roommate for years and best friend on the team, told me. "So when he was off, I'd visit him at the mound, and he'd go to me, 'Roomie, I got shit. Get in the hole.' That meant he wanted me to move away from my normal positioning at shortstop and move closer to third. So with the hitters still looking for his fastball, he would start throwing these little, bitty sliders that they would get out in front of and hit over to me. I'd catch them and throw the guys out at first. He kept doing that until he found his good stuff again. Then he picked up the rosin bag and tossed it on to the ground, which was our sign for me to move back to my regular position."

As the Cubs came up to hit in the top of the first, I could tell right away that Seaver had his best stuff. You had the feel after he struck out their leadoff batter, Don Kessinger, and their number three hitter, Billy Williams, that something special could happen. Just playing the Cubs was exciting enough, but throw in a dominating pitcher like Seaver going up against another budding All-Star in Kenny Holtzman, my old high school friend from St. Louis, and it was must-see baseball.

We would take it right to Holtzman in our half of the first. Agee led things off with a triple to right field and quickly scored after the next batter, Bobby Pfeil, doubled to left to give us the early 1–0 lead. Pfeil was seeing more time in the infield as Harrelson fulfilled his army reserve duties up at Fort Drum near Watertown, New York, just south of the Canadian border.

"I wanted so badly to be with the team during that time," recalled Buddy, "but the answer I got from an officer was something like: 'I don't give a shit if you're with the Mets!' I actually would get out early because I performed my duties so well. But then they would replace me with other Mets. There were a lot of us that had to go into the reserves. But it was better than going into the army, where you might end up dead."

After Seaver struck out all three batters he faced in the

second—Santo, Banks, and Al Spangler—he helped his own cause by belting an RBI single to score Grote to give us a 2–0 lead. Then Agee stayed hot by slicing a double to right field to score Weis for a 3–0 lead. For Agee, whose average climbed to around the .300 mark, it was a remarkable rebound from his lost '68 season.

"I think Gil had a big role in that," his friend Cleon said. "And the players were great—nobody ever put Tommie down. Even though he had that bad year in '68, everybody was so supportive. During that winter, I worked out with Tommie in Mobile and found some things he was doing wrong with his hitting, like striding too soon. He came back that spring a different player. He had a different attitude about everything. Once the season started, whenever things started to go wrong at the plate for him, he would look to the bench to see if we noticed anything. We all wanted to help him. I think that's what team unity can do for a player. He regained his confidence and ended up having a great year."

As Seaver cruised through the middle innings, it wasn't lost on anyone how Tom had so dominated the Cubs that none of them had reached base. It was also apparent that Grote was calling a magnificent game, helping Seaver keep a terrific Chicago lineup off balance all game long.

"We had some guys on that team that didn't get enough credit—most notably Grote," said Pfeil, who had spent eight years in the minors before getting called up that year. "He was awfully special. He was perfect for Seaver and the rest of the pitching staff. And with his difficult personality, I don't think he'd be perfect for a lot of other pitching staffs."

Oh yes, that personality.

"Grote was a bitch," Cleon said bluntly. "He was a bitch when he got in his car, a bitch when he went out the gate to go home, and a bitch when he came to the ballpark through the parking lot, where there were a lot of people. Everybody was a son of a bitch to him. Once he was inside Shea, he was like, *'Just get out of my way, I've got work to do!'* But once we got together as a family unit with our wives, he was the nicest guy you'd ever want to meet. He was gentle. It's only when he saw that ballpark that he got to be an angry man. Of course, that's the way he played. If anybody got in his way, he would try to hurt him. I saw Grote recently and asked him, 'Where did all that anger come from when you put that uniform on?' All he did was laugh. Everybody was a no-good son of a bitch to him when he put that uniform on, but once he put on his street clothes, he was the nicest guy."

But not Jones, or any of us that saw Grote play every day, ever questioned his skills behind the plate.

"He was the best defensive catcher in the game," Cleon praised. "And he really worked at it. Even Lou Brock had a lot of good things to say about him." The speedy Cardinals outfielder, en route to leading the National League in stolen bases for a fourth straight year, was one of the preeminent stolen base artists in the history of the game. "Lou also used to try to make him mad during warm-ups. He'd holler out, 'Grote, I'm going to run on you!' And Jerry would say something like, 'You son of a bitch! God, I really want you to try!' And Grote would really get upset about it, running into the clubhouse saying, 'I wish he would run on me!' But you know, you play with twenty-five different guys, and all of them have a different attitude and different ways of looking at things. When game time comes, we all approach it differently."

But with guys like Grote, some approach the game far differently than most. Maybe his orneriness was what he needed to pump himself up and be a better player. I guess you would have to talk to a psychiatrist about that. Joe Valerio of the *New York Post* once wrote colorfully, "Will Rogers never met Jerry Grote." Of course, it didn't surprise me that Valerio, as a journalist, would feel this way. Jerry was pretty brutal with the press. Our lockers were close, and one time a sportswriter came by and asked, "Jerry, what about that 3–2 pitch in the eighth inning? What were you thinking in that situation?" And Grote snapped, "What the hell do you mean?! You were there! You were in the press box! What are you asking me for?!" I believe, in the long run, Jerry actually hurt himself by not being friendly with the writers because they could have really given him the credit that he deserved as a superior defensive catcher. But that was just him, and he often wasn't much better with his own pitchers. During tense games, he sometimes threw the ball back to guys like Kooz and McAndrew extremely hard—to the point where it stung their glove hand. And God forbid someone shake off one of his signs. Grote was simply the kind of guy I loved having on our team for his fierce competitiveness, but if he played for another club, I probably would have despised him.

As the game moved into the later innings, Seaver continued to overwhelm the Cubs. It hardly seemed fair when Cleon slugged a home run to increase our lead to 4–0 in the seventh. It might as well have been 400–0. But instead of enjoying our comfortable lead, the tension of Tom's potential date with destiny increased with every Cubs hitter he retired.

"As an infielder that night," said Pfeil, who started at second but was moved to third in the top of the eighth, "there was added pressure because there wasn't room for any mistakes."

Said Krane, "There was a hush in the stadium—the fans and the guys expected something special to happen. We could just feel it. Tom was just mowing them down and dominated the game from pitch one. In the dugout, nobody talked to him at all. He stayed within himself, which was typical most of the time anyway because he concentrated all the time. He was a real professional with the art of pitching, knew how to get the most out of his body, and when he took over a game, there was no finer pitcher than Tom Seaver."

Now it was the top of the ninth. Seaver needed just three more outs to notch what would be only the eighth perfect game in the modern baseball era. *Nobody* in the ballpark was sitting down. Randy Hundley, the first batter, tried to bunt his way on, but he bunted the ball too hard right back to Tommy, who threw him out easily. The crowd's raucous cheers turned to merciless boos at Hundley as he jogged back to the Cubs' dugout. Mets fans saw his bunt as a cheap attempt to break up the perfect game.

Up next was a little-known rookie part-time center fielder, Jimmy Qualls. It's ironic, but with the rest of the Cubs lineup filled with stars, Seaver told me afterward that he was concerned about the young left-handed hitter in that situation because he didn't know much about him. Also, Qualls had lined out hard to right field in the third inning and gotten around on a pitch he grounded out to first in the sixth.

Qualls swung at Tom's first pitch, a sinker that came in waist-high over the middle of the plate, and hit a flare the other way into short left center field. Cleon and Agee both broke hard for the ball, but it dropped in for a hit to end Seaver's bid at immortality. I looked out at Tommy, who had his hands on his hips and his head bowed slightly—clearly dejected—and thought about the beauty of our sport. As badly as I felt for Seaver, we played a game in which one of the weaker hitters on the field that night could come through against one of the greatest pitchers of all time. At any given moment, *anybody* can get the better of you—even a career .223 hitter with just thirty-one lifetime hits.

Tom gathered himself and retired the final two batters to

complete his masterpiece and pull us to within three and a half games of Chicago. And while Qualls would hardly play after that '69 season, his name would live on forever in Mets history. In a sense, I've always felt that this so-called imperfect game took on mythical proportions as the decades have gone by—made even greater by the fact Seaver never did pitch a perfect game. And Tom once told me as much.

"It became a *bigger* game than if I had actually pitched a perfect game," he once affirmed. "With one out in the ninth, Qualls gets the hit to left field. Nancy was in tears after the game. But before sixty thousand fans, I pitched a one-hitter, didn't walk anybody, struck out eleven, and we won 4–0—and it was against the *Chicago Cubs*! It may have been the *best* game I ever pitched!"

And a game that has taken on a life of its own in Mets lore.

If there was one game in the history of that magical season that should be ranked at the very top, it was this one. As disappointing as it was for all of us to see Seaver lose the perfect game at the very end, it's a game that is still talked about and dissected almost fifty years later. Tom would go on to pitch a no-hitter with the Reds, but the feat paled in comparison to this game.

CHAPTER 8

ONE SMALL STEP FOR MAN, ONE GIANT LEAP FOR THE METS

– July 15–20, 1969 –

OUR NOW FIERCE RIVALRY WITH CHICAGO CONTINUED LESS than a week later at Wrigley Field. I absolutely loved playing there. Wrigley was a wonderfully vibrant and charming old ballpark, built in 1914. As a hitter, it was especially great, as the wind typically blew out during the summer months. And, of course, after the games— always played in the afternoon, because the stadium didn't add lights until 1988—you had a full night ahead of you hitting popular hangouts of Rush Street, eating at nice restaurants and enjoying the nightlife. Still, the best part of those Chicago trips was Wrigley Field, with its ivy-covered brick walls, manually operated scoreboard, and legion of loyal Cubs fans.

As an outfielder, I became very familiar with Wrigley's infamous "Bleacher Bums," a most rowdy and vocal group. One time during batting practice while shagging fly balls, I heard this screechy female voice shout out to me, "Shamsky! You suck! You can't hit! We hate you!" I kept repeating to myself, *Don't turn around. Whatever you do, just don't turn around.* And I didn't—at least not then. Fast-forward to the completion of the top of the sixth inning after I made the last out. This same fan had been riding me all game long, and as I ran to right field and began taking some warm-up throws, again I heard the same screeching voice, this time shouting, "Shamsky, I told you you *sucked*! You can't do *anything*!" That was it for me—I'd heard enough of this crap. So I whipped around, and here's this absolutely beautiful young girl wearing a bikini top and a Cubs hat putting suntan lotion on her arms. Noticing me looking at her, she goes, 'Yeah, Shamsky, it was *me*! You *suck*!' I couldn't believe it. In my mind, the person shouting was going to be this hideous-looking woman who probably had a few too many beers. Nothing could have surprised me more when it turned out to be the exact opposite. I learned from that point on that it didn't matter what Cubs fans looked like—they all hated us.

Well, except for maybe one. I'll explain. While in Chicago, the club stayed at the Executive House Hotel. One night after going out, Boz and I are just kind of lounging around our room in our underwear. The phone rings, Boz picks it up, and a man on the other end tells him how good he looks without his clothes on! The guy must have had binoculars and was peering into our room from the apartments across the inner-city canal. We couldn't believe he figured out our room number and called us. I'm guessing maybe he worked at the hotel, but it was one of the strangest things. Anyway, it was just one more indication that the Mets had truly arrived. And, by the way, Kenny hung up on him!

But getting back to those Bleacher Bums: they were the first fans to throw opposing teams' home run balls back onto the field. They did it to show their beloved Cubs that they were behind them to the point of giving up a great souvenir: *a home run ball*! Now, of course, that tradition happens at most every ballpark around the major leagues. But, you know, of all the home runs I hit at Wrigley, I really wish I would have gotten one of those balls back from somebody.

· · ·

After losing the opening contest of the three game series—a 1–0 pitching duel between Bill Hands and Seaver on July 14—to drop us to six games out of first, we would battle back to take the next two thanks to the unlikeliest of sources. In the first victory, with the game tied at one in the top of the fourth, I led off with a single and then moved to third on Krane's single. That brought up Al Weis, affectionately called Mighty Mite by Mets broadcaster Lindsey Nelson for his skinny six-foot, 160-pound frame. Weiso, as the players called him, was not a real good hitter—as he'd be the first to admit. At best, he was a singles hitter who didn't strike out a lot. Weis's value to the club was his glove, not his bat. But in this situation, he would hit his first home run of the season (and just his fifth in eight seasons) over the ivy-covered left field wall off our '68 Mets teammate Dick Selma to give us a commanding 4–1 lead en route to a 5–4 win. Then, in our second victory of the series, Al would come through again, this time with a solo home run in the top of the fifth off left-hander Rich Nye to give us a 7–5 edge. If I was shocked by the one he hit the previous day, for him to hit another in our very next game was simply *unreal*. I added a two-run blast in the eighth for some insurance runs in our 9–5 win—trimming the Cubs' lead back down to four games.

"It was a great experience to homer in back-to-back games, especially playing in my hometown of Chicago," Weis told me. "I had a lot of people I knew at those games. But the other big part of it was how each time we beat the Cubs, we would pick up a game. And whether it was me or one of the other guys, we were going to find a way to win. I credit Gil with getting the most out of all his players, whether on defense, offense, when to bring in different pitchers—stuff like that. Everyone was involved, and whether you played or didn't, you rooted for the guys that did. Remember the 1979 Pittsburgh Pirates had that slogan 'We Are Family'? Well, the '69 Mets were like that, too. We all got along well and accepted our roles."

Of course, accepting our roles as platoon players may have hurt our careers in the long run, but you couldn't argue with success. Gil's system was working. Besides, Hodges wasn't the kind of guy you could march up to and say, 'Hey, I got three hits last night. How come I'm not playing today?' He wasn't going to change his mind about the platoon system and playing the averages. But while I may have felt some frustration over playing time, Weis's words ring true: we still supported one another. I always pulled for Rocky, my cotenant in right field. And that was mostly because we genuinely liked each other. We were all friends who shared time in the locker room and time where we had dinner and drinks together. On any given night on the road, there could be eight to ten guys going out together. We usually talked a little bit about that day's game, but a lot of it would be anything friends would normally discuss with one another. And I think those bonds we had contributed greatly to the success of that team.

But for as well as we played against the Cubs that year, there was visibly something else working to our advantage as the All-Star break was approaching: our archnemesis was beginning to look a little lethargic.

"I've said for many years that while we remained fresh, the Cubs were wearing down," Garrett said, alluding to the dog days of summer. "We really had maybe only three everyday players: Buddy, Cleon, and Agee. The rest of us basically platooned. But their same starters were out there practically every day. And there was a heat wave in Chicago that summer. The days that we were there were over a hundred degrees. I once almost had heat exhaustion and stayed in the clubhouse as much as I could. I couldn't imagine being a Chicago Cubs player dealing with all their day games. Plus, they were older, more seasoned veterans playing in that kind of weather. The physical effect that took on them must have been tough. I remember thinking after that July series, *God, I could never play in Chicago.* But because they didn't have lights at Wrigley then, they had to play all day games."

Still, Wayne didn't dismiss at all the vast improvement of our ball club. "After that series in Chicago, I thought, *We can stand toe-to-toe and beat any team in this league.* Coming into that year, I had no idea how good or bad our team was. But now the confidence was there, and it continued to grow with each series we won."

What was also becoming clear was how we had an edge over the Cubs in certain areas. They may have had a terrific lineup, but their bench wasn't very deep. And while they had three good starting pitchers in Hands, Jenkins, and Holtzman, they didn't have much in the way of secondary pitchers to come in for doubleheaders or when they played a string of games without any days off. And lastly, they didn't have the great relief pitching we had. So I believe those deficiencies made a difference and really hurt them. And as Wayne pointed out, that realization only fueled our confidence.

July 17 was an off day for us, as we traveled to Montreal to take on the Expos in a four-game series. But while we enjoyed the emotional high of our surprising ascent near the top of the NL East standings, trouble was brewing just two hundred miles southwest of Shea Stadium in the small city of York, Pennsylvania. It was on that date that several days of rioting, fighting, and arson began after a white gang member shot and wounded a black youth, seventeen-year-old Taka Nii Sweeney. More than sixty people were injured in the rioting, with more than a hundred arrests. The next day, the life of rookie police patrolman Henry C. Schaad was lost after being fatally shot by an assassin. There were reports of officers turning on the black protestors, with one allegedly giving bullets to white gang members and telling them to "kill as many niggers as you can."

And kill they would.

Three days later, an African American woman from the South named Lillie Belle Allen, while visiting family in York, was shot and killed by white gang members. National Guard troops descended upon York as Pennsylvania governor Raymond Shafer declared a state of emergency. The violence was, at last, brought to a halt.

America, just a little more than a year after the assassination of Dr. Martin Luther King Jr., still had a serious race issue. And New York, like other cities around the country, was bracing for racial conflicts. Thankfully, it would never materialize—at least not in New York.

"I think the mayor and chief of police were expecting a really bad summer," recalled Gentry. "This is what I was told afterward. What we were doing on the field was actually helping matters. We calmed that damn town down. We had people pulling together. I remember getting all the 'Attaboys' and 'Thank-yous' from our city and state officials, as well as Governor Nelson Rockefeller and Mayor John Lindsay. You know, I don't think we knew what we were doing when we were doing it, but after it was over, I heard a lot about how we turned the town around."

As ballplayers, we were very much aware of what was going on around us. However, race never caused any friction between our four African American players and the rest of our diverse roster.

"I don't think race plays a part in sports," Krane once told me. "I grew up in the Bronx, and I had plenty of black and Spanish friends. You had all different types of nationalities in New York. And as teammates, we all got along great. To this day, I'm still very friendly with Cleon. I don't think sports has any color."

Still, it was Krane who was our player representative when we voted not to play our 1968 season opener in San Francisco four days after King's assassination. The decision was made out of respect for King's funeral the next day, and our opener was moved forward by two days. The rest of the major-league openers were postponed as well. So sports and society very definitely collide in times of tragedy.

"Baseball Commissioner William Eckert wanted us to play after Martin Luther King was killed," Rocky said. "But we didn't think it was right. I was proud of the fact we voted the way we did. We had conservatives and liberals on the team, but we came together and decided not to play."

And truth be told, even though the sensitive topic of the York riots never entered into the conversation in the locker room, everybody had a point of view on the subject of race. Some, naturally, were more sensitive to it than others. As a Jewish man, I think it was only natural that I fell into the more-sensitive camp. I didn't suffer any of the injustices that Hall of Famer slugger Hank Greenberg did during the 1930s and 1940s, playing for the Detroit Tigers, but I would occasionally hear some catcalls from the stands—particularly when I played minor-league ball in Macon, Georgia.

Others, like Swoboda, were sensitive to the black struggles as well. Growing up in the still-segregated city of Baltimore during the late forties and fifties exposed him to all kinds of racism. However, good parenting, an open-mindedness, and the love of baseball prevented him from becoming bigoted.

"We had a small section of black families whose kids didn't go to our school," Rocky recalled. "But during the summer time, if we were playing pickup baseball games and some black kids wanted to play, we were like, *'Let's play!'* We always needed guys. And with my mom, it was never correct to use the N-word when I was growing up because it implied that you were looking down on somebody. That was never okay with Mom. That didn't fly in our house. So I related to all people as, simply, people. I've always felt like once we all become the same shade of brown, that'll be the end of racism. But I won't live to see it.

"The notion that white people have some sort of lock on intelligence and creativity and everything else that's good and decent under the sun is the biggest load of shit in the world. You have to be ignorant to think that way. Unfortunately, we still have a large share of ignorance going around this world today, and it's angry and dangerous and becoming more so with this loony bird in the White House. I'd like it to be less so, but I feel like it is based on who elected him and the fact that he can say the most absurd shit in the world, and that's fine with some of the people that elected him. It's astounding to me that that's true because I don't understand it, and I can't get my little brain around it. I've tried to delve into it over the years and am just more or less convinced that I'm right about it. You relate to people as people, first and foremost, all the time. Our similarities are way more important and fundamental to who we are and what we are than our differences. Period."

Nobody knew racism on our team more intimately than the Glider. And while I had total respect for all four African American players on the club, as a student of the game's history, I had an especially profound appreciation for Eddie's journey. Racism stalled his arrival to the big leagues, yet he was never bitter about it. In fact, he took just the opposite approach.

"I can recall in the minor leagues when I was with the Jacksonville Braves Class-A team in 1956," Charles once told me from his apartment in Queens. The Braves were a farm team in the Milwaukee Braves' minor-league system. "We were playing in Knoxville, Tennessee, and it just so happened that I had an outstanding day. I hit a couple of home runs and fielded everything in sight. Well, there was this southern *gentleman*—I'm not sure if I should call him a gentleman—who was sitting right over one of the dugouts and had one of those voices that really carried. He was hollering all these slurs and put-downs at me—just calling me every name in the book.

But it seemed like every time he hollered and tried to put me down, I would do something outstanding.

"After the game, we had to go through this little gate and go around a corner to the clubhouse, and, lo and behold, there's this guy who's been on my case all day, standing there at the gate. All of these emotions are going through my head right about then. I thought, *Is he going to start a race riot?* By the time I had gotten up to him, I had made up my mind to just ignore him. But when I got within reach of him, he extended his hand and said, 'You know what, nigger? You is a helluva ballplayer!' Those were his exact words! I proceeded on my way toward the clubhouse, but when I thought about it later, I realized how he'd been taught all of his life one way of thinking: that people of color couldn't do nothing, that they were inferior. On that particular day, I thought, *I've made such an impact on that man that it's going to change his mind.* You just had to tear down that Jim Crow mind-set. We couldn't eat in the restaurants with our white teammates or stay in the same hotels with them. They had signs that said White Only or Colored Only for the restrooms. We had to obey the Jim Crow rules of the South all through my days playing in the minor leagues until I went to Vancouver in 1961. They didn't have Jim Crow signs or any of that stuff in Canada. They treated us like human beings."

I just loved Charles. During turbulent times, he was there when we needed a poet. When we needed that calming force, Eddie was the guy. If you needed some guidance in life, you could walk over to him and say, "Eddie, I'm struggling with something. Tell me what you think about this. What should I do?" And the Glider would always give great advice. He probably never went to college. And I'm not sure if he even graduated from high school. But Eddie Charles had wisdom—and you can't teach wisdom. There wasn't a better person to go to if you needed knowledge about real life or needed something that would make you a better person. He easily could have been a preacher or a minister. For a man to stick through all the things he went through, all the disappointments, all the racism, and to make it to the big leagues after ten trying years in the minors is a tribute to his wherewithal to stay with the times.

A few years ago, the film *42* about Jackie Robinson breaking baseball's color barrier was playing in the theaters. A young actor, Dusan Brown, accurately portrayed the Glider as a boy who idolized Robinson, even following him to a train station and putting his ears to the track to feel the vibrations of the train carrying his hero away. I was so happy that he was featured so prominently in that movie because I know how much Jackie meant to him.

Charles, who grew up in Daytona Beach, Florida, recalled, "I first saw Jackie when he was playing for the Montreal Royals"—the Brooklyn Dodgers' Triple-A team. "They had to finish their spring training in Daytona Beach because initially they were about forty miles away in Sanford but they were having problems over there because of Robinson's presence. So Branch Rickey moved the team to Daytona, and that's when I got the chance to see him. We used to run home from school to catch Montreal where they worked out before going to the pro stadium to play their exhibition games. It just so happened that their recreation complex on Cypress Street was situated right across the street from the house where I lived. I used to walk across the street and watch them practice. The funny thing was, when my friends and I first got wind of it, a lot of kids in the neighborhood that I'd pal around with would run up to get his autograph. But I was so shy that I just stood back and looked at him.

"So one day, the Royals were playing the Brooklyn Dodgers in a spring training exhibition game. I couldn't afford a ticket, so I hoisted myself up on the left field fence, just hanging on it while bracing myself on a flagpole, and watched the game from there. I recall *praying* for Jackie to get a hit every time he came to the plate and to not make any errors. It was quite a happening. I remember thinking, *They've got to make it different in terms of race relations.* I didn't get to see Jackie play in a regular-season game after he got promoted to the Dodgers. And by the time I got up and started my major-league career, he was already out. But I did have a face-to-face with him after we both were out of the game, in 1972.

"I had an appointment with a Small Business Administration office in Lower Manhattan, and, to my happiness, Jackie had an appointment after me! When the administrator was through with me, he said, 'Guess who's coming in next?' I said, 'Who?' He said, 'Jackie Robinson.' I said, 'I've got to stay here. I've got to thank him.' It was like I was that twelve-year-old kid again as I approached him. I was so nervous. When he appeared, I walked over to him, thanked him and shook his hand, and told him how glad I was that he was able to endure everything he did to make it to the major leagues. I opened my veins up to him. But he spun it, telling me, 'You're the first black guy that's approached me like this. I appreciate it. Thank you.'

"A couple of weeks later, I went over to his office in Englewood, New Jersey, where he was trying to get a little taxi business off the ground. Lo and behold, I had him all to myself. I'm just running my mouth like someone does when they meet their idol. And, again, he was very gracious. He sat there, listened, and we exchanged ideas on different things. But then maybe just three weeks later, I'm sitting in my office in the Greenpoint section of Brooklyn with the radio on, when the announcement came over that Jackie Robinson was dead at age fifty-three from a heart attack. *Tore me down!* It just hit me so hard."

We would split the four-game series in Montreal, to a team that would lose 110 games and finish in last place—a full forty-eight games out of first. But the Expos played relatively well against us, winning five of our contests that season. In the finale of a double-header against them on Sunday, July 20, DiLauro picked up his first major-league victory, in relief. We'd reached the All-Star break with a record of 53-39, .576—unprecedented in team history; heck, the Mets didn't win more than fifty-three games in a whole *season* until their fifth year—and were breathing down the necks of the first-place Cubs. Everybody was looking forward to a few days off—everybody, that is, except for Seaver, Kooz, and Cleon, who would be headed to the nation's capital to represent the National League in the All-Star Game.

Our charter flight back to New York was delayed, which actually had its upside. Sitting and waiting at the Montreal airport bar, we got to watch on live television as Neil Armstrong became the first man to set foot on the moon. Had our plane been on time, we would have been in midair when the Apollo 11 astronaut was planting his boot in the dusty lunar surface, and missed the historic moment.

"We couldn't take off because of an issue with our plane," Krane recalled. "Then they had a crazy rule you couldn't fly out after a certain time at the airport we were at, so we were stuck waiting for a ride to go to some other place so we could take off. I remember the writers commenting that summer how man would walk on the moon before the Mets win a pennant. But everything happened during that tremendous year of 1969. It proved miracles could happen."

As we watched the conclusion of the moonwalk by Armstrong and fellow astronaut Buzz Adrin, DiLauro came up with one of the all-time greatest baseball lines.

"I'm at the bar, having a nice, cold beer, watching a guy land on the moon—actually sitting at the bar watching it. I'm thinking, *Geez, there's a first!* And then there was my first win that day, too. It was kind of cool. So I turned to a couple of the guys and said, 'One small step for man, one giant win for DiLauro!' I was a little cocky back then."

Some of our guys had fun with it and created this retort: "When he gets his second win, man will walk on Mars!"

"I guess it's the history of me and then the history of the space program," DiLauro told me tongue in cheek with a chuckle recently. "Obviously, during the game, I didn't think anything about the lunar landing. But we knew it was coming later that day."

Indeed we did. Despite all the other problems going on in the world, here was this great and incredible moment in our history. Everything else took a backseat. I really felt it. I got this chill thinking how I was alive to actually see it happen. I recalled how John F. Kennedy had said in 1961 that we would send an American safely to the moon and back by the end of the decade. So many people I knew laughed at the idea. Some thought, *A man on the moon? Really?* So at that time, I instantly recalled the significance of Kennedy's vision. I think the whole team was caught up in the moment and wasn't thinking about baseball or catching the next plane home.

"Everything was possible in '69," Swoboda said. "The 'man on the moon' was a part of that season we could never forget. I lived out on Long Island, and the Grumman Aerospace Corporation was where they built the lunar lander. We had a tour of the place before it took off, and we saw that lunar lander. I had a model of it that they gave us from Grumman. So I had a personal attachment to it. We had also met the astronauts in Houston—one of the benefits of being ballplayers. When we were stuck on the ground in Montreal because our airplane had a malfunction, the irony wasn't lost. I thought, *We can't get back from Montreal to New York, and here's a guy stepping on the moon!*"

I saw the irony as well. But I think fate allowed us to see it happen live, and it counterbalanced the fact that the plane wasn't right for us that day. But a lot of things happened in '69 that both irony and fate brought into perspective. In a summer filled with racial strife, war, riots, strikes, assassinations, poverty, and a world in general upheaval, Armstrong's walk on the moon was very important for our nation's morale. And so were the Mets.

CHAPTER 9

GIL SENDS A MESSAGE

– July 30, 1969 –

IT WAS AS UGLY AS IT GETS. A WEDNESDAY DOUBLEHEADER at Shea against the Houston Astros started off badly and just kept getting so much worse. In the first game, the Astros put up *eleven runs* in the ninth to beat us 16–3. And then in the second game, a *ten-run* third inning put them comfortably ahead in another laugher Houston would end up winning 11–5. They were stealing on us, we were making errors in the field, we looked listless at the plate, Gary Gentry walked in a run and threw a wild pitch—it was just a real sloppy, lethargic effort on our part. We were a club in need of a wake-up call, and Gil was more than willing to oblige.

Near the merciful conclusion of that fateful third inning, Astros catcher Johnny Edwards hit a flare down the left field line. Cleon, nursing a bad leg, ran after it tentatively, and Edwards ended up on second base with a run-scoring double to give Houston an 8–0 lead. The fans were restless and booing us incessantly. Out of the dugout popped Hodges in a scene I will never forget as long as I live. Usually when he went out to the mound to talk to a pitcher, he skipped over the first base line—never coming close to touching it. Although I was in right field at the time, my eyes were pretty good then, and I noticed how this time he missed the line by just a half inch and didn't skip over it like he always did. I thought, *That's really strange. He's usually very superstitious about doing that.* As he walked toward

Nolan Ryan, who was out there in relief of Gentry, I just assumed he was going to make a pitching change. But then he kept walking past the mound in Buddy's direction. I thought, *Oh my gosh, what did Buddy do? Is he hurt?*

"As he came close to me," Harrelson recalled, "I said to Gil, 'Me?' And he goes, 'The *other* guy.' So I started walking out to left field with him, not all the way, maybe halfway to Cleon. I had no idea what was going on."

"Edwards hit the ball right down the third base line," Cleon explained. "There's no way you're going to stop him from getting a double on that play. I ran after the ball the best I could, but it was soaking wet in the outfield. Plus, I had a bad ankle. So when Gil walked out there, I was as surprised as everybody else. I thought something happened behind me."

When Gil got near Cleon, I said to myself, *Oh shit, Cleon's in trouble* and thought Jones would be wise to just dash through the visitors' bullpen gate in left field. That's because I had a feeling there had to be something stern that the hard-nosed, no-nonsense ex-marine wanted to say to Cleon. Or worse.

"We were getting waxed by Houston, and Gil was steaming," recalled Swoboda, who was on the bench near Hodges during this Mets meltdown. "So Cleon really got his attention when he didn't go hard after the ball. Gil usually walked *slowwww*. But that was just the longest walk."

"It was a *scary* walk," was how Kooz described it.

Eventually Hodges made it out to Cleon, our All-Star outfielder, and didn't mince words.

"He walked right up to me and said, 'What's wrong?'" Jones recalled. "I said, 'What do you mean, "What's wrong?"' Then he said, 'I don't like the way you went after that last ball.' And I said, 'We talked about this in Montreal. I have a bad ankle, and as long as I don't hurt the team, I could continue to play. Besides, look down.' When he did, he could see that his feet were underwater. It had rained for two days. So he goes, 'I didn't know it was that bad out here. You probably need to come on out of the ball game.' I said, 'Fine.' So he turned, and we both walked back to the dugout together. So the next day, we had a conversation, and Gil told me, 'I wouldn't have embarrassed you out there, but I look at you as a leader on this ball club. So if I can show the club I can take you out, it sends a message to everyone. Everybody seemed comfortable with this ball club getting its tail kicked and I didn't like it.' Gil did it to wake us up. That was his motive. If he could do it to someone hitting .360, he could do it to anyone."

"You bet your ass Gil was making a statement," Seaver told me. "His actions spoke volumes."

"But everybody misinterpreted at the time what really happened between us," recalled Jones.

And that would include Mrs. Joan Hodges.

"After the game, Gil called to tell me he was on his way home," Mrs. Hodges once told me. "I'd always try to have something ready for him to eat when he arrived. Gil really did leave the game in the clubhouse, although he couldn't hide his emotions when something happened—especially the night with Cleon, because he knew I was watching. I watched all the games, and when I saw him pull Cleon, I almost died! I called Rube before Gil got home and asked him, 'Why did you let Gil do that?' And he goes, 'I really didn't know where he was going. Besides, Joan, I don't think there's anyone on this earth that could have stopped him.'

"So when he arrived home, I had the TV on. Johnny Carson had a replacement on that night: Don Rickles. So he sat down to eat his sandwich and asked me to turn off the TV. I asked him why, and he said, 'Just turn it off.' So I did, and Gil goes, 'Okay, get it off your chest.' I told him I would rather not. But he insisted, saying, 'Go ahead.' We always discussed the games, but I had promised myself I wasn't going to discuss Cleon. Anyway, I said, 'I wouldn't care if you got Cleon in the office after the game, shut the door, and wiped the floor with him. But *whatever* possessed you to do it on the field?' And he goes to me, 'Do you want to know the gospel truth?' And I'm like, 'Yeah, I'm your wife.' And he goes, 'I never realized it until I passed the pitcher's mound. And I couldn't turn back!'"

I think it's hard to say if Gil had any regrets for embarrassing Cleon—intentionally or not—like he did. In hindsight, I don't think he was necessarily trying to show up Jones, but just wanted to make sure that, even though we were getting our butts kicked, we always hustled. And while the significance of Hodges's statement would no doubt act as a turning point to our season and make us a better, more focused team, I wish Cleon, a dear friend of mine to this day, would have just sat out that second game of the doubleheader to nurse his bad ankle instead of playing hurt. I think the incident with Gil affected him personally when fans perceived that he wasn't hustling for that ball. But to Cleon's credit, he never harbored any ill feelings toward Hodges about it. In fact, just the opposite.

"I'll say this anytime, anywhere," Jones confided in me. "Sixty-nine would never have happened if not for Gil Hodges. It would never have happened with any other manager. He was tough, but he was *thorough*. He was just the total package as a manager. If he went out there onto the field and felt like you didn't have it, you were out of there. He just did everything right. And because of him, *we* started to do everything right. We no longer beat ourselves. And when you don't beat yourself, it's harder for the other guy to beat you."

Aside from Hodges, an even earlier influence in Cleon's evolution toward becoming a winning ballplayer was the Glider during Charles's first year with the Mets.

"When I first got to the team in '67," Eddie recalled, "Tommy Davis, Cleon Jones, another black player named Tommie Reynolds, and I went out after a late night game to a little club on Astoria Boulevard in Queens named the Outfielders Lounge. As a matter of fact, Cleon and Agee would end up buying the place. But anyway, I recall when the four of us went to the club that night, our host announced to the other people, 'We got a few Mets here. I guess you know—they lost another one!' And everybody started laughing. But I get pissed off—all these people laughing because we lost. So Cleon goes to me, 'Take it easy, man. That's the way they look upon us.' I said, 'Shit, nobody's gonna laugh at me 'cos we lost.' So I got up from my chair and left. The others stayed, but they got my message that the old attitude wasn't going to be acceptable any longer. You really had to fight off that attitude."

What helped Charles in getting his point across to Jones and some of the other young Mets was what transpired following the season.

"Of course, the next big thing that happened was getting Gil Hodges as manager," Eddie said. "Oh boy! He took over for Wes Westrum, who was a lovely guy but couldn't handle us. We walked all over Wes. But Gil really shook things up. You knew who was in charge."

Aside from the bad ankle, Jones's injury woes would continue.

"Soon after the All-Star break," recalled Cleon, "I don't know how I did it, but I cracked a rib. I tried to play for a week with the pain, but it wasn't getting any better. They finally gave me a second X-ray and found the fracture in the rib cage. That was the injury that really hurt me. If not for that one, I have no doubt in my mind that I would have won the batting title. Before the rib injury, I was hitting the ball as hard as I wanted to. I would have great at bats. I found out what that meant through the tutelage of Gil Hodges—having good at bats each and every time you went to the plate. But when I got hurt and then came back, I just didn't have the same concentration."

As it was, Cleon would still end the season third in hitting in the National League with a .340 average, close behind a couple of guys named Pete Rose and Roberto Clemente, and finish seventh in the NL MVP voting. But if there was a silver lining in Jones's having to miss a few weeks of action, it was the reemergence of Rocky as an everyday force in our lineup.

"I got a little bit hot," Swoboda recalled. "And when Cleon came back, I was still in there. I got half my RBIs that season from that point until the end of the year. I had some pretty big games, including the one when I hit two home runs against Steve Carlton to beat him when he struck out nineteen. All that stuff happened after the incident with Cleon and Gil. Up until that point, I was reasonably disappointed in what was happening to me. I had struggled, but the baseball part was still exciting and carried me over a lot of vicissitudes—individual ups and downs."

By "ups and downs," Rocky was referring mostly to his openly tenuous relationship with Hodges.

"I had a little difficulty with authority," Rocky confessed to me after some soul searching. "It just seemed like the oddest thing in the world at that time. There was my ambition to become a regular in the big leagues, and here was this man who had control over that. I don't like being ordered about. Never did. And don't like it today. I do much better when I can craft my own path, whether it's right or wrong. So that kind of put me at odds with Gil, and it was a foolish thing. If I could have just shut up and did what Gil wanted, because all he ever wanted you to do was the right thing—play when asked, be ready when you're not in the game—it would have been fine. I wrestled with that whole notion in a way that was not to my benefit or anyone else's benefit. And, on top of it all, he was such a good manager and such a substantial character. But we did sort of rub one another wrongly. I missed a great opportunity to have a better relationship with one of the true great minds in baseball. I respected him—I really did. But I never ran out of ways to piss him off. And then I'd go to myself, *Christ, you did it again.* It was stupid and immature on my part. Of all the things that I felt regret from in baseball, that's number one right there. If I could fix that, I would feel entirely different about the game of baseball. But there's no way to do that now."

Kranepool who, like Rocky, also had his disagreements with Gil, additionally came to realize the genius of Hodges.

"It didn't matter who you were or how big a star you were, you were not bigger than the team," Krane noted.

"Hodges had a lot of guys bitching and moaning," added Charles. "Even the fans and media got on his butt, but he didn't say nothing. He stood tall and didn't waver. When we started winning, guys started showing him the type of respect he deserved."

"The team was always more important than an individual player," concluded Krane. "And Gil proved it to everybody."

Even to our star left fielder.

CHAPTER 10

THE COMEBACK

– August 16–August 30, 1969 –

OUR SUMMER SWOON CONTINUED FOR THE NEXT TWO WEEKS, climaxed by a three-game sweep at the hands of our archnemesis in Houston.

"We couldn't play the Astros worth a shit," Swoboda surmised. "They just wore us out, and it seemed to stay that way all year long. They did some weird things to us. We just couldn't seem to play those guys."

On the morning of August 16, the second day of the Woodstock Music Festival, we found ourselves a season-high ten games behind the Cubs with just six weeks remaining.

While nothing changed our belief that we still had enough talent to compete against any team in the league, as a collective unit, we were somewhat split on whether this could truly be a championship-caliber season. Some began to acquiesce to the idea that, while we might not win the pennant, it would, at least, still be a successful stepping-stone kind of season.

"I think we were just happy that we were playing winning baseball and were over .500," recalled Krane, who had endured seven losing seasons with the Mets. "We were competitive. I don't think we had any aspirations or any thoughts about winning a pennant. We just were playing the game as the game should be played and let the numbers take care of themselves. We didn't put any pressure on ourselves. Every day was a new game. We still came to the ballpark expecting to win."

"My general impression," remarked Rocky, "was that here we were finally putting a few things together by bringing up some guys, adding a few positive additions during the season, and would end up with the best year the Mets had ever had while *somebody else* had a Cinderella story."

"It was the first time I was on a winning team in the major leagues," said Cleon, whose days with the Mets dated back to the Polo Grounds, where the Mets played until Shea opened in 1964, with Casey Stengel at the helm. "And we were having fun. We weren't necessarily thinking about going to the World Series or even winning the World Series then, but we were having fun winning for the first time as New York Mets."

While there may have been a sense of realism in their feelings, which I shared, I think some of our guys probably got caught up in thinking that we had only recently been known as lovable losers. Our metamorphosis into a winning ball club had come so swiftly that any more of a jump in just one season almost seemed like fantasy. But not *all* of us felt that way.

After the sweep in Houston, Clendenon once told me, "Everybody started talking about 'next year.'" "I said to Cleon and Tommie, 'You guys ran track. Did you run looking over your shoulders? The Chicago Cubs appear to be looking over their shoulder at us. Why are we talking about second place? We still have a shot *this year.* We have the pitching. All we need is more timely hitting.' The great miracle for me was not winning the World Series but getting these kids to believe the New York Mets baseball team could not lose."

Maybe Clink was on to something. Right after we hit rock bottom following the Astros series, we started playing better baseball, and guys started believing again. And when you start believing you can win, anything can happen. Over a sixteen-game stretch, we would win fourteen, which included two separate six-game winning streaks. From the end of August through the remainder of the season, we were almost unbeatable, and would ultimately go 38–11 the rest of the way. Our formula was simple: we had terrific starting pitching, strong defense, and an ability to find ways to win close games with contributions from *everybody* on the ball club—from the stars to the last man on the bench. And it all started with back-to-back doubleheader sweeps of the San Diego Padres during a memorable weekend at Shea.

In the first game of an August 16 twin bill, Seaver pitched a gem: eight innings of shutout ball. Unsung utility infielder Bobby Pfeil, getting a rare start at third base, led the offensive charge with three hits in a 2–0 win. Pfeil, a rookie, was one of the classic, unheralded Mets that season. Plus, he could play multiple positions, making him an extravaluable asset. He was seeing his first big-league action after eight years in the minors, finally getting promoted in late June after Buddy went away to perform his military duty. He may have been only a .242 hitter coming into that game, but Gil played his hunches and batted Pfeil second against the Padres' Tommy Sisk.

"Hodges has to get a lot of credit for that," Pfeil explained. "He made everybody feel like they belonged. *Everybody* played. Even if you were a fringe ballplayer like myself, you'd still get at least two starts a week. That's the definition of a team. I thought it was amazing how Gil used so many people. You never got lost on the bench."

"Gil used to tell me," Mrs. Hodges said, " 'When they put on that Mets uniform and walk out on the field, they belong to me. They are my children.' And that's just how he felt about each and every one of his players. No one more than the other."

And that was a part of Gil's brilliance. He treated us all the same way. And, by using his entire twenty-five-man roster, it kept everybody fresh for the stretch run of the season. He foresaw that he was going to need bench players such as Pfeil, Gaspar, and Weis to spell guys that needed a day off or, in Buddy's case, someone to fill in while he fulfilled his military commitments. It was a testament to Hodges's ability to manage and assess talent.

In many ways, Pfeil was not your typical rookie, in that he fit in with everybody right away.

"I always felt like I was accepted," he told me. "I don't remember anybody thinking they were a big shot. I was married with no children, as were Seaver and Ryan, and we did a lot of things as couples with them. And I enjoyed being around you and Boswell. There were a whole bunch of guys you felt you could hang around with."

In the second game of that doubleheader, another talented yet unsung Met, Jim McAndrew, took center stage and thrived, giving up just three hits over seven innings in a 2–1 victory. Jim was just in his second big-league season and didn't receive the fanfare that our power pitchers like Seaver, Kooz, and Ryan did.

"I wasn't a strikeout pitcher," admitted McAndrew. "I was a 'contact pitcher,' and if you had confidence in your stuff like I did, you threw strikes and had hitters put the ball in play. And because of that, I never threw a hundred pitches in a nine-inning game. Typically, if the average guy is throwing well, he throws around a hundred thirty-five pitches over nine innings. When I was pitching, I threw anywhere from eighty-five to ninety-five pitches over nine, so I could come back and be successful time and time again."

Despite Hodges having, as McAndrew described it, "all kinds of confidence in me," Jim barely pitched during the first half of the season. Instead, Gil had given his big three of Seaver, Kooz, and Gentry the bulk of the starts. But that all started to change in August.

"Because of Gil's style and the depth of our pitching staff," Jim said, "all of a sudden our numbers four, five, and six starters—between myself, Ryan, and Cardwell—were beginning to get more starts. Teams were playing a lot of doubleheaders because we had some bad weather in the spring. Because our pitching was so deep, we were matching up so much better against our competition. Other teams were faltering because they were thin on pitching. That's when we started outplaying everybody over that final six-week time frame. It was kind of mind-boggling, in retrospect."

Unlike a lot of us, McAndrew saw his relationship with Hodges in an old-school father-son kind of way.

"During my generation and the way I was raised, Gil was a lot like my own dad, whom I loved deeply," McAndrew said. "Like my dad, Hodges didn't necessarily communicate much verbally but rather with body language, looks, and speaking loudly when he had to. He wasn't a man of many words. When he did say something, you definitely listened because he loved that you were still scared shitless of him. And when he did act, you usually got responses from him that were not necessarily positive ones. They were more disciplinary actions instead of the loving actions most parents give today. But I had the utmost respect for Gil because I thought he was an honorable man. Whether you liked it or not, he was doing things that he thought were best for you. He and Swoboda had a terrible relationship, but everything that Gil did with Ron was to make him a better person. When you find a personality that's honestly working to make everybody around him a better person, he is definitely worthy of my love and respect."

Few contributed more to our success late that summer than McAndrew. He went on a dazzling twenty-three-inning consecutive scoreless streak in which he won four games in a row.

"And the next game after the streak, I actually gave up a few runs in the first inning but then pitched another ten innings in a row without giving up a run," Jim recalled. "I really hit a streak there. But then after we went into first place for the first time, beating Montreal after I pitched the first eleven innings, I never really bounced back from the number of pitches I threw and hardly pitched the rest of the year. You learn things about yourself physically as you look back. Trouble is, with most of us, you find out what those limits are twenty years after you retire!"

The next day, with another doubleheader on tap, Kooz started the first game and went the distance, tossing a five-hit, 3–2, complete-game victory over Padres ace Joe Niekro. To have Seaver and Kooz pitch for your team on back-to-back days like that gave our club an overabundance of confidence. Although both were terrific, their pitching styles were so different. Tom was an artist, like Leonardo da Vinci out there on the mound, whereas Kooz was more like General George Patton, willing to throw at an opposing batter if their pitcher threw at one of us. Seaver was the great pitcher, while Kooz was the great battler, if you will.

Kooz saw the similarities and the differences with Seaver in his own way.

"We both challenged hitters," he told me, "but if Tom could get a strikeout, he'd work for that strikeout. So he threw more pitches that way. We would compete against one another on things like strike-outs, wins, and whatever. And we both worked fast—a lot of our games only lasted 2:08, 2:10, 2:12. The defense loved playing behind us. There was not a lot of up-and-down and full counts. They hate that. Get 'em in, get 'em out, and really go hard. If we just scored a run or two, you go out there and you shut them down as quick as you can to bring your guys back in. Don't go out there and start nit-picking and walking guys. They get pissed off at that. I always chal-lenged guys."

Incredibly, from August 16 through the remainder of the season, our dynamic duo would win seventeen of their eighteen decisions.

"I remember when that first cool air came at the end of August," Kooz said. "We got a breath of it, and it gave Seaver and me some extra stamina."

Again it would be an unlikely source supplying the offense in this latest victory, our third in a row: backup catcher Duffy Dyer. Down 2–0 in the bottom of the fifth, Duffy blasted a three-run homer that proved to be the difference. It was just Dyer's second home run of the season and the first since he went deep all the way back on opening day.

"That was another memorable day for me personally," Duffy told me. "I remember I got a ball up from Niekro and was able to pull it into the stands. That was such a thrill! And it was also always a thrill to catch for Koosman because he had great stuff. That's when we started thinking again, after three wins in a row, *Hey, we've got a chance.* We knew we were still quite a ways behind the Cubs but felt like anything was possible. It was another close comeback win."

In the second game of the doubleheader, now our fourth game in two days, yet another spot starter, the veteran Don Cardwell, stepped up and pitched seven shutout innings, as we finished off the four-game sweep of the Padres, 3–2. Cardwell was a terrific pitcher who had over a hundred career wins and had thrown a no-hitter at Wrigley Field nine years earlier as a member of the Cubs. With the victory, we were now eight games out.

Much of the attention from that '69 season is placed on the gifted arms of Seaver, Kooz, and Ryan, but Cardwell, McAndrew, and Gentry combined for twenty-seven wins. We would never have had the success we enjoyed in '69 without their efforts. Gil and Rube Walker realized they had a great overall pitching staff and really started to take advantage of that depth as Seaver and Kooz, in particular, started accumulating some serious innings. Hodges had no fear of starting any of his pitchers in important games—and that went for the occasional start by McGraw and Koonce as well.

"We all had our fifteen minutes of fame," is how McAndrew once put it.

As a kid who grew up in St. Louis as a big Cardinals fan, I was a student of the history of the game. And because Brooklyn battled my Cardinals for the National League pennant every year, I knew all about the players on those great Dodgers teams. Gil, a perennial All-Star first baseman and a leader on those championship clubs, was able to maintain strong ties with other Dodgers greats while managing the Mets. So throughout spring training and during the season, a steady stream of legendary Dodgers would visit our ball club and lend their assistance when requested. Guys such as Sandy Koufax, Gene Hermanski, Cal Abrams, Don Newcombe, Carl Erskine, Ralph Branca, Carl Furillo—the guys that still lived and worked in New York would come by the most. I also saw shortstop Pee Wee Reese fairly often—in fact, he signed me to a contract with the bat company Louisville Slugger. But one of my biggest thrills came at a Mets Old-Timers' Day where I met three-time MVP catcher Roy Campanella, who, sadly, was confined to a wheelchair due to a 1959 car accident that left him partly paralyzed.

I have to admit: I was in awe of those guys when Gil would invite them in. I guess I'm old-fashioned in my appreciation for the guys who came before me, the ones who paid their dues and were able to sustain their careers at a time when there weren't that many teams and jobs were scarce. And there is no question that some of what made them great rubbed off on us as a young team. Perhaps the greatest benefactor was Kooz.

"Sandy Koufax taught me how to throw my curveball," he once told me. "He was friends with Hodges, Rube, and Piggy, and he'd come by the clubhouse from time to time. Once in '68, Rube called me over to him and goes, 'Sandy, show Jerry how you threw your curveball.' He was working four seams, which you normally do anyway, but it's how you cock your thumb underneath that enables you to throw it at different speeds. So I learned from Sandy how to throw it slow and medium—a very effective combination."

In a way, it was symbolic of one iconic New York baseball southpaw passing the torch to another.

"We epitomized the word *team*," Clink observed many years ago about our '69 club. "We played together, we talked baseball together, and we went out together."

That summer, we became more than just a team; we were one big family. And it wasn't limited to just the guys but also often included our wives and children. On off-days, it was normal for much of the team to get together at someone's house for a picnic or some other type of gathering. We bonded more than any other organization I had ever been a part of.

"It was such a mixed bag of people from every corner of the earth," Boswell said. "Yet we all came together. And I think that's why we were so loose on the club. You know, in retrospect, I can't name one pitcher that I got a base hit off of at a particular time. But I do remember, on and off the field, the closeness of that team. All twenty-five guys and everybody else getting along. It was all fun times."

For some, the belief was that it started at the top.

"It was a close group," observed Cleon. "We did a lot of family things with one another. We'd go to plays, our wives played on a softball team, we had a fashion show, and other gatherings. I think we could attribute that to our leaders, Gil Hodges and Johnny Murphy. Johnny was probably the most caring guy of all of us. I know for a fact that he pulled me to the side, one-on-one, and we talked about family and about being happy and about winning. He was a guy I could go to anytime—he was kind of a hands-on guy. And Gil was responsible for that environment, too. Because of them both, we *all* started to be hands-on with one another and very genuinely caring for everybody. If there was ever any tension or issues between any of the players, I never knew about it."

It also helped that a lot of the guys lived near one another on Long Island.

"My wife was good friends with Jerry Grote's wife, and we would get together because they lived out in our direction," recalled Rocky. "Kranepool lived out on Long Island, too, and we would do things occasionally. It all seemed natural. We all lived in houses with back-yards and took turns hosting barbecues. Back then, players had more days off. I remember one time Kranepool had us over to his house, and a bunch of our guys came over to help sod his front lawn. We got loaded on gin and tonic and were lucky we kept putting the green side up! But the barbecues were no big deal. We'd just throw some meat on the grill. Grote was pretty good at it—he had a little barbe-cue touch.

"The one thing I missed out on was when Tommie and Cleon would go over to Louis Armstrong's house." The house where Satchmo spent the last three decades of his life, today a museum, was just a mile from Shea. "When I found out about that years later, I was like *'God dang, would I have liked to have done that!'* I wasn't invited, but wouldn't that have been amazing?"

• • •

We would remain hot, winning eight of our next ten games to quickly whittle the reeling Cubs' lead down to just four games as we began an August 30 game in San Francisco. In the annals of the '69 season, this was another of those dozen or so games where observers scratched their heads wondering how we pulled out a victory. It was truly bizarre.

With the game tied at two with one out in the bottom half of the ninth at Candlestick Park, Bob Burda singled to Rod Gaspar in left field. Rod had entered the game, as he often did, as a defensive replacement the inning before. Gaspar was another one of our young rookies who made the most of limited playing time—in his case, leading all of our outfielders in assists, with twelve, and the entire National League in double plays started by an outfielder, with six. In our crowded outfield of Jones, Agee, Swoboda, and me, Gil still somehow managed to get Rod into 118 games that year. But for the brash twenty-three-year-old, even though he was batting just .215 at the time, it wasn't nearly enough.

"At the time, I was a young, stupid, single, punk rookie," Gaspar enjoyed telling me. "I was talking to our minor-league pitching instructor Wes Stock one day on the bench during spring training that year and told him, 'I can play with all these people. I'm better than Jones. I'm better than Agee. I'm better than Rocky and Sham.' That's the kind of attitude I had. But you know, the way I looked at it, you had to think you were the best no matter who you were competing against. Even to this day, I always think, if I'm going to compete in something, I'm going to win."

The next batter to face reliever Tug McGraw was big first baseman Willie McCovey, who would win the NL MVP Award and lead the league in homers and runs batted in for the second season in a row. We put on our own version of the "McCovey shift," moving our infielders and outfielders more toward the right side of the field against the strong left-handed pull hitter. But instead of pulling the ball, McCovey took it the other way.

"I'm playing way over in left center," Gaspar recalled. "Tug throws a sinker, low and away, and McCovey just sticks his bat out and hits like a nine iron down the left field line, the ball landing right in front of the warning track. As soon as he had hit it, I took off from left center toward the ball. I knew that the game was over unless I made a play. Burda took off hard from first, knowing I wasn't going to catch it. I got to the ball, bare-handed it, rotated my body, and threw a line drive to Grote all the way in the air to get Burda at the plate by ten or fifteen feet to save the game for us. It was the best throw I ever made in my life.

"There were still only two outs, but I think the throw shocked Grote—who was usually a very heads-up ballplayer—to the point where he forgot how many outs there were. So, thinking there were three outs, he rolls the ball back to the pitcher's mound. But Clendenon, who was always very heads-up, saw what Grote did, charges in, picks up the ball, and throws it to Bobby Pfeil at third to nail Mc-Covey, who was trying to get there on Grote's mistake toss to the mound. Just your typical seven-two-three-five double play! That's one of the craziest double plays we ever made. Then the next inning, Clendenon hits a home run, and we beat the Giants 3–2 in ten innings. That's just the kind of team we had."

It was the kind of miracle baseball we were getting used to seeing practically every night during the comeback late that season. To have someone like Gaspar, who would get all forty-nine of his hits with the Mets in '69 (and only five more the rest of his career), start a play like that and have Clink finish it the way he did, it truly felt like something out of this world was taking place with us.

"You could see the younger players getting, I'm not going to say 'cocky,'" Weis noted, "but getting very confident in themselves. There were a number of times during that season where we'd be going into the ninth losing by a couple of runs, but we knew somehow, some way, we were gonna win the game."

It was a confidence that permeated the entire ball club as we entered the stretch run.

Gil Hodges shares a light moment with our three young superstar hurlers, Jerry Koosman, Tom Seaver, and Nolan Ryan.

Tommie Agee makes a spectacular backhanded catch in the top of the fourth inning of game three of the World Series to save at least two runs.

Agee makes his second circus catch of game three, this time saving as many as three runs.

Donn Clendenon gets a congratulatory pat from first base coach Yogi Berra after connecting on a game four home run.

A wide-grinned Ed Charles joins Jerry Koosman and Jerry Grote on the mound to celebrate our World Series victory.

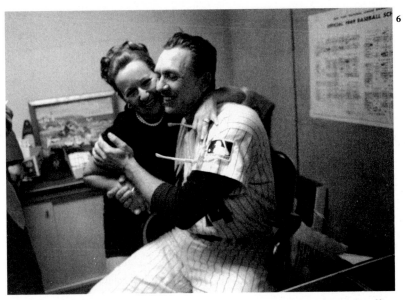

Joan Hodges gives her husband a warm embrace in the manager's office after we finished off the Orioles in game five.

After each title the Mets clinched at Shea in '69, including this one after we won the World Series, the fans stormed the field in celebration.

The Franchise (right) and Kooz dousing each other with champagne in our joyous clubhouse.

Shortly after the World Series, some of us performed in a Las Vegas singing act at Caesars Palace. From left to right: Art Shamsky, Tommie Agee, Tom Seaver, Donn Clendenon, Ed Kranepool, Jerry Koosman, and Cleon Jones.

Koosman proudly holds a copy of the October 17, 1969, edition of the *New York Times.* The Mets' victory was front-page news.

A recent photo of Al Weis gripping the "souvenir bat" he used in winning the Babe Ruth Award for the most outstanding player of the '69 World Series.

Adorning Seaver's home office are his three Cy Young Awards and game-used baseballs to commemorate some of his greatest achievements.

Seaver (right) discussing his vineyard with Rocky Swoboda.

Pictured on Seaver's terrace at his Napa Valley home are, from left to right, Buddy Harrelson, Jerry Koosman, Ron Swoboda, Nancy Seaver, Tom Seaver, and Art Shamsky.

Perhaps nobody had a bigger impact on Seaver's career than Gil Hodges (pictured with Tom in the framed photo).

Eating lunch at a restaurant near Seaver's home are, left to right, Harrelson, Koosman, Erik Sherman, Shamsky, and Swoboda, and Seaver in the foreground.

CHAPTER 11

THE BLACK CAT

– September 8–9, 1969 –

WE ENTERED A CRITICAL TWO-GAME SHOWDOWN WITH CHI-cago at Shea, now just two and a half games out of first place and surging—having won fourteen of our last sixteen games. All the pressure was now on the Cubs, as they came to New York losers of their last four straight.

"They were running out of oxygen," was how Rocky put it. "It wasn't them choking. I think they played all the baseball they could with a four-man rotation and basically the same regulars out there every day."

While every series with Chicago was something special, the added importance of this one was evident with only three weeks remaining in the season. For us, it was win both and move to within a half game or, God forbid, drop both and fall four and a half back. But no longer were the Cubs the darlings of the National League East. No longer did they have a big ten-game lead. And no longer were we seen as baseball's punching bag. The Cubs were now desperate. And desperate means called for desperate measures.

"When Bill Hands walked out to the mound that night for the Cubs," J. C. Martin observed, "he went out as a veteran who wanted to try to intimidate our young team."

And Hands wasted little time. In the bottom of the first inning, he faced Agee, our leadoff hitter, and vented a month's worth of

Cubs frustration with his very first pitch: a high-and-tight fastball just under Tommie's chin. The tone was now set for an evening of fireworks.

"Leo Durocher wanted to get into a throwing contest," Swoboda said. "And he was going to get one!"

When Kooz took the mound in the top of the second, we all knew what was coming with Ron Santo leading off. Nobody had to say anything to him. Given Koosman's fierce competitiveness and high intensity, there was no doubt that he was going to retaliate. The George Patton of our team was going to climb into his proverbial tank and flatten Santo.

"As Santo came up to hit, I thought, *God have mercy on your soul!*" recalled Swoboda, who was playing right field. "If you needed someone to get plunked, Koosman was the guy to do it. Seaver might have whizzed one by a hitter, but didn't go out there to plunk anybody. It wasn't his thing. That wasn't the case with Koosman."

"When Hands knocked Agee down, we absolutely knew it was on purpose," Kooz said. "It was like Hands was trying to show us who's boss. The Cubs were still flying high, still in first, Santo was still clicking his heels after they won, and they were still doing all kinds of stupid stuff like that. All they did with knocking down Agee was wake up a sleeping dog. It really pissed us off. Well, I always felt like I had to protect my teammates. Gil had a deal where he would never tell you to knock 'em down, but in a meeting one time, he said, 'You should know how to do your job out there.' That's all he said. He didn't say go out there and kill somebody. So when Hands knocked Agee down, I knew right away I was going to go after their best hitter. You mess with my hitters, I'm going after your best one. I'll go after him *twice* if I have to!"

Santo, the reigning NL All-Star third baseman, who was leading the league with 112 RBIs at the time, stepped up to the plate. Kooz's first pitch to him was a hard fastball up and in, sending Santo falling back, arms flailing, and unable to avoid getting hit squarely on the right wrist. Santo, in obvious pain, went straight into the Cubs' dugout to receive treatment from their trainer.

"I thought his arm was broken," Rocky said of Santo. "He was really hurting. But, in a way, he was lucky. If it didn't hit his arm, it would have hit him onside his head."

Surprisingly, Santo would stay in the game after enduring several minutes of agony inflicted on him by Kooz's purpose pitch. The significance wasn't lost on any of us.

"That was the turning point of the series," Krane told me. "Koosman showed that he was a real fighter. He was the guy I wanted on the mound in that spot. If he would have thrown the ball two feet over Santo's head or anybody else's head, it wouldn't have meant anything to us. But when he really intimidated the Cubs by hitting Santo, they stopped throwing at our hitters, which we were really pissed about. They were an older ball club and would try to intimidate you with Leo Durocher's style of play. But Koosman put a stop to it. When he threw at Santo like he did, he really could have hit him between the eyes. That really made a statement that we were there, we weren't going to be intimidated, and that was going to be the end of it. That's why I wanted him on the mound—even more so than Seaver. Tom came up as a star. As soon as he joined the ball club, he had that halo around his head. He was the best pitcher, obviously, in the Mets organization. Koosman was also outstanding, but he was also the toughest guy of the lot. He was an intimidator, and he would fight for you. Jerry was the guy you wanted to go to war with because he was going to be there for you. He came out of the trenches with you, arms swinging. He did everything."

"Koosman never got the credit he deserved," McAndrew said. "As far as I'm concerned, Kooz should be in the Hall of Fame. Seaver laughs every time we all get together and tells him stuff like, 'You'd be in the Hall of Fame if you hadn't been with the Mets for so long. You should have gotten traded earlier. Instead of losing twenty games a year in the late seventies, you would have been winning twenty games on other clubs.' But Kooz was like a lot of the pitchers in the expansion years that lost twenty games. They were usually great pitchers. You don't go out there every fourth or fifth day unless you're better than everybody else." Koosman would remain a Met through 1978, their second year in a row of finishing in the cellar. But traded to the Minnesota Twins, he won twenty games in 1979—at the age of thirty-six.

Kooz's toughness on the mound and innate makeup to protect his teammates at all costs should never be misinterpreted as him being a mean-spirited guy. In fact, just the opposite. As anyone from our club will tell you, he's a wonderful man with a heart of gold.

"He's just a fun-loving country boy," J. C. Martin said. "I was a country boy, too, and he reminded me of guys I grew up with. But that son of a gun could pitch. It was just a wonderful thing to see him rise to the occasion. I remember him at the beginning of his first full season with the Mets: a game against the Giants in Shea Stadium. In the first inning, he quickly loaded the bases. But that son of a gun took his hat off, rubbed his forehead, and got them out without them scoring a run. I think from that day on, he realized he could pitch in the big leagues."

There's no doubt in my mind that Koosman's message resonated not only with our ball club but also with the Cubs, the fans who were at Shea, and the rest of the fans all around New York and Chicago. That pitch, that inning, that moment will live on in Mets history forever. Kooz proved that he was the warrior I always thought he was. And everybody on the team respected him for it.

Piggy took it even one big step further, saying, "Koosman won the pennant for us that night."

Years later, after Kooz was out of baseball, he was on a flight with a bunch of other former players—including Santo.

"Ron and I were sitting in seats close to one another," he recalled. "Pretty soon, after the plane is in the air, we're off our seats sitting on the armrests, BS-ing with one another. He says to me, 'Hey, Kooz, you know you damn near broke my arm that time. I know it was an accident, but you damn near broke my arm.' I said, 'Well, I thought I did. I kind of felt a little bad about that.'

"He said, 'I know the pitch got away from you.' And I said, 'Well, Ron, I've got to tell you: it didn't get away.' He said, 'Really?' And I said, 'Well, think about it: Hands knocked down Agee—he threw right at his bleepin' neck! What am I going to do? My job is to protect my players. You were up next. Boom. I've gotta get you.' Well, he was shocked that I threw at him on purpose. In fact, he kind of acted a little upset. All those years, he never thought I did it on purpose. I thought, *Geez, you gotta be thinking it was intentional, don't you?*"

Lost in all the commotion was the true grit displayed by Agee. Just as he had done in the previous night's game after getting brushed back by Phillies pitcher Bill Champion and then homering off him, Tommie again dusted himself off after Hands knocked him down. This time he went deep in the third inning to give us a 2–0 lead.

But the Cubs would tie it at two in the sixth when Kooz gave up consecutive singles to Don Kessinger, Glenn Beckert, and Billy Williams, and then a sacrifice fly to Santo.

There would be more fireworks and rising tempers in the bottom of that inning. Agee stayed red hot by lashing a leadoff double and then scored on a single by Garrett just slightly ahead of a sweeping tag by Cubs catcher Randy Hundley in what would become yet another iconic play in Mets lore. Hundley argued so vehemently that

Agee was out that he jumped high off the ground in outrage. I was honestly surprised he wasn't kicked out of the game. Randy was always a hard-nosed, fiery guy. He was a poor man's version of Grote in that respect, though not quite as unlikable to opposing players as Jerry was. From my vantage point, Agee was in there safely, and I think part of Hundley's explosive reaction was due to his club's pressing and starting to sense things falling apart all around them. Still, Hundley and Durocher screamed and yelled, as you would expect. You're always going to see a bang-bang play like that the way you want to see it. There would have probably been an argument either way. Getting that call just seemed pretty typical of the year we were having. We were winning in the game of inches.

"To this day, Hundley still argues that he tagged Agee out," Kooz recently said to me with delight.

Kooz held on to the 3–2 lead and would go the distance, striking out thirteen Cubs—including three in the ninth to finish off Chicago. We were now just a game and a half out of first place and feeling invincible.

The next night, a Tuesday, both clubs sent their respective aces to pitch in this huge game for both clubs before nearly fifty thousand fans. Seaver was vying for his twenty-first win, while Fergie Jenkins was trying to notch his twentieth. Fergie was a terrific pitcher—as good as any other in baseball. The funny thing about Jenkins was that no matter how hot it was when he pitched, he always wore this 100 percent wool shirt under his jersey and never perspired. I used to get on him all the time about that. He once answered back with a grin, "Well, I'm from Canada." But on the mound, he was a surgeon, consistently painting the black on both corners of the plate. One of his greatest attributes was an ability to induce hitters to swing at pitches they didn't like. I actually had decent success off of him over my career by working the count and waiting for a pitch to drill.

Even though we were facing a future Hall of Famer, I liked the matchup in this game for us. As a team, when a right-hander like Fergie would pitch, we could put out a pretty good lineup of left-handed hitters. And on this night, we jumped on Jenkins right away in the bottom of the first inning. After Agee and Cleon worked walks, I moved them both into scoring position with an infield groundout. Boz followed with a shot to right for a two-run double to give us an early 2–0 lead. Then the party was really on in the third inning after Clink took Jenkins deep for a two-run homer to put us up 4–0.

If the Cubs weren't demoralized enough by this point, what was to follow in the top of the fourth surely would do the trick. With one out, Glenn Beckert on second and Billy Williams at the plate, a black cat mysteriously dashed onto the field.

"I was watching from the dugout," Kooz remembered. "That black cat came out from right underneath the home plate side of the Cubs' dugout. There were these flaps under the stadium for when they moved things around for football games, and this cat went through one and ran right beside their dugout. The fans were all hollering and screaming—just going *berserk*!"

The cat had the presence of mind to stay on the third base side of the field, circle around Santo in the on-deck circle, and then stop and peer inside the Cubs' dugout, staring straight at Durocher. At the very least, it was an ominous sign for Chicago, and, at worst, it was as if this black cat was putting a hex on them. As someone who is very superstitious, I thought it was one of the most eerie things I've ever seen in my life. I would have freaked out had that cat come over and peered into our dugout.

"I was *loving* it! *Loving* it!" Kooz exclaimed. "I knew the beliefs and superstitions of black cats. Like a crack in a mirror or walking under a ladder. So I just thought, *Hey, something else in our favor. The black cat is working for us!* It was beautiful; absolutely *beautiful!* You couldn't have made a better movie scene than that."

"It was like we hired him from central casting," Swoboda said. "I kept thinking, *How do you train a cat to do that?* This cat acted like it had been trained. It wasn't a calico or a tiger, it was a solid-black cat that came from nowhere underneath the stands, probably scared shitless, running back and forth in front of their dugout. I'm not superstitious about that crap, but when you've got a stadium full of people and everybody saw it, it became a thing. And for it to happen during a crucial game against the Cubs was unbelievable."

Everybody was riveted and stunned by the cat's display.

"I don't think the umpires even called time-out," Kooz recalled. "Everybody was just watching that cat."

Eventually, after a minute or so, the cat disappeared back under the stands, and the game continued. Pete Flynn, the Mets' Irish-born groundskeeper since 1962, told me he had never seen that black cat before or after that day. Over the years, occasionally you would see a bird flop down in the outfield or read about someone seeing a rat, but never a cat—much less a black one.

In retrospect, it was another incredible moment in our season. It went from strange, to bizarre, to eerie, to "Somebody's watching over us. Somebody got this black cat to stare down Leo." The Cubs already knew we were coming at them. They already knew we were a viable team. Now *this* happens! I remember talking with Jenkins about it years later. He told me, "Thank God he didn't stare at me, because I would have freaked out!" A lot of people, especially ballplayers, are superstitious by nature. Many drive the same route to the ballpark, eat the same food before games—things like that. So I wouldn't be surprised if that black cat affected some of the Cubs in the days and even seasons to come. After all, it would take fifteen years before their organization won as many games as they did in 1969.

We would continue to have our way against Jenkins. When I homered off him in the fifth, it gave us a commanding 6–1 lead. And as Seaver finished off the Cubs in the ninth inning with a five-hitter to cut their lead over us to just a half game, Durocher really began to hear it from the chorus of the near sellout Shea Stadium crowd that joyously sang their own rendition of "Goodbye, Leo," yowled to the tune of "Goodnight, Ladies."

"Most of the fans were also waving white handkerchiefs, as if to tell Leo it was time to surrender," recalled Kooz.

In a sense, you almost had to feel a little sorry for the guy. *Almost.* Durocher got blamed for everything, even when Santo clicked his heels after Cub victories because we assumed it was a "Leo thing." Funny thing about Santo clicking his heels that year: late in the season, he stopped doing it. And Pignatano took credit for it.

"I just told him, 'Ron, you're too good a player to be acting like a clown,'" Piggy told me. "And he said, 'You know, Joe, I think you're right.' And he stopped."

The thing was, even though we hated to see Santo click his heels, Ronnie was a guy you had no problem talking to or looking at. In fact, once you got to know him, he was a terrific guy. Durocher, however, was a guy you didn't want anything to do with. All you wanted to do was beat him, and when you did, it made the victory a little sweeter.

But I think there were a number of stigmas at play with Leo, and that's why he was a lightning rod for how vehemently our fans reacted to him. His roots in New York baseball ran very deep. As a player, he began his career in 1925 with the Yankees and finished it twenty years later with the Brooklyn Dodgers, where he was also a player-manager for seven seasons. After his managerial stint with Brooklyn ended unceremoniously near the midpoint of the 1948 season, due, in part, to his outspoken personality and poor results, he jumped to pilot the archrival New York Giants, where he remained for eight seasons through 1955. Once beloved by Dodgers fans, he quickly became the enemy to them—many of whom would later become Mets fans.

"I was always kind of a fan of his as a kid," Cleon once told me. "The Dodgers and Giants were my favorite teams growing up. He was a good manager. But everybody loved beating Leo, I think, simply because he was Leo. I think his only flaw as a manager was that if he had a horse, he was going to ride it until it dropped. And that's what he did to some of his Cubs pitchers."

Some of us got to know the future Hall of Fame manager better later in our careers and found him to be a little mellower and even, dare I say, a nice guy. When I joined the Cubs as a free agent for a brief time in '72, it was Leo's last season there. He was sixty-six. When I saw him on my first day with the club, he smiled, put his hand out, and said, "Hi, Art, I'm happy to see you. I'm glad you're here." It was a very different persona than the fiery, win-at-all-costs demeanor of previous years.

Kooz had a similar experience.

"One winter, I was out in Scottsdale at a golf tournament," he recalled. "A few of us players went out to a nice restaurant, and, by God, Leo Durocher is in there sitting at another table not too far away—probably with his wife and some other people. After Leo finishes eating, he gets up and comes over to our table, puts his arm around my shoulder, and says, 'Let me tell you about this guy. We tried to trade for him, but we couldn't get him. The Mets wouldn't let him go. But I wanted this guy on our team.' I thought, *Holy smokes.*

Then he stayed with us, and we talked for a long time. He was pretty nice with us—a very friendly guy."

But I think it's safe to assume that Leo must not have been too pleasant to be around after losing two more pivotal games to us that September—and getting stared down by a black cat.

CHAPTER 12

LOOK WHO'S NO. 1

– September 10, 1969 –

IT WAS TRULY SURREAL. EVEN THOUGH WE HADN'T CLINCHED anything yet, and even though it was only September 10, with three weeks still remaining in the season, our Mets team had, after seven long years, climbed into first place for the very first time. As the crowd loudly chanted repeatedly, *"We're number one!"* a message on our giant scoreboard in right center field lit up to tell the whole Cinderella story.

LOOK WHO'S NO. 1

NL East	Won	Lost	Pct.
NY Mets	84	57	.596
Chi Cubs	84	59	.587

"It was like walking on the moon," Krane, an original Met, said. "You're in a different stratosphere at that point. We had never been that high in our life. We didn't know whether we were going to fall off the cloud, but it was a great feeling, and we felt we were invincible at that time. The way we were playing down the stretch run of the season, we didn't fear anybody. They were fearing *the Mets*, finally. The league knew that our organization had arrived."

This most celebrated and historic moment in Mets history to that point occurred just moments after Boswell hit a two-out seeing-eye base hit to bring Cleon home with the winning run in the bottom of the twelfth inning of a 3–2 victory over the Expos.

"My mama always used to tell me, 'Hit it where they ain't,'" Kenny said. His game-winning single "was a low, outside breaking ball that I hit through the middle. And that's when we had a little celebration at first base, knowing that we were now number one. But to be honest, we were so hot that we felt like first place was inevitable. Our mindset was to play as hard as we could and see what happened. And obviously, the rest is history."

Boz getting that momentous hit was of little surprise to me. While Kenny was best known for his defensive skills and would ultimately go on to establish a major-league record for second basemen with eighty-five consecutive errorless games the following season, it was his bat that was as responsible as anything in getting us into first place after being ten games back just four weeks earlier. After returning from military service, Boz would hit .407 from August 23 through the end of the regular season.

Kenny was enjoying a perfect existence—the epitome of a guy who was living life to the fullest. Not only was he a terrific all-around ballplayer on the hottest team in baseball, but he was also a young, handsome, vibrant, and charismatic single young man who was enjoying every moment that the nightlife of New York City could possibly bring. As one of the few married guys living in the city, I would drop him off at places on the East Side where we both lived, just hoping that I would see him the next day—especially in time for day games! Simply put, Kenny never lacked for female companionship.

"It was a dream come true," Boswell once gushed to me. "Living in the city was like one big party—there's no question about it. And you know, it's been said that people from New York love people from Texas. So playing for the Mets was doubly good for me. And when you're twenty-one, twenty-two, or three-three years old, your recuperative powers are a lot better than they are when you get a little older. So I didn't have a lot of problems with staying out late and getting to the ballpark and being ready to play. I would do anything to go back to 1969 and relive some of those nights on the East Side—we had so much fun! And it was good, *clean* fun! Near the end of the '69 season, as a Met, you could walk into a place, and you might get a standing ovation. Or sit in a restaurant, and people might put a bottle of whiskey or a bottle of wine on your table. When we started winning, everything just steamrolled. You couldn't go anywhere without the cook coming out of the kitchen or people telling you how proud they were of you and to go get 'em! They were really behind us. I wish I could shake hands with everyone I met that year. And go back and see *every girl* I met, too! It all went by so fast. From August on, it was a blur."

But for as much as Boz enjoyed Manhattan in '69, he noted to me how things had changed for the worse soon thereafter.

"The drug scene in New York is what changed everything," Kenny believes. "I can now go on the record that I never did a drug of any kind—*ever*. And if others around me did, it was hush-hush. But in '69, you could go up and down First Avenue, Second Avenue, Third Avenue, and it'd be jumping. Lots of places to go, lots of people on the street. Everybody was just abusing alcohol—nothing else. But after that, the bars kind of emptied out, and the New York scene became a kind of hidden culture. You'd have to go to people's apartments and stuff like that, so it wasn't as much fun in my later years there. Still, I made so many friends, *genuine* friends, that if I went back there now, I guarantee they would still be friends today. I miss that part of it."

But it wasn't just wine, women, and song that made the second baseman from Austin fall in love with New York. Like many of us on the Mets, Kenny enjoyed his celebrity in other ways.

"We were friends with many of the Jets, the Rangers, and the Knicks, especially guys like Dave DeBusschere and Walt Frazier," Boz recalled. "I went to a lot of their basketball games. Of course, we had little privileges at Madison Square Garden. You could get tickets or sit on the photographers' bench and then go into the clubhouse after Knicks games. It was just a great time. Where else but New York City? I mean, c'mon! It's just the best of everything in the world in New York."

For those of us on the Mets that lived in Manhattan, it was as if we were princes of the city. I used to go to this diner right around the corner from where I was living in the East Sixties. I would walk in, and *everyone*—even the owners, who were from Greece and weren't into baseball at all—knew that we were the talk of the town. With all the bad news that was going on around the world, we were a ray of hope for New Yorkers because of the surprisingly great baseball we were playing. We were all so recognizable because we were in the news so much now. Bruce Stark, a renowned sports artist with the *Daily News*, was doing special caricatures of us, the front pages of the newspapers around the country were following us, and we were all over television. And remember, this was still a good ten years before cable television came along. We were just so visible for that time.

So when we at last reached first place, the idea that Vegas had us pinned as a preseason 100-to-1 long shot to win the NL East was a distant memory. We were playing great baseball, we had confidence, things were falling our way, and everybody was contributing to the effort.

Eddie Charles, a veteran of eighteen professional seasons, reflected on Kenny's game-winning hit that put us in first: "In all my years in the game, I never saw a team blessed with so many guys throughout the lineup that, when you really needed someone to step up and get a big hit for you, would come through. To that point in the season, you can talk about Weis, Bozzy, Shamsky, Agee, Jonesy, Clendenon, Kranepool, and just keep going down the line, and they all delivered big hits for us. It was incredible."

"I felt if I didn't do it," Boz said, "somebody else would have. But I'm glad it was me!"

There was a second game of the doubleheader to play that night, and what a luxury it was to have a "spot starter" like Nolan Ryan take the hill for us. I was back in right field again that night, just the way I liked it. While Ryan would turn out to be every bit as successful as Seaver and even more so than Kooz, it was a much different dynamic playing behind him. With both Tom and Kooz pitching, you always had to be on your toes. They threw a lot of strikes and worked fast—getting the ball back and pitching in a quick rhythm. But with Nolan pitching, you had a tendency sometimes to be back on your heels.

In one typical Ryan game, I was playing first base, and he was going 3–2 on virtually every hitter. And then, because Nolan had great stuff, the opposing hitters couldn't square up on him—so they kept fouling off pitches. Our bachelor Boz, who was playing second base, came halfway in toward the mound and yelled out, "Hey, Nolan, I've got a date tonight! I got to get out of here!" And Ryan said, "Get the hell away from me!" It was really funny to watch. But while Nolan had the least control on the entire staff, he had such overpowering stuff that when Gil would start him in second games of doubleheaders like this one, he was hard for hitters to pick up.

True to form in this game, Ryan threw a ton of pitches in striking out eleven Expos and walking four, though he still went the distance in pitching a three-hit 7–1 gem. Although the opening game that put us into first place got all the attention, Nolan's performance was hardly anticlimactic. It gave us our sixth straight win and moved us a full game in front of the fading Cubs. After the game, some of us toasted Boz and Ryan—the two heroes of the day—with champagne and sparkling burgundy that Seaver poured into paper cups for us.

"Coming on like we did and catching the Cubs from ten games back made us feel great . . . really proud," Kooz said.

Now we had a lead to pad.

CHAPTER 13

EXPECTING THE UNEXPECTED

– September 12–15, 1969 –

OVER THE NEXT FOUR DAYS, TWO OF THE MOST UNLIKELY occurrences that could ever take place on a ball field played out for us in a big way. But then again, it had long since felt as if the uncommon was now commonplace in the season we were having.

On September 12, a Friday, we were in Pittsburgh for a doubleheader against the Pirates. The Bucs were throwing two right-handers that day—Bob Moose and Dock Ellis—and I would most assuredly be penciled into the lineup and playing right field in both games. But prior to the doubleheader, I decided to observe Rosh Hashanah, the Jewish New Year. Sandy Koufax had famously skipped a game one start in the 1965 World Series because it landed on Yom Kippur, the holiest day in Judaism—just as another Jewish superstar, the Detroit Tigers' Hank Greenberg, had done thirty-one years prior when he opted to miss a key, late-season game against the Yankees. Nevertheless, this was a tough time for me. It was a decision that, for whatever reason, I needed to make at what was certainly a crucial time of our season. So I went to Gil to talk about it.

"Look, you do what you think is best. I'm okay with it," Hodges told me. "I'll back you up."

I didn't have a close relationship with Gil, but he was always fair in matters like this. But while he made my difficult decision a little easier, I still had my doubts. I remember thinking to myself, *Oh my gosh, we can't lose the doubleheader now. If we do, I'll definitely get some hate mail.* Fans can be cruel. They might write things like "How can you do that to your team?" Or, of course, much worse. And then I thought, *Well, if we split the two games, then the letters won't be that bad.* I was really dealing with a strong internal struggle over the whole thing. The reality is that I still have no idea why I chose that particular day, in that particular year, and at that particular time to take a day off for a Jewish holiday. I had never done it before. But part of the reason I never had was that it often fell on an off-day or a day game, which meant we were off that particular night. But that wasn't the case in every instance, which leaves me perplexed as to why I chose a day in September 1969—one of the most thrilling months of my big-league career—to observe this Jewish holiday. I guess you can't explain certain things that happen to you in your lifetime. Something just made me want to do it then.

Over the years, what I did that day has taken on a life of its own. Many people who weren't even born yet in 1969 have come up to me and talked about how my decision influenced them in a positive way. Parents come up to me all the time telling me what a good example I set for their children. And I've always said if I can influence somebody in a positive way, I've done something really good. But the reality of it was I was hoping the entire day that we wouldn't lose the doubleheader because I would have really felt the brunt of fans hating me if it happened. As it turned out, Koosman and Cardwell, our pitchers that day, each single-handedly made sure it wouldn't.

"Cardy and I were in Pittsburgh a day before the rest of the team," Kooz recalled. "Gil flew us ahead a day early so we could get our rest. That really helped us get settled in."

And settled in they were.

In the first game, Kooz went the distance, pitching a three-hit shutout against a superb Pirates lineup that featured sluggers such as rookie Al Oliver, Willie Stargell, and, of course, the great Roberto Clemente. Kooz also drove in the game's only run: a single in the top of the fifth inning that scored Pfeil. For a pitcher to toss a shutout and drive in the lone run in a game is rare enough—a feat that might not be repeated for years.

The Mets, however, in our wacky season, wouldn't have to wait nearly that long. That's because Cardwell, a tough competitor and quality pitcher, was also up to the task, putting up nothing but zeros in the second game after he drove in the only run with a single to score Harrelson in the top of the second. McGraw came into the game in the ninth to preserve Cardy's four-hit masterpiece.

"We both hit singles over second base, Cardy and me," Kooz recalled vividly. "Little did we know they would both be game winners."

I firmly believe that the two of them, like most pitchers would be, were far more proud of their RBIs than their shutout performances. The two of them later argued over which of them hit the ball harder ("I hit mine better; yours was a fluke"—and things like that), which was hysterical. Cardwell, to his credit, was actually a pretty good hitter for a pitcher and even hit some home runs in his career. Kooz might not want to hear it, but he was not much of a hitter, though if you ask him, he'll say he was a *great* one!

In any event, it was another day that would go down in Mets folklore, a phenomenal story line that will live on forever. Not only did we beat a Pittsburgh team that hit us as well as any other in baseball, but also we shut them out in both games, with our pitchers producing the only runs off two very good pitchers in Moose and Ellis.

Duffy Dyer, who caught Kooz's shutout, recalled, "Of everything that happened to us during the season, I remember those back-to-back shutouts the most."

When I returned to the club the next day, there was a sign by my locker that read "We Won the Doubleheader. Why Don't You Take Off the Rest of the Year?" I didn't know for sure who was behind this latest bit of clubhouse humor, though it had to have been Clendenon. We all had a good laugh over it. And why not? After all, the most important things to me were that we won that doubleheader, and I was back in my element, ready to help the team win in any way I could.

That afternoon, Seaver would pitch yet another complete game victory for his twenty-second win of the season, 5–2. It was our tenth win in a row to move us three and a half games ahead of Chicago. We felt unbeatable.

On September 15, the second of the two incredible happenings that week occurred in a game at St. Louis's Busch Memorial Stadium. Steve Carlton, the future Hall of Fame pitcher who could, on any given night, pitch as well as anybody in baseball, was on the hill for the Cardinals. Then just a twenty-four-year-old southpaw, Lefty would strike out nineteen Mets to set a new all-time major-league record for strikeouts in a game—*yet we still won 4–3!*

But that was hardly the only extraordinary occurrence that evening. What was just as uncanny was how Swoboda led the charge with a couple of two-run homers, while also striking out twice. Rocky gave some of the credit for his big game to one of our broadcasters—Hall of Fame slugger Ralph Kiner—and explained how he could be so good in some at bats and so overmatched in others against Carlton.

"Before the game," Swoboda recalled, "I went to Ralph and said, 'I'm struggling a little. And I've never done much against Carlton. Is there anything you might suggest?' So Kiner takes me down to a batting cage they had at Busch Stadium behind the left field fence. He fed me a bunch of balls off an old pitching machine they had there, then looked at me, and said, 'Get your hands higher. Take a couple of hacks and let me know how it feels? Let me know if you're comfortable that way.' So I started hitting some balls real good, and he said, 'I liked the way that looked. Let's go with that.' I don't know if it was the attention Ralph gave me, the extra swings, or both, but I went into that game with Carlton, who had extragreat stuff that night, and got some good swings off him—even if the end result wasn't always perfect. Because against a Hall of Famer like him, you could get some good swings and still not find the ball.

Anyway, I can't help but think, *Why didn't I go to Ralph before, and why didn't I do so on a continuing basis?* I think the whole team would have been fine with Ralph talking a little hitting and just looking at us. You think about the metrics in today's game and the studio study and accentuation. Every team in the big leagues has two hitting coaches, for crying out loud! Back then, we had Yogi, who would say something like, 'If you can't hit it, don't swing at it.' And you'd be like, 'Well, what about with two strikes?' And he might say, 'Well, then you might have to swing at it.' That was hitting advice from Yogi. As a player, he could just do it. As a coach, I don't think he could explain it. Ralph, on the other hand, had a little idea about what a hitter ought to look like up there."

Kiner was, indeed, a student of the game. He flat-out knew hitting and faced some great pitchers over his career. In retrospect, like Swoboda, I wish I would have grabbed him and said, "Ralph, sometimes I struggle with this pitch," or "I'm struggling in this situation. What should I do?" Just pick his brain and utilize his baseball intellect. After all, Ralph would be down on the field on occasion during batting practice, so it would have been easy to do. But prior to my work with him as a broadcaster, I was really too shy to walk up to him and ask him about hitting. I wasn't the type to intrude on anyone's space. But I really should have. He was a slugger I watched as a kid when he played first base and the outfield for the Pirates. I used to think, *This guy's such a great hitter on a bad team.* In fact, Kiner held the mark for the most home runs by a right-handed batter over a ten-year period until Phillies third baseman Mike Schmidt came along and broke it. And he led the National League in homers his first seven years in the game, from 1946 through 1952 (hitting more than anyone in both leagues in six of those seasons), before injuries ended his career prematurely. I always thought it was odd that it took fifteen years—in Kiner's final year of eligibility—for him to finally be voted into Cooperstown.

In this unlikeliest of victories, Rocky struck out with two men on to end the top of the first, but then gave us a 2–1 edge in the fourth with a deep home run to left. Swoboda would again strike out before hitting his second homer of the game in the eighth to put us back in front, 4–3. Carlton fanned the side in the ninth, including an inning-ending punch-out of Amos Otis for the fourth time of the game, to get his record nineteenth K. But for all his dominance, Lefty wouldn't get rewarded with a win, as Tug closed out the bottom of the ninth for a three-inning save. The win propelled us to a season-high four-and-a-half-game lead over the Cubs.

"I was a guest on a postgame show with Harry Caray," Rocky recalled. "I walked into the room and thought, *Holy smokes!* when I saw Steve Carlton sitting there. He looked like somebody had just run over his dog with a car—he was pretty desolate. And I'm thinking, *Well, this is uncomfortable.* So I did the postgame interview with Harry, and when I was done, Carlton talked to him. How about the fact that Steve Carlton talked to Caray after a loss like that? You think some of the guys today would do that?"

Rocky used that big game against Carlton as a springboard for the remainder of the campaign, easily becoming one of our more dangerous hitters.

"That stretch run was the easiest baseball I've ever played in my life," he told me. "Something gets into your nervous system—something clearly chemical, and you're making chemistry. We were manufacturing our own performance-enhancing drugs, and it came from nothing other than the excitement of realizing what we were accomplishing. We were now in the driver's seat, and it was scary and exciting all at the same time. I was a feel hitter and felt really good down the stretch. I was able to keep the fire of the moment. I was not a technically complex player. I was really more of an emotion-of-the-moment kind of player—never 'heady' or intellectually into the game. There were guys who were true students of the game. If I even pretended to be a student of the game, I don't think you'd want to see my report card! But I was into it—we were all into it—and nothing will get you more focused than playing great baseball."

It was a game where we could have been excused for thinking, *We're overmatched today. Carlton's got great stuff. We'll be lucky to get a couple of hits. How can we possibly win?* But Rocky comes up big with two home runs, Gentry limits the defending National League champion Cardinals to just three runs over six, and McGraw closes it out with three near-perfect innings of relief. That's the kind of baseball we were playing. Plus, fate was clearly working on our side. In other words, this game was just another microcosm of our magical season.

CHAPTER 14

THE CLINCHER

– September 24, 1969 –

FITTINGLY, THE OPPONENT FOR OUR FINAL HOME GAME OF the regular season and our only chance to clinch the division title at Shea Stadium was St. Louis, then mired in fourth place. That's because just prior to this three-game series, word had spread that long-time, legendary Cardinals announcer Harry Caray, still incredulous over our miracle season, had made the stunning proclamation that not a single Met could start ahead of any of the two-time defending National League champions. For some of us, it just further fueled our motivation to sweep the three games and end their two-year reign on our own turf.

"Well, you know Harry Caray made his living out of talking," J. C. Martin surmised, "and he evaluated players in his own mind. But he didn't know what players could do, and he didn't know what it was like to compete in a ball game. The Cardinals had a tremendously talented ball club. We went into St. Louis and had to face Gibson and Carlton and all those seasoned veterans they had. But if you went down our lineup and looked at our pitching staff, he should have seen just how competitive we were with Koosman, Seaver, Ryan, and Gentry, even if they were young and still learning how to deal in pressure situations. Harry had a famous team—the Cardinals—for whom he had called games for many years. But he evaluated those players way above what they could really do. They may have been good players, but some days you just don't hit the ball or you don't throw it where you want to. He saw the Mets as a bunch of no-names. But we could compete and give teams a lot of trouble—we could play with anybody. Harry didn't want to understand that and certainly didn't want to broadcast it. He was so dead wrong."

Of course, J.C. was correct about this. Right off the top of my head, we had Cleon, a .340 hitter that year, who could have played on any team. And as good as Tim McCarver was as an all-around ballplayer, his catching skills couldn't compare with Grote's—who also could have played for any club. Then you had our starting pitching and bullpen, which may have been the best in baseball. I think that for Caray, and many others in the press boxes around the league, it was a perception issue. They saw us as just a year removed from being longtime lovable losers, and frustration over our meteoric rise abounded.

And then there was the idea that if you looked at other clubs' offensive numbers our success didn't add up. Because of Gil's platoon system at five positions, it was easy for someone to say, "Well, this Met or that Met couldn't play for me." But if you combine, for example, my statistics with Swoboda's in right field, we collectively had a terrific year. The same with Clink and Krane at first. And defensively, we were very strong up the middle—something else that doesn't jump out at you in statistical analysis. Clearly, Harry and others didn't really stop and think about what they were saying. Instead, they just thought, *This is all hard to believe. We're missing something here.* But while people like Caray were still downplaying all the success we were enjoying, I'm glad we proved them wrong. But I'll say this: ill-advised statements like Harry's made for great, and highly motivating, clubhouse bulletin board material.

Ironically, we were all rooting for the Cubs in their game earlier that day at Wrigley, because a Chicago win over the Expos would keep us from backing into a division crown. Thankfully, they obliged, and their victory gave our 54,928 fans at Shea a chance to party along with us that evening should we defeat the Cardinals. And the significance wasn't lost on the twenty-two-year-old Gentry, our rookie starting pitcher that night.

"I knew full well that the Cubs winning that day made it possible for us to clinch on our own instead of backing in," Gentry said. "So that made it *much* more exciting. I understood the magnitude and was just so happy about getting the ball. The game wasn't life-or-death, as we had still had five games after that, but I was glad we had a chance to win it with me pitching."

But if he was to succeed, he would have to do it against Steve Carlton.

"It seemed like I always pitched against Carlton every time we played the Cardinals," Gentry said. "But I wasn't too concerned. I don't think I ever really had any problems with them. Even the night Carlton struck out nineteen against us, Swoboda hit two home runs—so we still won. So I didn't have any particular strategy that I can recall. I just did what Grote told me to do."

"Gent," as I liked to call him, had become a terrific pitcher for us, though naturally he kind of got lost behind Seaver and Koosman. At six feet and 170 pounds, he was slight of build but had a great arm and even better stuff. The right-hander's delivery always came right over the top and featured a live fastball, a decent curve, and a good slider. Gent was the perfect third starter on that team, in much the same way that Claude Osteen complemented Sandy Koufax and Don Drysdale on the Dodgers teams I faced earlier in the decade. And like many of our young arms, Gent didn't lack in the confidence department and would often get frustrated with Gil for removing him early from games.

"I always wanted to win every game I ever started and finish every game I ever started," he told me. "I once said something in the papers about it, and I got called into Gil's office. He questioned me about my comments, and I said, 'Gil, I promise you if you let me pitch every game until it's over, I'll win you twenty games a year.' And he just laughed. I think I could have done better statistically, but that's just the way the Mets pitched me."

As my teammates took the field, it was a classic night at Shea. We had our usual big crowd that was revved up from the time the national anthem was played. There was a tremendous media presence, with writers and photographers in from all over the country. There was so much tension in the air because of all the ramifications of closing it out that night. And as meaningful as it was for me and many others on the club, it was especially so for guys such as Swoboda, Tug, and Krane, who had been with the club for so many of the down years. They were now in uncharted waters. After all, this was the first season the Met veterans played important games after the middle of July, much less one with a division title in play.

"We never celebrated anything but rainouts in the earlier years," Krane would always tell me with a grin. Can't lose another one if your game gets canceled.

Gentry would show little signs of nervousness in the top of the first, going right after and retiring a veritable trio of All-Stars in Lou Brock, Curt Flood, and Vada Pinson in short order. And then our offense went right to work against the masterful Carlton.

After Buddy led off with a single and Agee walked, Lefty came back to strike out Cleon for the first out. But then Clink positively brought the roof down with a three-run blast over the center field wall to give us a quick, commanding 3–0 lead. An understandably stunned Carlton then walked his old nemesis, Swoboda, to bring up the Glider—our thirty-six-year-old leader.

"Being the eldest guy on the team," Charles explained, "I had to send a message and show the young guys that 'Oh man, I still got a little left in the tank!' I played that way the whole year. I thought that'll motivate them because they don't want to see that 'old man' outdo them! As such, I really didn't go out and socialize with any of them because I knew I only had a little time left in the majors. I had to keep my body in shape, and I had to produce. Some of the black players would get mad at me and say, 'That son of a bitch . . . ' and everything under the sun. But I had a plan. And sure enough, it worked!"

Carlton would deliver his signature slider to Eddie. Willie Stargell once compared trying to hit it to drinking coffee with a fork. Others called Carlton's slider the toughest pitch to hit in the league. But as the phrase *"Never throw a slider to the Glider!"* had become part of Mets folklore by that time, Eddie planted the ball beyond Flood's outstretched glove over the right center field fence for a two-run homer and a 5–0 advantage. The game had quickly become a rout and, as Eddie rounded the bases clapping his hands in delight, the crowd erupted in a deafening uproar even as cannonlike sounds of fireworks boomed in the distance from the parking lot. As the jolted Carlton was removed from the game, we could taste victory.

But back to that famous phrase and how Eddie got his nickname.

"It was Jerry Koosman," Charles explained. "We were playing one Sunday afternoon in a shaded area, and a guy hit a bullet down to me at third base. I just scooped it up and threw him out at first. Kooz was so impressed that he ran off the mound all the way over to me and said, 'That was one hell of a play.' I just looked at him like he was crazy to run over to me on the field like that. And then he said, 'You don't move like the regular infielders. You sort of glide to the ball. That's it! You're the Glider!' And that's how it came about— and it really stuck. Now you had all the announcers on the air and old Tug McGraw start saying, 'Never throw a slider to the Glider!' I remember Ralph Kiner twice had me on his *Kiner's Korner* postgame show after I hit home runs. He'd say, 'What pitch was it you hit for the home run?' I never said what the real pitch was, because nobody knew the difference. So I would just always say a slider. Even if it was a fastball up in my eyes!"

Clink would make the score 6–0 with his second dinger of the night: a fifth-inning home run off reliever Dave Giusti. Meanwhile, Gent cruised through the Cardinals batting order like a seasoned veteran. Admittedly, the big start by the Mets in the opening inning helped put him at ease.

"When you get an early lead like that," Gent explained, "you don't have to worry about being too perfect. You can just go out there and throw and hope for the best. Even one run would have been enough to make things easier, but we scored a bunch early that night."

With the game never in doubt from the very first inning, Shea Stadium took on a carnival-like atmosphere throughout the evening, with confetti, banners, fireworks, and one last rendition of "Goodbye, Leo!" by the throngs of fans—to mock the loathed Chicago manager whose Cubs had held a ten-game lead over us less than six weeks before. To this day, it's still a season that is very painful to Cubs fans.

"I live in Arizona," Duffy Dyer told me recently, "and there are *a lot* of Cubs fans there. When they notice my '69 World Series ring, they'll usually say stuff like, 'Oh, you broke my heart! Aww, the Cubs blew it!' And I'll say something like, 'No, we won it! We won it! We won the division by eight games! How can you say the Cubs blew it? It's not like we beat them on the last day of the season.'"

I would add to Duffy's take with how I always tell people it wasn't so much that the Cubs blew it, it was just that we were unbeatable down the stretch. We beat them head-to-head and just blew by them. They just didn't have the balance we had. Unable to resist, I'll joke with Cubs fans and say, "That's why they call Chicago the Second City!"

In the ninth, Gentry, pitching a magnificent two-hit shutout, walked out to the mound to a standing ovation. With nobody warming in the bullpen, the game was his to finish—an honor our slender right-hander had resoundingly earned. The sellout crowd was on their feet, many standing on top of their seats, while thousands of others jammed the aisles—ready to storm the field after the final out. The famous "Sign Man of Shea," Karl Ehrhardt, was just beyond the third base dugout, getting the fans even more revved up. It was the moment we, as players, and our loyal fans had waited for.

I couldn't help but think how far we had come since the previous season when we finished ninth, just one game out of last place. And how Gil had led us to this point, exactly one year to the day from a mild heart attack he had suffered in Atlanta, at just age forty-four, that sidelined him for the last few games of the season. And how, since August 13, we had gained a remarkable sixteen games in the standings. And how, during those awful times for the city and our country, this moment was giving the crowd something to hold on to—to give them some excitement and make them forget, if only for a time, all the calamities taking place outside the ballpark. *Everybody* was caught up in this moment: the players on the bench, on the field, and in the bullpen, and the fans in the stands.

The boisterous crowd chanted "We're number one!" in unison as the inning began. Back-to-back singles by Brock and Vic Davilillo opened the top of the ninth for the Cardinals but did little to dissipate the enthusiasm for the inevitable outcome. Gentry would come back to strike out Pinson for the first out. Now Gary had to face first baseman Joe Torre, easily the Cardinals' most dangerous hitter, and a guy who could hit to all fields with authority—and hardly ever strike out.

"Joe Torre had this incredible way of hitting against me," Gentry recalled. "He always hit the ball back up the middle. He even hit me in the foot a couple of times that year."

But this time, thankfully, was a little different.

"Torre hit it a little farther to the left," Gary said. "When I saw the ball hit the ground, I thought, *Oh, that's perfect. He's not gonna beat it—he's not gonna beat that throw to first.* I was just thrilled to see it happen."

The result was a perfect double-play ball—Harrelson to Weis to Clendenon—to end the game and clinch the NL East Division title. An unbelievable scene followed—*pure bedlam*—as thousands of fans poured onto the field like locusts while our guys raced for the safety of our clubhouse. Crowd control? Crowd control then was the police saying, "Go ahead, do whatever you want." In a matter of moments, the fans tore up the field and grabbed anything—bases, home plate, hats, sod—whatever they possibly could get their hands on. They wanted mementos of this incredible time after they had no reason to think, as late as the middle of August, that we were going to be anything much better than a second-division team. But now everything had changed: the dream of a division title had become a reality. It wasn't a pennant or a World Series championship, but it was an accomplishment the Mets had never been close to before. Thankfully, for the ground crew, it was the final home game of the regular season, so they had a week to get the field ready for the very first National League Championship Series (NLCS) in baseball history.

"Oh God," recalled Pete Flynn. "That was a disaster because we had to come in the next day and fix it. I mean, they really ripped the field up. And then some fans broke into the stadium late that night because security wasn't that tight at the time. They took the team

emblems, so everything had to be replaced in time for the next series. We had fourteen guys on the ground crew between extras and
steady guys. But the excitement was still there the next day—it was
unbelievable. We were all so young and excited about the team. We
were true Mets fans."

You had to be impressed with those guys. Pete and his crew had
suffered through some lean years, too, and there's no doubt they
were as excited as we were. And they were really good guys. We got
to know them well because they got to the ballpark early and were
always out there working on the field. Even while we took batting
practice, they were out doing something to make the field nicer.
They became a part of our lives, and I was so happy for them.

So while the fans rushing the field as aggressively and destruc-
tively as they did was a little scary, we were all wrapped up in this
division-clinching victory and defying the odds. In fact, Gentry
would go as far as to say, in reflection, that he wished he wasn't so
quick to vacate the field.

"Over the years," Gary told me, "I thought instead of running off
the field and trying to hide, I should have stayed out there and talked
to some of the fans—shake their hands or something. But the whole
team was running to get off the field, and it might have been a mistake to stay out there; maybe a little dangerous. But I always think in
my mind that I should have celebrated a little with them. I think it
would have been kind of fun to stay out there a little bit."

The clubhouse celebration was epic, with shaving cream and
cases of Great Western champagne sprayed and poured on everyone
from the players, to the reporters, to the announcers, to His Honor
himself, Mayor John Lindsay. The moment was literally intoxicat-
ing—pure pandemonium.

"We drank a lot of that champagne, too," Krane recalled. "We really partied. We were just so happy to be in the playoffs. September

for us had always been a training period to bring up young players. You had nothing to play for, so the game of baseball now became really fun to everybody. And being as young as we were, with the exceptions of Eddie Charles and Donn Clendenon, we were a club that grew up together. So we had a lot of things to celebrate."

Said Dyer, "It was just a terrific scene in that clubhouse. Of course, you had Tug running around like he had his head cut off—never knowing what he was going to do or say. Those six months of the season went so fast that I just didn't appreciate it as much as some of the other guys that had been in the big leagues for a few years. After we won it, I realized how big an underdog we were and thought, *This is unbelievable!* Now I look back and appreciate what we accomplished even more."

The next day was an off-day before heading down to Philadelphia for a series with the Phillies. A day to reflect—and recover from the greatest victory and celebration most of us had ever experienced.

CHAPTER 15

A BRAVE NEW WORLD

– October 4–6, 1969 –

IT WAS A SERIES OF THE UNEXPECTED. OUR STELLAR START-ing pitching, easily the greatest strength of our ball club, would take a pounding at the hands of a relentlessly power-hitting Atlanta Braves lineup that featured the likes of Henry Aaron, Orlando Cepeda, Rico Carty, Clete Boyer, and Felipe Alou. It would, instead, be our hitting, and near-perfect relief pitching, that would carry us through the NLCS and into the World Series.

"We went into that series thinking, *It's going to be a pitching duel,*" mused Koosman. "Both clubs had good pitchers. What it turned into was 'a hitters' duel!' The starters were getting raked over the coals."

With the Braves having a predominantly right-handed pitching staff, Gil would go exclusively with his left-handed-hitting platoon. This meant that I would be in the lineup each game along with Boz, Krane, and third baseman Wayne Garrett.

"I felt our best-hitting lineup was with our left-handed hitters," Krane told me. "And we proved it by dominating the Atlanta Braves. We scored a lot of runs, and we had a good time doing it. We would have never gotten to the World Series if we didn't score all those runs in the three games against Atlanta. And where the right-handed hitters did well in the World Series, the left-handers played in just one of those games and scored six runs. The right-handers were scraping out runs in some of those games—you know what I mean? But that's why Gil didn't fool anybody; he managed in a set way of doing things, and he continued to do that all the time."

Another benefit we had going into the series was how relaxed and confident we felt. The club's average age was just twenty-five, yet we weren't overwhelmed in the least by all the veteran stars on the Braves roster. I think that had a lot to do with Hodges and all the success we had during the regular season. Hodges was a cool, calm, and collected manager. He just made out the lineup and never panicked over it at any time. And winning all those close games like we did built a tremendous amount of confidence in ourselves. So, as far as we were concerned, it was pretty much business as usual.

"We checked into the Marriott the night before the series," my roommate Boz recalled. "And my dad, who came along on the trip, was putting on his pajamas while Art and I were getting ready to go out. So my dad says, 'What are y'all doin'?' and I said, 'Art and I are going out. We can't change anything now.' And he goes, 'You got a big playoff game tomorrow; a *day* game.' And I said, 'Dad, you can either stay here or you can come with us, but we're going out.' So we came dragging back in—I don't know what time it was—but we weren't going to get up earlier than usual because it was the playoffs."

According to Cleon, "We had maybe one or two guys that were a little uptight, but even they felt good about our chances. Personally, I don't ever remember being uptight, intimidated, or frightened by anything. After all, we knew for a fact that we were a team to be reckoned with." A 100–62 (.617) win-loss record, surpassed only by the Baltimore Orioles, will tend to do that. "When you have that kind of confidence in your pitching staff, your regular players, and your bench," he continued, "you have to love your chances. Every player on the team had a hand in our success—every one of them."

Personally, I felt really locked in going into game one against future Hall of Fame knuckleballer Phil Niekro. Throughout my entire career, I always considered myself to be a self-taught hitter, rarely working with hitting coaches. I typically made my own adjustments. You talk to any really good hitters, and they'll tell you how they constantly adjust in accordance with what kind of pitcher is out there, what the count is—those types of factors. What I did with Niekro was move up in the batter's box a little bit. I knew he wasn't going to throw anything by me, so in each at bat, I'd cheat and move up two or three inches toward him. All I wanted to do, like against other knuckleball pitchers, was to just try to hit the ball right back at him. You never want to pull a knuckleball, but just put it in play.

My strategy worked, as I collected three hits in four at bats off Niekro. But as much success as we had off him as a team that game, we found ourselves trailing 5–4 after seven innings. The Braves were having their way against Seaver, who had given up a practically unprecedented eight hits, including home runs to Aaron and Tony Gonzalez. But we never lost hope for a second. Even Seaver never got down on himself or the team, maintaining a conviction to us all in the dugout that we would come back and win.

And that's exactly what would happen.

Our bats came to life in a big way in the top of the eighth to save the day. Garrett doubled to lead off, and Cleon followed with a single to tie the game at five apiece. I then singled to give us runners on first and second. After Boz hit into a force-out at second to put runners on the corners, Krane hit a one-hopper to first baseman Cepeda, who threw errantly to home, allowing Jones to score and giving us a 6–5 lead. Grote grounded slowly to Boyer to move Boz to third and Krane to second. With two outs now, and Seaver due up, Niekro intentionally walked Buddy to load the bases. That's when Gil made a brilliant decision to pinch-hit for Seaver and bring up J. C. Martin.

J.C. is one of the nicest and most decent men I've ever met. Boz and I used to try to trick him into saying swear words, but he never took the bait. I always thought it was an interesting coincidence that he went by the initials *J.C.* and had strong Christian beliefs. But he was also a tough competitor, one of our few veteran presences on the club, and a great guy to have come off the bench in big spots like this one.

"With Gil, you always had to be ready on the bench to hit," J.C. said. "He used anybody at any time. So when he called on me in that situation with the game on the line—bases loaded and two outs—it really perked me up. As I began walking to the plate, the on-deck batter, Tommie Agee, goes to me, 'Hey, J, he's throwing that knuckleball—you know. Go up there and just look for a changeup. Because that knuckler looks just like one. That's how slow it is.' That was great encouragement to me, and when I got up to the plate, that's what I was looking for. And when I got it, it was like batting practice, because I felt like I knew exactly what was coming."

Martin ripped a single to right center field to score Boz and Krane, and then, on the same play, Buddy would come around to score on an error by center fielder Gonzalez, to break the game wide open—giving us a commanding 9–5 edge.

"I had a different philosophy coming off the bench from when I first came up to the big leagues," J.C. told me. "When I was a younger player, I thought I had to hit a lot of home runs and stuff like that. But then during spring training one year, I drove a single to right field. As I stood on first base, Stan Musial was there and said, 'Boy, it feels good to hit a line drive down the right field line, doesn't it?' And I said, 'Yeah, it really does. I like to hit the ball hard and pull it.' And Musial said, 'You know, J.C., I found out there's just as much room in left to hit the ball as there is in right.' It was the greatest tip anyone had ever given me. I wish I had taken it to heart earlier in my career. But as I got older, I found out if I just put the ball in play, it was often just as good as hitting home runs. I actually became a better hitter as

I got older because of that way of thinking. And it certainly worked for me in that playoff game in Atlanta."

Taylor would come in from the bullpen to collect a scoreless, two-inning save to preserve our 9–5 victory. It was a tremendous feeling to outscore a terrific Braves offense on a day when the Franchise had less than his best stuff. The fact we were able to overcome Seaver's subpar performance just reinforced to us all how talented and mentally strong we were.

Despite all the offensive fireworks in the first game, most of us again were anticipating a pitchers' duel for game two. We had as good a big-game pitcher as there was in Kooz on the hill for us that day, while the Braves gave the ball to eighteen-game winner Ron Reed. Koosman initially performed as we expected, holding Atlanta's fearsome lineup to just one run over the first four innings. By that point in the game, Reed was long gone, having yielded four runs in just 1 ⅔ innings. We then went to work on their bullpen, first pounding Paul Doyle for two runs in the third inning, and then tacking on four more off my former teammate in Cincinnati, Milt Pappas. When the dust cleared, we held a 9–1 lead heading into the bottom of the fifth inning.

"It was unbelievable," Kooz recalled. "We'd never scored so many runs in a series as we did in that playoff series."

I can honestly say I wasn't too surprised by our left-handed hitting output. We obviously had some pretty good hitters in our right-handed lineup, and probably even more power in it with Clendenon, Swoboda, and Charles, but I also knew very well what our lefties were capable of once we got going, especially against a good, but not great, Braves pitching staff and bullpen.

I would pick up three more hits in the game off a trio of Braves pitchers—Reed, Pappas, and Cecil Upshaw—to give me a total of six in the first two games of the series. While I felt a sense of satisfaction after batting .300 during the regular season and now .667 in the NLCS, I honestly was just happy that I was able to continue contributing to the team's success.

Kooz's job now, in the bottom of the fifth with an eight-run lead, was to just go right after the Braves' hitters. We all figured it would be the easiest W of his career.

"In that situation," Kooz said, "you don't want to pick, pick, pick. You want to make them hit the ball. But it puts a pitcher in a bad position because you're throwing fastballs, fastballs, and more fastballs. You don't want to even mess around with a curveball and all those other pitches. The problem is now you're giving them something more to hit. That's the downside of pitching with a big lead. I learned later in my career that you've still got to pitch your own game—but just don't walk anybody."

After Kooz retired the first two Braves hitters in the fifth, he was now just one out away from qualifying for the victory. But he gave up a single to future Mets star second baseman Felix Millan and then made the fatal mistake of walking Gonzalez, to bring up the ever-dangerous Aaron. Henry would make him pay by hitting a three-run homer to cut our lead to 9–4. And what made Aaron's second homer against us in two games even more impressive was what Kooz learned afterward.

"Clink would tell me after that game," Kooz recalled, "that Aaron went home the night before, and his wife had locked the door on him. So he took his fist and rammed it through the door window. I don't know how many stitches he had, but he cut his hand all up from it. That's why he played with a glove on it that game—to cover it up. But it didn't stop him—he was having a hell of a series."

Carty followed with a walk, and Kooz was clearly on the ropes.

"The thing I remember about Carty," he told me, "was how he always played with his billfold in his back pocket, because he didn't trust anyone to leave it in the clubhouse. Of course, he was a great hitter with all the rest of those guys."

Cepeda would come up and promptly double to left, moving Carty to third. Kooz, like Seaver the previous day, was getting hit hard.

"Besides their tough lineup," Kooz recalled, "it was hot down there. Seaver and I didn't like that friggin' hot humidity. But give the Braves credit: they ripped right through us. We may have been off, but they also did a good job and showed us what a good-hitting team they were."

Boyer delivered the knockout punch to Kooz: a single to center to score Carty and Cepeda, and our lead was now 9–6. Koozman just couldn't get that final out of the fifth, and Gil had seen enough. Hodges knew he had the personnel out of the pen that could shut the door on the Braves, so he brought in Taylor to attempt to hold on to the three-run lead. Ron wouldn't let us down, getting the final out of the fifth and then pitching a scoreless sixth to keep the game at 9–6. To that point in the series, Taylor was the only one of our three pitchers to shut down the Braves.

We tacked on a couple of insurance runs in the top of the seventh when Agee drew a one-out walk, stole second, and moved to third after Garrett hit a long fly ball to center for the second out. That brought up Cleon to try to drive in Tommie, but Agee had other ideas. He wanted to steal home! Gil gave some of our guys like Agee the green light to steal whenever they wanted without giving any signs, especially in '69 because we often had leads. But Cleon was intent on swinging away.

"I saw him coming home," Jones recalled. "But when I saw him, I had already started my swing. I wasn't worried about hitting him because I wasn't the kind of hitter that pulled a whole lot of balls foul. I waited longer to swing and tried to use my hands more. After fouling off the pitch, I stepped out of the box and told Tommie, 'You just stay right there. I'll get you in!' Tommie figured he could just steal home and take my RBI away from me. But I would get him in. A couple of pitches later, I hit a home run! Afterward, Tommie said to me, 'What are you trying to do, kill me?' And I said, 'No, I was driving you in. I need the RBI!' But really, I couldn't hurt him. I could have swung and missed the ball to try to keep the catcher back, but if the catcher saw him coming, all he's got to do is just come up, lay over the plate, and he'd be out. I've had a lot of time to think about that since it happened. I felt like it was good at that time, but maybe I wouldn't do that again."

Now leading 11–6, Hodges brought in McGraw to pitch the bottom of the seventh. Besides being a great reliever, Tug was also one of baseball's greatest characters and kept everybody around him loose. Enzo Limongelli, a member of the Mets' ground crew for forty-six years and keeper of Pignatano's tomato plants in the bullpen while the club was on the road, drove our relief pitchers to the mound in the bullpen cart. While he loves to recount the days when Tug would order pizza or ribs to be delivered to the bullpen during games, those short drives with McGraw were some of his fondest memories.

"He was always so loose," Limongelli told me. "Driving Tug into the game, he'd sometimes ask me, 'How's this guy I'm about to face hitting? Is he hitting good?' He was such a cutup. But then he would go about his business on the mound."

And in game two of this NLCS, Tug was nothing short of superb, hurling three innings of one-hit ball to earn the save in our 11–6 victory. We were now just one win away from the unlikeliest of World Series berths.

· · ·

Under a perfectly cloudless blue sky and bright sunshine, we would look to finish off the Braves in the first-ever postseason game at Shea Stadium. We had become accustomed since around the middle of July to playing before large crowds, but this was like none we had ever seen before.

"I remember the people jamming the subway ramp out there in right field," Boz said. "You couldn't have squeezed another person on there. It was the same inside the ballpark—there weren't enough seats, so many people had to stand. I think the announced attendance was over fifty-four thousand, but the estimate of everyone there was sixty-five thousand. Those fans had waited a long time for the Mets to get to this point."

But it wasn't just fans that were fighting to get a glimpse of history in the making. The media circus surrounding us was unprecedented for a baseball team at that time.

Said Matt Winick, who dealt with the press for the Mets during that period, "The media requests kept going up through the end of the season. But the postseason was uncharted waters for us. Nobody in our front office other than one or two people had ever been involved in postseason baseball before. So you had to start thinking about where we were going to find extra seats for the media. And then the other thing was, it was the first year of the NLCS, so we couldn't even go to another team and ask them how they approached it because nobody had ever been through anything like it before. We just had to wing it and somehow figured out how to get the additional seating. But despite it all, it was wonderful. You went to work with a high every day. I had been around the team since 1963 and saw a lot of bad baseball, so now you're involved in something that's different and exhilarating. You came to work every day, and you were charged up!"

Gentry would again get the call to pitch in a potential clinching game, while the Braves countered with the workmanlike Pat Jarvis (13–11, 4.43 ERA)—a decent number three pitcher.

"When I took the mound to pitch in game three," recalled Gent, "I was feeling pretty confident because Seaver didn't do well, Koozy didn't do well, so I thought, *Shoot, I'll show them. I'll go out there and pitch great.*"

But just like our two aces, Gent struggled early. In the first inning, after Gonzalez hit a one-out single to left, Aaron would take Gary deep, blasting one well beyond the 410 sign in center field for his third home run of the series to put Atlanta up 2–0.

"I made one bad pitch to Hank Aaron," Gent lamented, "and he hit it off the center field flag pole. Prior to the pitch, I kept thinking about throwing the curveball again, because he had swung and missed badly at the last one I threw to him. So I did—I threw him another curveball and he hits it off the flagpole. I should have come back and thrown him a fastball instead, because, at that time in his life, Hank was a guesser. And he guessed right about that one."

Said Cleon, "The Braves didn't have the best pitching, but with Hank Aaron and some of the other guys they had, if you didn't play your best baseball, nobody could outscore them. But the way we were hitting in that series, even when we were down, we weren't out, because we felt like we could always come back."

Still ahead 2–0 in the top of the third, the Braves would threaten again. Gonzalez led off with a single to right and the unstoppable Aaron followed by ripping a double to left to put runners on second and third. That would bring the dangerous Carty to the plate with a chance to break things open early for Atlanta. Midcount, Rico smashed a laser off the left field wall about two feet foul, barely missing a three-run homer. Gil wasted no time, walking slowly to the mound and removing Gent from the game despite having two strikes on Carty. It was a perfect example of Hodges's premonition as a manager and his feel for the game. He saw something—or better yet, *felt* something—he didn't like about the way Gent was pitching and made his move. It was one of the great abilities that Gil had as a manager. Still, the move surprised me and everyone else. Removing a pitcher with two strikes on a batter was unconventional, to say the least.

"I was kind of flabbergasted," remarked Gent. "But I think the way the first two games went with Seaver and Koosman, he just didn't want to see this one get out of hand. I'd never been taken out of a game on a foul ball. But I didn't have a choice in the matter. When Gil comes out, you're done."

The other surprise was which pitcher Gil summoned to relieve Gent: Nolan Ryan. While Nolan could overpower anybody back then, the issue was over how he hadn't yet developed the control he would have later in his career. So if you're in a close game like that one—still just 2–0—the one thing you can't do is walk players or pitch from behind in the count. Whenever Nolan came into games in these situations, I thought, *I hope he's got control today.* Even Nolan was a little stunned by the move.

"I had no feel that I was going to get in that game whatsoever at that point in time," he told me. "But I do remember the ball Rico Carty hit. Still, I was as surprised as anybody when Gil went to the bullpen."

But Gil knew his players, and Nolan would get the job done in short order.

"I came in and made a pitch on Carty that was exactly the one I wanted to make," Ryan said. "It was a fastball low and away to strike him out."

After Nolan walked Cepeda intentionally to load the bases, he fanned Boyer and then got catcher Bob Didier on a routine fly ball to left to end the inning. Ryan had performed masterfully to hold the Braves scoreless in that critical frame.

———

"I knew I *had* to throw strikes, so that was my focus for sure," Nolan said. "I was just trying to hold it right where it was and give us a chance to win."

Ahhh, what could have been.

It's a phrase that has been uttered countless times by Mets fans and the New York media alike for decades now. Of course, it pertains to how the fortunes of the Mets organization would have been altered in a most profound way had it not traded Ryan to the California Angels following the 1971 season. That's because, *immediately* after the trade was made, Nolan would embark on one of the most storied Hall of Fame pitching careers in baseball history. Ryan would ultimately win a career total of 324 games, set the all-time strikeout mark, and throw a record seven no-hitters.

"You could tell in '69 how good Nolan was gonna be," Jack Di-Lauro opined. "We knew if he ever could consistently throw strikes, there wasn't anybody that would ever hit this guy. He just had way too much talent."

But while the Mets saw great potential in their young right-hander while they had him, control problems early in Nolan's career had given them pause. Initially, it was blister problems that affected his accuracy.

"The reason I developed blisters on my fingers," Ryan explained, "was because of an old childhood injury. There was scar tissue from it on my fingertips, and that created a problem for me. Well, the Mets' trainer at the time, Gus Mauch, had trained fighters earlier in his career, and those fighters ran a lot for stamina. So they would soak their feet in pickle brine to toughen their skin and keep from developing blisters. Mauch tried that with me for my fingers, but it didn't work because there'd be tissue buildup, and then it'd blister under that. So then we started taking a scalpel and trimming my fingers right before I would go out and warm up to pitch—removing as much skin and tissue as possible without it becoming an irritant. Because there wasn't anything left to blister, it worked. As it turned out, I did that the rest of my career."

Once that problem was resolved, another control-related challenge arose: the difficult task of pitching on an irregular basis. This also adversely affected his command.

"I was in a top-priority reserve military unit, and I had to go back to Houston every other weekend," Ryan recalled. "Gil and Rube worked me into the rotation when my time came up, but if my rotation spot came up over the weekend, they didn't juggle the rotation for me. Instead, they would just insert Jim McAndrew or Don Cardwell into my spot. And if they were going to use me in long relief until my turn came up again, there was a window of about two days in which I might be able to throw. So I think the biggest challenge I had was dealing with the inconsistency of when I was going to pitch and when I wasn't. It didn't make my situation a very good one. But Gil and Rube were patient with me because of the fact that I didn't pitch on a regular basis and had to leave on Fridays and come back Sunday nights. They *hoped* I would become more consistent with my control. Of course, it helped the situation having Seaver and Koosman—obviously the leading two pitchers in that rotation—be so durable that year, as well as the contributions from other guys like McAndrew and Cardwell."

But it was precisely that strength in the pitching department that ultimately held back Ryan's career in New York.

"With Seaver, Koosman, and Gentry, we had three great starters," recalled Krane. "They were so good, in fact, that Nolan Ryan wasn't really guaranteed a slot in the rotation. He had to wait a lot of times and got pushed back. That probably affected his effectiveness.

You can't have control if you don't pitch regularly. And they always pushed him back. He never developed in New York and probably would have never developed with the Mets."

Ryan also attributed developmental issues, like throwing too hard, in an attempt to impress Gil and Rube, and to compensate for all of his time away from the club.

"I had always been an overthrower from the time I was a kid," Ryan reflected. "All I knew was to throw as hard as I could for as long as I could, and that affected my control, too. But with my military obligation limiting my opportunities to pitch, I had a tendency to just continue to be an overthrower."

But everything changed for Nolan after the trade to the Angels for twenty-nine-year-old third baseman Jim Fregosi—likely the *worst* trade in Mets history. Jimmy, a six-time All-Star, was a terrific player but sort of at the end of his career. The Mets were looking for a third baseman ever since they'd let Ed Charles go. I guess they didn't want to play Wayne Garrett every day and an experiment in making outfielder Amos Otis a third baseman didn't work out. Neither did a trade with the Kansas City Royals for Joe Foy—another third baseman acquired shortly after the '69 season for Otis and Bob Johnson.

"I know that some scouts liked Fregosi," Herzog told me. "At the time, I was a minor-league director and Mets general manager Bob Scheffing called me to tell Leroy Stanton he's been traded to the Angels." Stanton was a highly touted outfield prospect. "I asked, 'For who?' And Scheffing said, 'For Fregosi.' I said, 'I wouldn't trade Stanton for Fregosi. I just saw Fregosi play in three games in Kansas City, and Stanton's going to play in the big leagues. I wouldn't do that trade.' Shit, I didn't even know Ryan, catcher Francisco Estrada, and a pitcher, Don Rose, were also a part of the deal. He didn't even mention them. I just told him I wouldn't trade Stanton for Fregosi. Nothing against Jim—he was a good guy and everything, but I was not in favor of that deal at all. Then the next day, I picked up the paper and read about it. Christ, I almost died! I thought, *God almighty! That's terrible!* But you know, the greatest thing that ever happened to Nolan Ryan was getting traded to the Angels from New York."

Ryan could only agree. Although, ahhh, what could have been . . .

"Now, would it have been fun to have been able to stay with Koosman and Seaver and have Jon Matlack come in and join us?" he mused. "Yeah, it would have been just to see how that would have gone. But things don't always work out as we would hope at times."

Another question that Mets followers have long pondered is whether or not Ryan would have still had a plaque in Cooperstown had he remained with the Mets.

"Oh, those things are hard to predict," Nolan told me. "People said when I got traded to California that it fit my lifestyle better. They said I didn't like living in New York—which I didn't because it was a little confining for me with the way I grew up. But was that so detrimental to me? No. But I'll tell you what: being a teammate of Tom Seaver was a great influence on me. As a young kid and not really being focused on my career, watching Tom go about his work on a daily basis and *his* approach to his career—I took notice. But to think about what would have happened if I had stayed with the Mets? Who knows. That's all speculation, so I don't really give it any thought."

Invigorated by Nolan's Houdini act in the top of the third inning, Agee hit the first pitch he saw in the bottom half for a home run, cutting the Braves' lead to 2–1. Then, after Ryan mowed down Atlanta in order in the fourth, I led off our frame with a single to right, and Boz followed with a two-run homer into our joyous right field bullpen to give us a 3–2 edge. It was Kenny's second home run of the series, and he would finish the NLCS with a .333 batting average.

"I was hot," Boz said. "I hit .400 the last part of the season, so it didn't surprise me that I stayed hot. I was seeing the ball good. The main thing I remember was how my father was at all the playoff games. I was very happy to be able to do what I did in front of him. It meant so much to me in my life."

Ryan would make a mistake in the top of the fifth. After issuing a two-out walk to Carty, he gave up a long home run to Cepeda that landed well beyond the temporary stands beyond the left center field wall to regain the lead for the Braves, 4–3.

But we would again battle back in our half of the fifth. Ryan opened the frame by helping his own cause with a single off Jarvis. Then, one out later, Garrett connected on a belt-high, inside fastball that stayed just inside the right field foul pole above the auxiliary scoreboard for a two-run homer to put us up 5–4. For Wayne, who had hit just one home run throughout the entire regular season, it was the biggest thrill of his young career and just so typical of the good fortune we had that season.

"I was just lucky at the time that I got a pitch that I could hit out," said the soft-spoken Garrett. "I mean, when you hit one home run during the whole course of a year, it's not like I knew I was going to hit this one out."

Wayne was just another of our left-handed hitters to have a superb series. Although he batted just .218 during the regular season with just the one dinger in 400 at bats, he elevated his game in the NLCS with a .385 batting average and a .467 on-base percentage.

"I played against the Braves pretty well that whole season," Garrett recalled. "That was the organization I came from. Not that I knew or faced any of their pitchers when I was in their system—I hadn't. But it was fortunate that I had a good playoff against them."

Wayne and I have been friends ever since he came over to the

Mets as a twenty-one-year-old from Atlanta in the 1968 Rule 5 draft. The Rule 5 draft was composed of unprotected players that didn't have major-league contracts. Wayne, a Triple-A player in the Braves' system, wasn't protected by them, which meant the Mets could draft him but could keep him only if they signed him to a major-league contract. So if Garrett hadn't made our big-league roster out of spring training, the Mets would have had to send him back to Atlanta and lose half the investment they paid for him.

"When they started making cuts at spring training in '69," Wayne recalled, "I had to hold my breath every day. As long as your uniform was still in your locker at the end of the afternoon, it meant you were still on the team. If it wasn't, that was a bad sign. Thankfully, my uniform was still hanging in my locker at the end of spring training. That's when I knew I was heading north with the team."

And that's how close Garrett, who in ensuing years would become a prominent everyday third baseman with power—and a critical part of the Mets' '73 pennant winner—came to never coming to New York. And as for his becoming a home run threat, he credits Hodges for working with him the following spring.

"Gil came up to me during batting practice and goes, 'Who taught you how to swing down at the ball?'" Garrett recalled. "I told him, 'Charlie Lau,' who was the last manager I had at the Double-A level with the Braves. One of Lau's theories on hitting is to hit down at the ball. So Gil said, 'I don't want you hitting down anymore. I want you swinging on a little upward plane. You're not a home run hitter, but you have home run power. The grass is too thick in New York and in some other places around the league like Chicago. It's hard getting ground balls through those infields. So swing up a little bit.' In '70 we had traded for Joe Foy, and I didn't play much until probably around July of that year. But I still ended up with twelve home runs in a half season. And in '73 I hit sixteen home runs after not playing the first two months after we got Fregosi. So Gil's advice really helped make me a more powerful hitter."

After Garrett's big home run, Cleon knocked Jarvis out of the game with an opposite-field double to right. One out later, Boz would come through again with an RBI single off future '73 Met George Stone to give us a 6–4 lead. An inning later, Agee drove home Grote with a single to pad our lead to 7–4. In the meantime, Ryan continued to shut down the Braves' lineup as the game moved to the later innings. At no time did Hodges or Walker say anything to Nolan for the balance of the game.

"They didn't talk to me at all," Ryan recalled. "So my attitude was that as long as I was throwing well, they were going to stay with me. But would it have surprised me if they'd have gone to the bullpen? No, it wouldn't have."

As the Braves came to bat in the top of the ninth, the packed house was on the edge of their seats, eager for us to win the second leg of our championship journey. They had already tasted the first clincher the last time we played at Shea—now they wanted an even bigger party if we closed out this game and moved on to the Fall Classic. The final pitch, a nasty twelve-to-six curveball from Ryan, was hit meagerly by Tony Gonzalez on three bounces to Garrett, who flipped the ball across the diamond to Krane for the final out. Our team and scores of fans converged triumphantly at the mound where Ryan had just completed a magnificent seven innings of three-hit relief.

"It was very exciting, and everybody just got wrapped up in that moment," Ryan recalled. "The realization was that we were going to the World Series. It was a dream come true."

Said Krane, "Your whole dream is to play in the World Series, and it's finally arrived. It was a long, uphill battle, but we got there, and you're in seventh heaven. And we got to celebrate it on the field again with thousands of Mets fans. Of course, it was very scary. I mean, you'd better be off the field fast. Fortunately for myself, being a first baseman, I got to the dugout in a hurry because with all those fans, you never know what could happen. So then you're like, *Let's go back for more champagne!* It tasted even better the second time!"

"I was actually never concerned for my safety," Nolan said. "It was just amazing that the fans were so excited and so involved in the moment. We were all just taken aback and just observing it."

"My dad and I went out on the field long after the clubhouse celebration," Boz recalled. "It looked like a moonscape the way they tore everything up. It was actually pretty impressive. The New York fans are special. They were very knowledgeable, and they were for the home team. If you did something wrong, they booed, but if you did something right, they cheered. But they were behind you all the way."

And for Limongelli, there was work to be done.

"Fixing the field was a big challenge, a lot of hard work," he said. "Our ground crew worked through the night—over most of the field, we had to put sod down. But we were really happy for the players because we were big fans. We were hugging and kissing one another! I never thought it was going to happen."

To me, the celebration was déjà vu—another championship of sorts at Shea. First the one in September, and now another one in October. And, hopefully, another one later that month. During our joyous clubhouse celebration, we began to understand the significance of what we had accomplished: a three-game sweep of a terrific Braves team. And for me personally, while it was the team victory that mattered the most, I was thrilled I could contribute the way I did during the NLCS, finishing with a series-leading .538 batting average. I still get fan mail today from people that show my stats from that NLCS and write things like "Oh, you had a great series against the Braves!" It's really nice that people remember after all these years. And it's also something for me to talk about with fans and answer an often-asked question with "I don't know if I would have won the NLCS MVP of the series if they had one to give back then, but it's a nice thing to think about."

Next up for us would be a World Series date with a historically good Baltimore Orioles team in the midst of its own mini-dynasty. We would have to overcome big odds once more.

CHAPTER 16

DAVID VERSUS GOLIATH

– October 11, 1969 –

NOBODY GAVE US A CHANCE. NOT THE MEDIA. NOT THE ODDS-
makers. And certainly not the Orioles. Baltimore had one of the
most dominant regular seasons in baseball history, winning a staggering 109 games. Then they steamrolled over a dangerous Minnesota Twins club in the ALCS. They had a defense that had earned
enough Gold Gloves to build their own Fort Knox, a starting pitching staff that was the envy of baseball, a supremely deep bullpen, and
an overpowering, balanced lineup that was, on paper, much better
than ours. Not only didn't we have a shot at winning the World Series, they would say, but we would be fortunate not to get swept.

"The writers all talked about Baltimore being a great team," Krane
recalled. "They talked mostly about all of their pitching and the two
Robinsons, Frank and Brooks. To them, the Mets were a big underdog with a lot of young players. Nobody knew what to expect of us.
All the national writers knew was that we had Tom Seaver, and that
was about it."

Said Cleon, "All we kept hearing about was how Baltimore was
one of the greatest teams of all time and how we weren't at all like
that."

Maybe it was the exhilaration of youth at play for us, but we were
excited about our chances in this World Series. There was really little
apprehension about taking on the Orioles. Not for a moment did any

of us think we would get blown out. Quite the contrary. We believed we could win any kind of game—a slugfest or a pitchers' duel—against anybody now, including the big, bad Birds of Baltimore.

"They had great players," Boz said. "But what's a great player? He puts his uniform on just like we do. We were a red-hot ball club and weren't scared of them at all. It probably helped that we were all twentysomething years old. But we also knew we had guys like Seaver, Koosman, Gentry, and Nolan out there. I mean, c'mon! Plus, we didn't make mental mistakes, we didn't make errors, and we capitalized when the other team did. We weren't in awe of them—let me put it that way."

Said Al Weis, "Obviously, the Orioles were *heavy* favorites. They had us outgunned at just about every position, I would say, with the exception of left field, where Cleon Jones played. The only thing comparable on paper we had with Baltimore was in the pitching department. Our big two were Seaver and Koosman; they had Dave McNally and Mike Cuellar. Still, we had high hopes. We won a hundred games that year, so we were no slouches."

So although we were clearly outclassed on paper, we were the very definition of a team, and we were confident that would serve us well.

"All twenty-five players on the Mets contributed to our winning," Krane said. "Everyone knew their job. We all played as a 'professional group,' and we did very, very well with that formula. We didn't have the experience that Baltimore had, but we were going to show them!"

"I certainly wasn't thinking about losing!" Cleon exclaimed. "We were thinking about going out and playing good baseball and being as good as we could defensively, knowing that the pitching staff we had always kept us in ball games. All we needed was a hit here or there, and we could win. We weren't intimidated by Baltimore at all."

Jones was right: we had beaten up on enough strong teams

through the year to not fear anybody. But we did have a tremendous amount of respect for an Orioles team that featured an All-Star-caliber player at nearly every position and three future Hall of Famers in the two Robinsons and hurler Jim Palmer. And, personally, there wasn't a player in baseball I admired more than Frank Robinson, their power-hitting right fielder. Having come up with the Reds, I already had a personal relationship with Frank. So impressed with his talent, I've often stated how I believe the trade of Robinson from the Reds to the Orioles for pitcher Milt Pappas following the 1965 season started the demise of the National League versus the American League. The NL had been far more embracing of the African American player following Jackie Robinson's breaking of the color barrier in 1947. But now with Frank—a star whose name is right up there with Willie Mays and Hank Aaron in the annals of baseball history—in the AL, the tide was beginning to change. It was utter lunacy on the part of Reds owner Bill DeWitt to come out and defend the trade by saying that—after Frank hit 33 home runs and drove in 113 runs in '65—Robinson was "not a young thirty." The next year, perhaps more driven than ever before, Frank won the AL Triple Crown and led Baltimore to its first-ever World Series title.

Aside from his immense abilities in all facets of the game, Robinson was also one of the most fiery, hard-nosed, and intense players I've ever seen. He hated making outs and would scream at pitchers that threw up and in at him—which occurred relatively often.

So imagine what someone of Frank's stature and temperament thought about our late-inning defensive replacement right fielder, Rod Gaspar, predicting publicly after the NLCS that we would take the Orioles in four straight. The boldness of Rod's statement infuriated Robinson and the rest of the Orioles, prompting Frank to shout out, *"Who the hell is Rod Gaspar?!"*

"I didn't think," Gaspar told me. "I was just flapping my jaws. My dad always used to tell me, 'Think before you talk, Rodney.' But at the time, I was so excited after winning the playoffs that I just started mouthing off. I just blurted it out! Well, they got hold of that quote and started making comments like 'Who is this guy? He's a punk rookie!' Stuff like that. But I think we all expected to win because we were too young and inexperienced to know any better."

Not surprisingly, nobody enjoyed Gaspar's gaffe more than Clink. In Clendenon's infinite wisdom, he saw Frank before game one by the batting cage and brought Gaspar over to make an introduction—an extremely uncomfortable situation for Rod.

"Our 'buddy' Clendenon yelled over to me, 'Rodney, come over here! I want you to meet somebody,'" Gaspar said. "So he introduces me to Frank, and I said 'Hi.' But he barely even looked at me. Didn't even shake hands. He was such a tough guy. So, that was a really 'pleasant' meeting. But that was Clendenon for you."

Later on, when a reporter asked Robinson about our club, he said, "Who should I be afraid of on the Mets—*Ron* Gaspar?" The mistake wasn't unintentional. Frank was both mocking Rod by deliberately getting his first name wrong, while downplaying the Mets. Upon hearing about the whole Gaspar-Robinson affair, Hodges grinned and told a different reporter, "Don't tell the boys [as he always referred to us] any different. They think they can win this thing."

Gil shared our confidence that we could pull off a miracle.

Nobody epitomized our David versus Goliath challenge against the Orioles more than Mighty Mite himself, Al Weis. Throughout his entire ten-year big-league career, he was a backup infielder with a good glove, but as his .219 average and career home run total in the single digits would indicate, Al represented little threat at the plate. But now, because of Gil's platoon system, he would be the starting second baseman in most World Series games, facing off against the vaunted Orioles lefty pitching staff. It promised to be a mismatch of giant proportions if there ever was one.

But if the national spotlight of the World Series can do anything, it can make little-known players like Al into household names overnight. And for Weis, a terrific guy who always played his heart out, nobody was more deserving of that kind of recognition. But how in the world was Al going to make his mark offensively against a pair of twenty-game winners in Cuellar and McNally? The revelation he gave me was nothing short of stunning.

"I have a little story to tell you about going to Baltimore," Weis began. "The day we arrived, the bat companies put souvenir bats in our lockers. One was black from Hillerich & Bradsby, which produced Louisville Sluggers, and one was a regular-looking bat by *Adirondack*. So I get there, I look at the bats, and I took the one made by *Adirondack* and used it in batting practice. Remember, even though this was a regulation bat—thirty-five inches, thirty-three ounces—it was a *souvenir* bat, intended only for autographs. But I liked it and decided to use it throughout the whole World Series. But the only thing was, *Adirondack* had a blue label around it to show that it was their product. So after the first game, Louisville Slugger had a representative there, a real nice guy named Frank Ryan, and he said to me, 'You can't use that bat.' I was signed with Louisville Slugger and was only supposed to use their bats. But I said, 'I'm going to use it.' So he says, 'Well, okay, but do me a favor: take pine tar and black out that blue band around the bat.' I did, and, as it turned out, I had a *fantastic* hitting series with a souvenir bat!"

As a player, participating in a World Series is the kind of thing you've thought about—even dreamed about—since childhood. When it begins, if you say you're not nervous, you're just kidding yourself. Unless you were one of those wily old veterans from one of those great Yankees teams during their forty-plus-year dynasty, from 1921 through 1964, it was a new experience unlike any other. So while the Orioles had actually won a World Series just three years before, we had exactly one player, Ron Taylor, who had ever played in a Fall Classic before. As the Orioles took the field to start game one on a sunny and unseasonably warm day, we found ourselves in hostile territory at Memorial Stadium—up against a star-studded team that had dominated every opponent it had faced throughout the season.

But I believe that because we were so confident in everything we had accomplished to that point, it overrode our nervousness. Collectively, we were thinking, *Hey, if we just play our natural game, we can compete. We've got Seaver on the mound. We've got great defense, a solid bullpen, and good hitting.* I think our nervousness was simply a natural reaction to the enormity of the World Series and less about facing a team that, on paper, looked far superior to us.

Personally, I may have been a little more anxious sitting on the bench that day than if I was playing in the game. That's because if you're in the field, once the game starts, you're into the action. You're perspiring even though it might be a chilly autumn day. By not playing, it brings on the worst kind of feeling because you're always anticipating. You think, *Well, am I going to get in there? Am I going to pinch-hit?*

There was another emotion at play for me and other left-handed hitters like Boz as well. We were coming off strong regular seasons and an even bigger playoff series and were totally frustrated that we would be sitting out most of the World Series—except when right-hander Jim Palmer started—because of Gil's platoon. What you look for in any sport is consistency and it's hard to play three games in a row and then sit out, in this case, the first two games of the World

Series. Although we couldn't knock Hodges's system—*because it worked*—we couldn't help but be extremely disappointed.

"It absolutely drove me a little crazy," Boz exclaimed. "I actually hit left-handers as well or better than I did right-handers. But we were winning as a team, and we still pulled for one another. And if someone had to start over me, I'm happy it was Al Weis because there's not a better guy in the whole world than him. But years later, when I reflected on it—which I very rarely ever do—I thought, Gosh, I wish I would have walked into Gil's office and said, 'Look, I can hit this guy! I hit all these left-handers!' But that's not the way we were."

Even Weis had empathy for his second base counterpart.

"Ken played at the top of his game in the series against Atlanta," Al said. "I kind of felt sorry for him."

And to be clear, I would never disparage Swoboda, my right field peer, because he was having a decent year, and I was glad he was going to get a chance to start most of the games in the Series. But in a way, what was happening to me was so typical of my career. I once hit four home runs in a row with the Reds and didn't start the next day. But like everybody else on our Mets team, there was no way I was going to confront Gil about it. In a way, I was fortunate to have Kenny Boswell as a roommate so that we could vent our frustrations with each other.

Of course, Boz and I were hardly alone. For as productive as Rocky and Clink were throughout the regular season, neither of them had had even a single at bat during the NLCS. I'm sure that was just as difficult on them then as it was for us heading into the World Series.

"Clendenon was used to being an everyday player, hitting against both left-handers and right-handers," Cleon said. "But it wasn't easy for Gil, either, which is why his coaching staff was so important. When they thought a guy was down about not playing and needed a boost, a coach like Rube Walker might come up to him, talk to him, ask how he was feeling, blah, blah, blah. It wasn't just a coach talking to a player—it was a coach talking to a *friend*. You'd be surprised what kind of lift that gives to a guy, making him think that he really belongs. But that's the kind of team—and year—it was."

So it would be our right-handed-hitting lineup going up against Cuellar, the Orioles' starter. Cuellar, 23–11, 2.38 ERA, was a finesse-type pitcher who didn't throw very hard but might surprise you with a pretty good fastball once in a while. Primarily, he featured a curveball and a screwball—his bread-and-butter pitch—that could be very tough on right-handed hitters. He had been an effective pitcher for a long time with Houston but now was on a perfect team for him to win twenty games: one with great defense and a strong lineup.

In the top of the first, the thirty-two-year-old veteran gave off the aura of a man strolling through a park on a Saturday afternoon. He induced Agee and Harrelson to ground out to Brooks at third and then, after giving up a single to Cleon, struck out Clink to end the inning. We could tell right away that Cuellar, who had more victories in '69 than any other left-hander in the American League, possessed his usual pinpoint command.

However, we had Seaver—the winningest pitcher in baseball—an equal, if not supreme, counterbalance to the Orioles' ace. But Baltimore immediately made its presence felt, as leadoff hitter Don Buford hit Tom's second pitch high and deep to right field. Rocky kind of drifted back on it instead of racing directly to the wall and timed his jump late as the ball left the yard. In Swoboda's defense, when it was hit, I thought it was a fairly routine fly ball to right. I didn't think there was much wind blowing, either. It really looked like Rocky had a bead on it, but the ball kept drifting deeper and deeper before it disappeared.

"I remember being so nervous running out onto the field that first game of the World Series," Rocky recalled. "Just nervous as shit.

So when Buford hit the ball, I never really tracked it. I did everything wrong you could do on a fly ball. You can see in videos how I move a couple of different ways, don't get back there quickly enough, jump up, and just miss it. That ball was catchable, but I messed it up."

This was clearly a bad omen that Tom didn't have his best stuff. Buford was hardly a home run hitter, yet he had squared up on a Seaver fastball. However, instead of just keeping his head down as he trotted around the bases, Buford made a reckless move.

"Buford rounded second base," Buddy said, "and all of a sudden, he looked at me and goes, 'You ain't seen nothing yet.' I thought, *Yes! Wait until I tell the guys in the dugout!* So after the inning ended, I came in and said to them, 'You know what that fucking guy said? "You ain't seen nothing yet!"' Everybody was like, 'Fuck him! Who do they think they are?' They were so cocky. You don't piss people off like that. As I sat down, I thought, *This is going to change things right away for everybody: the pitchers, the guys on the bench. What the fuck was he doing? Why would he do that? How stupid can you get?* Buford had just woken up a sleeping giant!"

Seaver would escape the inning without further damage to hold the Orioles lead to 1–0. But the emotional Swoboda was still ticked off at himself for not making the grab on Buford's home run ball.

"I came in, and I was yapping and moping and jumping on myself over how I should have made the play," Rocky said. "But then Kranepool came over to me in his New York kind of way and said, 'Shut the fuck up and catch the next one.'"

"Swoboda should have caught it," Krane explained, "but Ronnie had played so well during the course of September when Cleon was out that I didn't want him to beat himself up over one play. Besides, we knew we were going to come back because we never gave up."

· · ·

A three-run Orioles fourth inning would give them a 4–0 lead. Seaver would last just one more inning, and his line was most uncharacteristic for the imminent Cy Young Award winner: five innings pitched, six hits, one walk, and just three strikeouts. But Krane was right about one thing: we never stopped battling. Cardwell entered in relief and pitched a perfect sixth inning. Then Taylor threw two hitless innings in the seventh and eight, while we picked up a run to pull within 4–1. And then in the ninth, Rocky led off with an infield single and would later move to second when Weis reached on a two-out, four-pitch walk to bring the tying run to the plate. Taylor was the scheduled hitter, so Gil needed to go to his bench for a pinch hitter. And that pinch hitter was going to be me.

Hodges was looking to tie the game up with one swing and had confidence in me to hit one out of the ballpark. But I must admit, while I was grateful he sent me up to the plate in that situation, a part of me thought if I was good enough to bat against the lefty Cuellar with the game in the balance, then why wasn't I good enough to start against him? But with Gil, you never really knew what he was thinking in those situations. He was predictably unpredictable—like when he brought Ryan in to relieve Gentry after a foul ball in the NLCS. But anyway, here I was in the most surreal of moments: the World Series, two outs in the ninth, with the game on the line. All sorts of things were racing through my mind in the thirty to forty seconds it took me to grab a bat and take some swings in the on-deck circle. I reflected on all the things that I had done to get to this point, like all of those practices with my friends in the park as a boy, all those Little League games, playing American Legion ball, and then those minor-league games and grueling bus trips. It all flashed before me because playing in a World Series is every kid's dream, and now, with a point of Gil's finger, I was living it. In this brief moment, I thought, *You can't get any higher than this.* And with two men on base, I actually had a chance to be a World Series hero.

Cuellar started me out with a curveball down and out of the strike zone that I swung at and missed for strike one. I was so nervous on that first pitch, but, in a way, swinging the bat relaxed me, and I was now more focused for the next one. Working quickly, Cuellar then threw me a slider right down the middle of the plate that I hit hard on the ground to Davey Johnson at second base for the final out. It was the kind of pitch that I could have just as easily hit out of the ballpark for a home run. I had missed a golden opportunity to be a hero. Even though we would go on to win the World Series, I can say without any exaggeration that barely a day has gone by when I don't think about my failure to come through in that spot. To say that I'm haunted by it would be an overstatement, though how many players get a chance like that? I would do anything to have that pitch back— even trade the four-in-a-row home runs that I hit to have come through in a situation like that.

Years later, I saw Cuellar several times at various charity events, and I once teased him by saying, "Mike, that pitch was *right there.* I can't believe I didn't hit it out of the ballpark." And he replied, while putting his hand out to show me, "I know: it was right there." But that's part of the beauty of the game. I just wasn't meant to be the hero that day. Cuellar was.

Once back inside the clubhouse, there was absolutely no panic. I would venture to say there wasn't anybody on the Mets that didn't think we could win game two, and for one reason: Jerry Koosman. I think part of Kooz's legend was how he was the guy that always followed Seaver. But make no mistake, Kooz was such a big-game pitcher that he easily could have started game one for us. So there was certainly no drop-off in the pitching department going into the second game.

"A bunch of us had a quick little meeting after the game," Clink recalled years ago. "We kept Gil and the coaches out and just talked amongst ourselves. We knew Seaver was really nervous—like we all were—in the first game. That was not the same Seaver that brought us down the stretch; he was pretty tight. That game, he could have hit you in the eye with his fastball and not given you a black eye! But we all talked about how we were going to come back because we had Jerry Koosman coming up next."

We left the ballpark programmed in the belief that game two would be ours, and then we would have Gentry and Seaver going for us back at Shea. Earlier in the season, we might have been on our way to being swept—but not now. There was no way we weren't going to fight back.

"Even after losing the first game," Cleon said, "we still felt like we were the best team. A bunch of us got together that night, went out, and had a relaxing dinner. And everybody knows what happened after that."

CHAPTER 17

KOOZ TO THE RESCUE

– October 12, 1969 –

IN REFLECTING ON THIS GREAT WORLD SERIES, OUR PLAYERS have long debated over which game proved to be the most pivotal: game two in Baltimore or game three in New York. Most of us have come to believe it was game two because, had we lost, our two best pitchers would have been taken down by the Birds, and it's highly conceivable that with Jim Palmer on the hill the next game, Baltimore could have gone on to sweep the Series.

"We couldn't go two games down to that team," Glider said. "Game two was big. We knew what type of lineup they had. And they had outstanding pitching, too. So it was very important to win that game."

But for Kooz, it was always about that next game.

"All the games were pivotal," he said. "Each game changes the mood of the club. It's how well you pick yourself up if you do have a loss that is important. A loss doesn't carry as much weight if you really believe in yourself and you've got confidence. And we believed."

That confidence and belief in ourselves would prove critical. After the game one loss, some of the Orioles tried getting into our young club's psyche by baiting us through the media. Frank Robinson commented how he saw little life on our bench, intimating that we may have been overwhelmed by the specter of playing on the big stage. Upon hearing this, Gil told reporters smugly, "Oh, it's real nice for Frank to notice what's going on in our dugout."

"All those guys were running their mouths in that series," Kooz recalled. "They said stuff like they were going to kick our ass or whatever. But those were little things that just amounted to waking up a sleeping dog."

Of course, Kooz didn't need any waking up. Always the warrior, he was eager to take on the Baltimore juggernaut. It's funny, even though Koosman didn't pitch well in his last outing during the NLCS, there was never a doubt in my mind that he was going to pitch well in game two of the World Series. I think we all just had so much confidence in him as a big-game pitcher, and that was all that mattered.

"Koosman had that 'don't care' attitude; he just wanted the ball all the time," Cleon said. "In my opinion, he should have been a Hall of Famer. Everybody that I've talked to about Jerry praised him—some even saying he was the best pitcher on the staff. I would never argue with that because, most of the time, he drew the most outstanding pitcher on the opposing team."

In game two, Kooz cruised through the first three innings, yielding only a walk to Davey Johnson, in holding Baltimore scoreless. By contrast, Orioles starter (20-7, 3.22 ERA) Dave McNally navigated through some early wildness—two walks, a wild pitch, and a Weis single—to keep us at bay. But that would change in the top of the fourth.

Clink led off with an opposite-field home run that barely cleared the fence to give us our first lead of the Series, 1–0. The run stopped McNally's impressive postseason streak of twenty-three consecutive scoreless innings that went back to the Birds' 1966 World Series four-game sweep over the Dodgers.

Kooz and McNally would pitch masterfully behind stellar defense as we maintained our 1–0 lead into the bottom of the seventh. But there was something more at play than just a great pitchers' duel: Kooz was flirting with a no-hitter.

"I had good control, a lot better than I thought I would with seven days' rest between starts," he said. "My fastball and curveball were working really well."

So dominating was Kooz, in fact, that Johnson was still the only Oriole to reach base. But his quest for immortality—and the only other World Series no-hitter aside from Don Larsen's perfect game in 1956—would end abruptly when Paul Blair led off the bottom of the seventh with a clean single to left field.

"That pissed me off to no end," Kooz told me. "I shook Grote off on a fastball, threw a curveball, and Blair hit a bomb between third and short. It was the *only time* I shook Grote off all game. God, it just ate me up that I did that! But I didn't know better then that the American League is a curveball-hitting league, and the fastball was your best pitch against those teams. That stupid league: they throw curveballs on 2-2 and 3-2 pitches. Those games last forever."

Koozman's expectations of himself in this game—and in every game, for that matter—were lofty ones, to say the least.

"My goal was to outdo Don Larsen," Kooz said. "Larsen may have thrown a perfect game in a World Series, but he didn't get a hit. My goal since boyhood was to throw a perfect game in a World Series *and* get a hit every time up to bat! I had to one-up him."

Now with no chance for a no-hitter, Kooz's lone objective was to hold our narrowest of leads. And initially, he succeeded, first retiring Frank Robinson on a fly ball to Agee and then inducing burly Boog Powell to pop out to Harrelson. But, still a little rattled over having lost his no-hitter, he admittedly lost his concentration.

"Earl Weaver was no dummy," Kooz said of the Orioles' irascible, wily skipper, then in his first full year of a Hall of Fame managerial career. "He knew my state of mind. So he had Blair steal while I'm still thinking about this other stuff, and I wasn't ready for it." With Blair now in scoring position, the ever-opportunistic Orioles tied the game when Brooks Robinson grounded a single through the middle.

"All this happened so quickly, and I really hadn't settled down from that no-hitter-type game," Kooz said. "And then it got away from me. After the third out, Seaver told me when I got back to the dugout, 'Pitch your game. Don't have a letdown. Don't let giving up that hit mess up the rest of your game.' Of course, he was talking about his own experience with the Jimmy Qualls hit that broke up his perfect game."

Kooz heeded Tom's advice, settled down, and resumed his dominating performance, retiring the Orioles in order in the eighth.

"I thought, *Oh, there's no way I'm gonna lose this game! I'm not going to let those guys embarrass me!*" Koosman said. "My biggest concern was not to disappoint my teammates or be embarrassed. I always pitched scared because I didn't want those things to happen. That was always in the back of my mind. That's why I pitched aggressively. Don't embarrass myself and don't embarrass my teammates. That kind of thought was always with me in all my starts."

I honestly don't think I've ever met anybody like Kooz. It's hard to find somebody with such a good-natured personality combined with his brand of toughness. He was a fighter on the mound, yet when he came back into the dugout, he was liable to say something funny that happened six weeks earlier to somebody. Nobody embraced life more than he did—and still does. Kooz breaks all the rules. You're not supposed to smoke, and he smokes. You're not supposed to drink, and he drinks. You're supposed to watch your weight, and he eats whatever he wants. Yet, despite all of this, he'll probably outlive us all!

Before the top of the ninth inning, the Baltimore crowd behind home plate became loudly agitated when some of the Mets' wives—Mesdames Ryan, Seaver, Pfeil, and Dyer—unfurled a large Let's Go

Mets! banner they had made out of a Sheraton hotel bedsheet. It was a pretty courageous thing for them to do in enemy territory.

"I saw them carrying that banner and thought, *Who in the world is that?! Why would they do that in Baltimore?!*" Nolan Ryan recalled. "Then I realized who it was, and I couldn't believe it! I had no idea that was planned and didn't know where that idea came from."

As it turned out, maybe it helped us. With two out, the Glider and Grote both singled to left to give us runners on the corners with Weis coming to the plate. This brought up an interesting decision for Weaver to make: intentionally walk the light-hitting Weis to load the bases and most likely force Gil to pinch-hit for Kooz? Or pitch to Al? Personally, I figured that with first and third, the Orioles wouldn't walk Weis and put two runners into scoring position. Earl felt the same way, choosing to pitch to Al. But Mighty Mite made him pay, belting the very first pitch—a high slider from McNally—to left field to score Charles and give us a 2–1 lead.

"We were going all the way with Weis," Weaver would tell reporters after the game. "After all, he's just a .215 hitter."

Said Al of Hodges's decision to leave him in: "This is just another example of Gil instilling confidence in me. We're talking about the ninth inning of a World Series game, with runners on the corners of a tied game. With other managers, I might very well have been taken out in that instance. Was I nervous? Even during the season, you're nervous playing. I always had to—excuse the expression—take a nervous pee before every game we played. Everybody's nervous; I don't care who you are. But when you get to the World Series, it's inflated a little bit. And in '69, televised World Series games were getting really big, and they had just started doing press conferences before and after games. But once the action starts, all that nervousness goes away, and you just react to what you've been doing for the last fifteen years. With McNally, I remembered he had struck me out on a breaking pitch earlier in the game. So I was looking for one there and got it."

Weis's hit did more than give us the lead. It also enabled Koosman—who was so locked in—to stay in the game.

"When Al got that hit," he recalled, "I knew I was going to hit and then go out for the ninth. Al was a big lifesaver."

Weis was having quite a game for himself off the Orioles' twenty-game winner: two singles, a walk, and this huge RBI. It surprised me, but then it really didn't. Al may not have been a real good hitter, but he was swinging a good bat, and baseball can be a funny game. Where else can a guy bat .215 during the regular season but become a hero in the World Series? Plus, in 1969, anything that could happen to help us win ball games inevitably happened. We had a number of individuals like Weis who just came out of nowhere to accomplish extraordinary feats. And to hit like he did with a *souvenir bat* makes his story even more unbelievable.

Kooz ended the top of the ninth by grounding out to Mark Belanger at shortstop and would now face the top of the Orioles' lineup in the bottom half of the inning with no room for error. After retiring Buford on a short fly ball to Rocky in right and getting Blair to ground out to Buddy at short, Kooz pitched ever so carefully to Frank Robinson—ultimately walking him on a 3–2 pitch. The adage "Don't let the big man beat you" was never more relevant than in Frank's case, so there was no sin in pitching around him. But after Kooz walked Boog Powell to move Frank into scoring position, Gil had seen enough and brought in Ron Taylor to try to nail down the final out. Though he was maybe a little gassed by this point in the game, being the fierce competitor that he was, Kooz was deeply disappointed by the move.

"I can never remember a game that I ever wanted to come out of," he told me. "And if I could have made the decision in that situation,

I never, ever would have pulled myself out. A reliever hardly ever helped me. Now, I can see why, once I didn't get Boog out, Gil would take me out with a right-handed hitter like Brooks Robinson coming up. So here comes Taylor, my roommate—the only guy on our squad that signed all of our team baseballs upside down. When he was hot, he'd go *boom, boom, boom* and get 'em out! But there were other times when he struggled. At least I knew that Ron was smart and knew what he was doing out there. And even when he struggled, Ron had confidence in doing his part."

What Taylor also had was phenomenal success in postseason play. As a reliever for the St. Louis Cardinals in the 1964 World Series against the Yankees, he didn't yield a hit in 4 1/3 innings over two appearances. Then in the NLCS against Atlanta, he did what Seaver and Kooz could not—stymie the Braves—and saved game one with two shutout innings and earned the victory in game two by blanking Atlanta over 1⅓ frames. And even in game one of this World Series, he didn't give up a hit to the Orioles, striking out three over two innings of work. The bright October spotlight clearly ratcheted up his game a notch.

"I just felt that I was the person to do that," the mild-mannered Taylor said. "I was very cocky at the time, had good control, and had no fear at all." In other words, Ron had all the ingredients for a successful closer.

Taylor would face Brooks Robinson, one of the great clutch hitters of the era, with the game—and, perhaps, the World Series—on the line.

"I didn't really think about what was at stake," Ron reflected. "Again, I didn't fear anything. I just wanted to throw strikes, make the ball move, and keep it low against Brooks. And it worked."

But that at bat would cause our hearts to skip a few beats. Brooks worked the count full and then, with the runners going, ripped a short hop to the Glider at third. Charles made an exceptional play to snag it cleanly and then made a tough throw over to Clendenon, who had to dig it out of the dirt to end a thrilling 2–1 Mets victory. For the Glider, who started our ninth-inning rally with a single, scored the go-ahead run, and then topped it off by making a game-saving grab at third, it may have been the most meaningful inning of his long professional career.

"Naturally, I was happy to contribute to the victory," Charles said, "but it wasn't like we had just won the World Series. We still had a ways to go. It would have had a greater impact on me had that inning won the World Series. That being said, I got to show our young guys that the old man could still play!"

Said Kooz, tongue-in-cheek, "That ball was really *smashed* to third! We couldn't believe 'Lucky Glider' caught it! And then he had a little something on his throw to first—more than usual. Usually, he never got in front of balls unless he got handcuffed or couldn't get out of the way of them. Instead, he reached for ground balls, kind of gliding over toward them like he was in slow motion. That's how I came up with his nickname, the Glider."

One thing I've always found apropos about that final out was how three of our oldest veterans were involved in it: Taylor, Charles, and Clendenon. But ultimately it was our biggest of big-game pitchers, Jerry Koosman, who turned the Series around when we needed him most.

CHAPTER 18

AGEE PUTS ON A CLINIC

– October 14, 1969 –

THE FIRST-EVER WORLD SERIES GAME AT SHEA STADIUM was everything we expected it to be: an amped-up sellout crowd with all the pomp and circumstance the city could muster. There were luminaries from the political world such as Governor Nelson Rockefeller, Mayor John Lindsay, recently retired US Supreme Court chief justice Earl Warren, and former first lady Jackie Kennedy Onassis and her children, Caroline and John Jr.; show business elites like Broadway star Pearl Bailey, opera singer Robert Merrill, and comedian Jerry Lewis; and baseball royalty Casey Stengel and Roy Campanella. It was the kind of star-studded affair that only New York could produce.

Once again, we found ourselves pinned as heavy underdogs by the oddsmakers, as Baltimore was sending out its future Hall of Fame right-hander Jim Palmer. The twenty-three-year-old, already in his fourth season, pitched to a staggering 16–4 record, with a microscopic 2.34 ERA, and had an excellent repertoire of fastball, curveball, and changeup to go with great command. Gary Gentry, still relatively unknown on the national stage and just one week past his twenty-third birthday, would face the same potent lineup the Orioles used when they took the Series opener.

"The Orioles were told not to underestimate me," Gentry said. "But I guess they did. I think they probably relaxed a little bit. Maybe they thought, *Okay, we got the two big guys—Seaver and Koosman—out of the way, and now we'll take care of this runt! We've got 'em now!* Plus they were just about as good as any team I'd seen, winning a hundred and nine games that year. But it was just nice and comfortable to be back at Shea Stadium; the crowd was great. And it helped that I watched the Orioles for two games. I had my own game plan, and Grote did a great job calling it. I was just hoping I would be on that day, and I was."

The O's simply never saw Gent coming—and you almost couldn't fault them for it. Gary's record was a pedestrian 13-12 on a 100-win team, but the bullpen blew a bunch of his games. With a 3.43 ERA, he easily could have won 20 games for us that year if he didn't pitch in tough luck at times. But truth be told, the Orioles had scouting reports on him, so you'd think they would have realized how he pitched in some tight games that he ended up losing. I know for a fact that there were a lot of hitters in the National League that didn't like facing him because he truly had great stuff.

Meanwhile, Gil went with our left-handed-hitting lineup, inserting Krane, Boz, Garrett, and me for the first time of the Series. But not Weis, who was putting together a great Series at the plate.

"Gil stuck to his plan of platooning," Al said, "despite the success some of the right-handed hitters had in the first two games. I had no problem with that, even after driving in the winning run in game two. Incidentally, I also drove in the only run in the first game, which set a record that nobody can ever break: it was the first World Series RBI in Mets history."

Admittedly, we were all a little nervous at the start of the game, played on an overcast and gusty afternoon. The magnitude of the first World Series game at Shea wasn't lost on any of us. But after Gent mowed down the Orioles in the top of the first, Agee wasted little time putting us on the board in our bottom half, belting a 2-1 pitch from Palmer well beyond the center field wall for an early 1–0 lead. Gent's scoreless inning and Tommie's blast was our best possible scenario because it took the pressure off us and set the tone for the game.

I was hitting cleanup that day—my twenty-eighth birthday—and after Palmer retired Garrett and Cleon, it was my turn at bat. After taking ball one, I got a real good pitch to hit and *just* missed it, sending a long fly ball to Robinson on the warning track in right field for the last out of the inning. I was under the ball by a fraction of an inch, or else I would have had a most momentous World Series home run. But it's funny: I don't think nearly as much about that missed opportunity as the one I had against Cuellar in the first game. Maybe it's because there were still eight more innings to play in game three.

We would add to our lead in the second when, with two outs, Palmer walked Grote, and Buddy singled to center. With Gent coming to the plate, the Orioles probably figured they would get out of the inning unscathed. After all, Gary had gone hitless in his previous 28 at bats and had driven in just one run the entire regular season, sporting an .081 batting average. But this, of course, was 1969, and the unlikely was commonplace. So with the Baltimore infield up and the outfielders shallow, Gent drove the first pitch he saw—a high fastball—to deep center field over Blair's head. The ball rolled all the way to the wall for a two-run double and a 3–0 lead. Our longtime sign man in the third-base side box seats, Karl Ehrhardt, held up one that read simply, *Incredible*. The roar of the crowd, the plastic long horns blaring, and the confetti cascading onto the field from the upper deck made it feel like New Year's Eve at Shea.

"Palmer was missing mostly high," Garrett recalled. "He was really off that day. I don't think I even swung the bat more than once or twice against him because he walked me twice, both times on four pitches."

Gentry would encounter some of his own problems in the top of the fourth, giving up singles to Frank Robinson and Powell to put runners on the corners. Then, with two outs, catcher Elrod Hendricks slugged what looked like a sure opposite-field extra-base hit between Cleon and Tommie in deep left center. Agee had been playing the lefty hitter to pull in right center, so he raced about a hundred feet in the other direction and made a spectacular backhanded catch in the webbing of his glove before colliding with the fence at the 396 sign. You could actually see the white of the ball peeking out the top of his glove. I always thought the fact that he held on to it after hitting the wall was almost as impressive as the catch itself. Tommie's magnificent grab saved at least two runs and was instantly being compared to the other great catches in World Series history, such as Willie Mays's over-the-shoulder basket catch off the bat of the Indians' Vic Wertz at the Polo Grounds in the 1954 World Series.

Interestingly, Gentry had a slightly different take on one of the most celebrated catches of all time.

"I was a little surprised, to tell you the truth, that Agee wasn't parked under that ball," Gary told me. "My instructions were to pitch Hendricks away, so that means your outfield shifts over. When he hit it, I thought the outfielders would be shaded that way, but they weren't. I always considered it a beautiful play and great effort by Tommie, but then again, I always thought my job was to keep the ball inside the ballpark, and it was their job to catch it. Still, it was a wonderful play. I guess that's the luck of the draw. Maybe it was my lucky day."

Gent would use Agee's catch as a springboard to keep the Orioles scoreless through the top of the sixth. In our bottom half of the inning, Grote ripped an RBI double down the left field line to increase our lead to 4–0. But just when it looked like Gary would work his way through another shutout inning in the Baltimore seventh—retiring both Hendricks and Johnson on fly balls to Agee—he began to battle with wildness and walked the next three hitters. Gil came out of the dugout and motioned for Nolan to face the always-dangerous Blair.

"I was so disappointed in myself that I couldn't get that third out in the seventh inning," Gent told me. "I always wanted to try to finish every game I ever started, so with two outs and nobody on, to walk three guys in a row, there's definitely some regret there. But, you know, I had another regret that's bothered me a little bit, too. Jackie Kennedy Onassis and her kids were there. When I was coming off the field when Gil brought in Nolan, I should have thrown Jack Jr. a ball or something, just to acknowledge them. I keep thinking about that. I don't know why I think about that, but I do."

The move to bring in Ryan, just like in game three of the NLCS, was an interesting one by Hodges. In both cases, we needed a reliever to throw strikes, and Nolan, while overpowering, could be wild. At the time, I thought that, *sure, a strikeout would be nice, but why not bring in a control pitcher like Jim McAndrew or Cal Koonce? Or even Tug, who was warmed up and ready in the bullpen?* But, again, Gil had a feel for the game and didn't go by the book with his pitchers.

Ryan would initially make Hodges look like a genius, throwing a first-pitch called strike and then blowing one by a swinging Blair to get ahead 0–2—electrifying the crowd. But then instead of wasting a pitch, Nolan gave Blair a good one to hit a long way to deep right center field.

"I left a fastball out over the plate that Blair had an opportunity to drive, and he did," Ryan said. "When the ball left the bat, I had no feel for whether it was catchable or not, but Tommie was such a good defensive player, with his speed and the jump he got on balls. As it turned out, he made an excellent catch on it."

Playing right field, I had a perfect vantage point of Agee's catch. It looked certain the ball would pierce the gap between us and plate three runs for the Orioles. But Tommie's speed got him in the vicinity of the ball, and, at the last possible moment, he dived headlong and made the catch just in front of the warning track for the third out. Later on, Agee would tell reporters, "I thought I had it all the way, but the wind caught it, and it dipped suddenly, so I had to dive for it."

"I was shocked when Blair hit that ball off of Nolan, because he was not easy to hit," Gentry said. "But he hit a rocket out there. I thought to myself, *Oh my God! All of this for nothing*. But then Agee makes that diving catch. It kind of worried me for a moment, but maybe it was just my day."

It was common for Agee to pat his glove with his right hand just before making a catch, and this one was no exception despite his having to dive for the ball.

"The reason he did that was to test the seam," said Cleon, his longtime buddy from Mobile. "Sometimes the glove will fold up, so he would test it so the ball wouldn't bounce out. It was bullshit, but he felt like he needed to do that, and you knew when he pounded his glove that he had a chance to catch the ball. To me, he was our MVP that year. I say that because he played center field so well. As a matter of fact, he played center at Shea better than anybody that I've ever seen. Every outfielder—I mean *every* outfielder—that came to Shea had problems. Curt Flood, Willie Mays—you name him—they had problems. The seats and the way they were colored made it hard to pick the ball up out there. But nobody did it better than Tommie."

I remember running back in with him after that catch. You could see and feel the adulation and excitement from the fans. As we reached the dugout, all of our teammates came up to congratulate him. And in a way, because I was right near Tommie as he approached the ball, yelling out to him that he had room, it felt like I was a part of the play, too. I used to kid Tommie all the time, "You know, you made an easy play look hard. You really did. You have all these people fooled that it was a great play. But I know because I was right there: it was an *easy* play! You made it look hard, and you've reaped the benefits all these years from making an easy play look hard!" The two of us used to laugh about that all the time.

We would score our final run of the game in the bottom of the eighth with a truly beautiful moment: an Ed Kranepool home run to dead center field off Orioles reliever Dave Leonhard to put us up 5–0. Eddie had seen the good, the bad, and the ugly going all the way back to the Mets' inaugural season in 1962 as a seventeen-year-old, so for him to hit a World Series home run was like coming full circle—something out of a Hollywood script. As he rounded the bases, it looked like he was floating on air, and he couldn't help but break into a smile.

"Normally, you didn't smile back then after hitting a home run," Krane told me recently. "The game today, guys will laugh and throw their bats up in the air—it's altogether different. Back then, you were kind of serious about it. But I had a smile that I will never forget to this day. I can still remember running around the bases; it was like I was flying around them. It was like being in seventh heaven, like walking on the moon tenfold."

Ryan would make quick work of the first two Orioles hitters in the ninth, but then a walk to Belanger, a Clay Dalrymple infield single, and a free pass to Buford loaded the bases. That brought Gil out of the dugout for his trademark slow stroll to the mound, where he had a prolonged discussion with Nolan while Taylor and McGraw were vigorously warming up in the bullpen. Hodges elected to leave Ryan in there to face Blair. Again, Gil's confidence was rewarded. After Nolan fired two fastballs by Blair, he followed with an ungodly, knee-buckling curveball for a game-ending strikeout. As Grote and our teammates rushed out toward the mound, Ryan was grinning and laughing under the bill of his cap at how ridiculously tantalizing that last pitch was. And who could blame him? After a couple of hundred-mile-an-hour fastballs, a twelve-to-six curveball was just unfair!

But for as well as Gentry and Ryan pitched, game three was truly the Tommie Agee Show. With his homer and two incredible catches, you could easily make the case he represented a difference of six runs. An argument could also be made that he enjoyed the greatest all-around game by an outfielder in World Series history. It was the kind of game you dream of having as a kid. The only thing better would have been to end it with a walk-off home run. But it was his day to shine and was so well deserved after all the trials and tribulations he endured when he first joined the team. I loved Tommie and was devastated when he died in 2001, because we had become very close friends. He was a guy you always liked being around and whose antics with Cleon kept us all laughing. Like Tug, Gil, Koonce, and Cardwell, Agee died way too young.

Now up two games to one, and with our ace Seaver going in game four, I think many fans around the city were just assuming that we were going to win the World Series. In fact, many believed we weren't going to lose another game. I can't begin to describe how caught up New York was in what we were accomplishing. We hadn't even won yet, and the city was treating us like we already had. It was as if they were "willing" us to win. And we felt it as ballplayers. To a man, especially with the latest exploits by Agee, we were starting to think, *Hey, something really special is happening here.*

CHAPTER 19

THE CATCH

– October 15, 1969 –

"BOMB THE ORIOLES—NOT THE PEASANTS!" READ A SIGN held by a young man outside Shea Stadium as Vietnam War protesters gathered in droves for the Moratorium to End the War in Vietnam while other peaceful demonstrations were also held around the country, drawing an estimated two million marchers. Even Seaver, our starting pitcher that afternoon, in spite of his own US Marine service, was outspoken against our country's involvement in Vietnam—which was both daring and courageous when considering how most of the Mets' sponsors supported the war effort. Tom said famously at the time, "If the Mets can win the World Series, we can get out of Vietnam." He would then tell me years later, "I just decided to say it. And history proved that Washington couldn't figure a way politically to get out."

However, Tom didn't want any direct association with the anti-war protesters because he was agitated by their use of his name and picture in unauthorized leaflets throughout the World Series. Inside Shea, in a directive from Commissioner Bowie Kuhn, flags were not lowered at half staff for the Moratorium, despite the urgings of Mayor Lindsay. This differed from elsewhere throughout New York City, where the flags atop other city-owned facilities were, in fact, lowered.

On the ball field, under crystal-clear skies, game four would be a rematch of the opener between Seaver and Cuellar before a record crowd. The two aces wouldn't disappoint, with a solo home run by Clink in the second inning representing the only run scored through eight innings of play. Tom had uncharacteristically struggled over his last two outings, but he was back in vintage form.

"It was like night and day between the first and fourth games," Tom said. "I felt much stronger in game four."

Along the way, a frustrated Earl Weaver, perhaps trying to inject some life into his stymied Orioles offense, got tossed from the game by home plate umpire Shag Crawford for arguing balls and strikes. It marked the first time a manager had been ejected from a World Series game since the Cubs' Charlie Grimm was bounced way back in 1935. In some ways, Earl's fiery approach to managing was similar to Durocher's, though we didn't dislike him as much as we did Leo. We understood that his hard-nosed style was just his way of getting his team going. And nobody could argue with his success: the Orioles were a top-notch organization in large part due to Earl.

Baltimore finally broke through against Tom in the top of the ninth when, with one out, Frank Robinson and Powell both singled to put runners on the corners. And that's when what was easily the play of the game—and likely the entire World Series—happened before our awestruck eyes. Brooks Robinson, always a dangerous hitter in the clutch, smacked a screaming, sinking drive to right center field. Instead of going back on the ball to take it on a bounce, Rocky cut across the outfield, dove, and miraculously caught it just as he landed hard on the grass. He then rolled completely over and fired the ball back into the infield to keep Powell at first. It wasn't just a catch—it was the *greatest* catch in World Series history and likely saved the game for us. Frank tagged up from third to score the tying run, but it hardly mattered—the play positively deflated the Orioles.

"This was a game where we're trying to protect the lead," Rocky told me. "You've got first and third, one out, and you're in a little bit of trouble. And here comes Brooks. I know he's got a little bit of power the other way, so I'm extra heads-up. Sure enough, he hits a line drive to right center. I broke hard to my right and didn't do anything but run as hard as I could to where I thought that ball was going to come down, taking the best instinctual angle I could take. I didn't really think I was going to get there, but if I had only one chance in a hundred to make it, I was going to try. There was no room for error. If I miss it, and if Agee's not backing me up, Boog scores from first, and the Orioles take the lead.

"At the last second, I just kind of laid out fully, and that damn thing hit me right in the web of my glove. And balls that hit me in the web weren't going anywhere! I really think my grasp exceeded my reach. What's kind of amazing is how nobody ever considered me acrobatic. One sportscaster said the only way I'd make a living with my glove was to cook it and eat it! I thought that was funny. But my mom, who heard it on television in Baltimore where she lived, did not."

What a lot of people may not know is that Rocky actually worked hard on his defense, particularly that very same kind of play he made so spectacularly against Brooks.

"I probably wore Eddie Yost out hitting me line drives and ground balls," Swoboda recalled. "I never took fly balls. I think in a lot of ways, that's the biggest waste of time because the balls that are tough to catch are the ones that you have to make quick decisions on and that if you're wrong, you're in trouble. With line drives and ground balls where you're charging in, you've got to get your footwork correct so you can catch them in rhythm and get off a good throw. I practiced that all the time, and I think it contributed to the jump I got on that ball hit by Brooks."

Said Cleon, "I watched Swoboda try to make that same catch for three or four years, but he missed it all those times. But he finally got it right. I told him afterward, 'You *finally* made that catch! You certainly tried often enough!' But for him to do it on the biggest stage in the world—during the World Series—was incredible. It was the things like that all year that made the difference for us: different players doing extraordinary things to help win ball games."

Clink, in the way only he could, called it "the greatest, dumbest catch I've ever seen in my life." He then went on to say, "Anytime you run and dive at the ball and don't even look it into your glove . . . I mean, his head was turned around looking at the scoreboard. If that ball gets by, the whole complexion of the game changes. The tying run and maybe the winning run score. At the very least, the go-ahead run advances to second. But that play put another nail in the Orioles' coffin. We were destined to win."

And maybe it was destiny for Rocky to make "the Catch."

"You've gotta remember, it was the Age of Aquarius," DiLauro joked to me. "And Swoboda had the beads hanging from the front of his locker, and he'd sit back in his chair all curled up."

After retirement, Rocky gave one of baseball's all-time best quotes in describing his time in the game, saying simply, "Some players had a career. I had a catch."

"When you're a pretty average player, and your numbers are not spectacular, and you never made an All-Star team, you're just 'a guy,'" Swoboda told me. "And that's what I was. I had a couple of nice little runs, but I didn't play every day. I had one year when I hit .281, and that was the high point. But just think about how many autographs I would have been paid to sign if we had never played in that World Series, and I didn't make that catch. I think that catch, in a sense, gave me an identity—a brand, if you will, that people can latch on to a little bit. So, I've been lucky. When somebody once asked, 'Hey, how long are you going to keep making a living off that one catch?' I answered,

'How long have I got?' So, yes, some people had a career, I had a catch. That says it about as succinctly as possible. But what I find amusing is when people ask me if I kept that ball. The ball was *in play*! So, no, I didn't keep the ball, though I probably should have called time-out and got it back! That would have been worth something today."

The game remained deadlocked at 1–1 heading into the bottom of the tenth. Grote led off against six-foot-six veteran reliever Dick Hall and, although jammed on a 3-2 slider, managed to bloop the ball into short left center field. Buford, as if by fate, got a late break after temporarily losing sight of the ball, and as it dropped in front of him, Jerry hustled all the way into second base with a double. The Orioles then walked Weis intentionally to set up the possibility of a double play. Gil, in turn, sent up J. C. Martin to pinch-hit for Seaver, who had pitched ten masterful innings, and replaced Grote with pinch runner Rod Gaspar. The Orioles countered by sending in southpaw Pete Richert to face the left-handed-hitting Martin.

J.C., one of the backup catchers along with Duffy, couldn't have been any more different from Grote with his warm and friendly demeanor. I don't think he ever got enough credit for being the truly terrific defensive catcher he was because of how everybody gushed over Grote's skills.

"I think we're just born with our own personalities," he told me recently. "I just felt like if you treated players like you wanted to be treated, you're going to have a good rapport with them. You don't begrudge them because of their talent; you play the role that you have. And that's what I did. I thought Grote did a super job with the Mets, but you still needed guys like me to come into the game and do what's called for. I was a catcher that liked to work with pitchers—I had that reputation with the White Sox. When I started,

Chicago had a young staff, and I really worked hard with them to call games. I would explain to them why we were doing this and why we were doing that. So after my career ended, I thought, *Hey, I did all I could do to help those pitchers.* And as a matter of fact, a sportswriter called me a couple of years ago and informed me that the pitchers I caught combined for a sub-3.00 ERA when I was behind the plate. That was the lowest ERA among catchers who have caught over four thousand innings. I thought there was a reason for that: I helped the pitchers, and they wanted me to catch them."

Now Martin was about to embark on the most important at bat of his fourteen-year career and a chance to be a World Series hero. It would be his only plate appearance of the entire Series.

"They had called me in from the bullpen to pinch-hit for Seaver in the playoff game in Atlanta, so it was the same situation here—nothing earthshaking," J.C. said. "It was another pinch-hitting opportunity with a game on the line. By that point, I had been in that role for several years, so I had become accustomed to it.

"So after the Orioles brought in the left-hander, Gil walked out of the dugout, came over to me at the on-deck circle, and goes, 'Hey, they're bringing in Pete Richert. Let's change our strategy. We've got a man on second base and nobody out. Let's bunt the ball down the first base line and keep the ball away from Brooks Robinson. Then we'll get a guy to third base and have two opportunities to get him in to win the game. What do you think?' I said, 'Gil, if that's what you want done, let's do it.' To me, it was just like any other game. When I went to the plate, there was absolutely no pressure, no trembling, and no trepidation. I'd been there before."

The professional that he was, J.C. laid down a beautiful bunt on the first pitch, a fastball up and on the inner portion of the plate, and hustled up the first base line as Richert and catcher Elrod Hendricks converged on the ball. Both reached for it simultaneously, but it was

Richert who picked up the ball and fired toward Davey Johnson, who had come over from second to cover first base for the charging Powell. But Richert's throw hit Martin on the left wrist and caromed past Davey, allowing Gaspar to come all the way around from second and score the winning run.

"The play happened right in front of me," J.C. recalled. "As soon as the ball ricocheted between first and second, I knew the winning run was going to score because there was nobody there to pick up the ball. I didn't even have to look back toward the plate to know it was over. It was pure jubilation. It was just a fantastic feeling knowing that my lousy bunt not only got the guy over to third but also won the game for us. Baseball is all about execution. You execute, and you make them execute. Most games are lost on the easiest, little old nothing plays that you don't execute. You put the pressure on the other team to make a play."

However, controversy swirled the next morning after newspaper photographs appeared to show Martin stepping illegally inside the baseline. But it wouldn't have made any difference even if those photos were available right after the play. Baseball didn't use instant replay back then, so an umpire's call was final.

"The umpire gave me his version of the play, and I accepted it," Bowie Kuhn told reporters. "It's a judgment call like any close play at first base. It can be argued, but not protested. If this were not so, we'd be playing all games over."

"In those days, you only had the foul line—you didn't have three-foot-wide restraining lines that they put in after I made the bunt," J.C. explained. "After that World Series, during the winter when the rules were looked at, they put in a forty-five-foot line that the runner had to run within. So when I ran down to first base, I was not even thinking of the foul line because the base was right on it. I was just running to the base. Nothing else was even on my mind."

Like Swoboda and his catch the inning before, the bunt was the pinnacle of Martin's baseball life.

"That had to be the highlight of my career," J.C. said. "Matter of fact, things happened to me after that that were absolutely unbelievable. I remember going to an Old Timers' Game at Shea Stadium, and they honored players that had contributed something in a World Series. So they invited me to come. In from center field come Duke Snider, Willie Mays, Joe DiMaggio, and Mickey Mantle! I said to myself, *What in the devil am I doing here?* Well, I was there because of that lousy bunt that I had in the World Series. It's put me in a situation where I was rubbing shoulders with Hall of Famers. That's a kind of privilege and honor you don't get every day. I had a tremendous amount of fun with the Mets. They gave me a chance to be a world champion, and it has gone a long way. I'm eighty years old now, and it doesn't get too old to talk about. It changed my life."

Martin's life wasn't the only one to change on that play. Gaspar will forever live in Mets lore as the runner who crossed the plate with the winning run before being mobbed by his teammates.

"I'm looking at that picture right now," Gaspar told me recently during a phone conversation. "I was just getting ready to step on home plate. My daughter found it, got it, and sent it to us. I remember I was on second base, and Shea Stadium was packed like it always was that year—especially during the playoffs and World Series. As you know, it got pretty loud. When J.C. bunted the ball, I took off. It was an excellent bunt. Those were the days when guys actually knew how to sacrifice bunt in baseball. Anyway, I just took off for third, figuring now either a single, ground ball, or fly ball could score me. As I reached third base, Eddie Yost was probably two feet away, yelling at me. But I couldn't hear him because the crowd was so loud. Then I turned to look over my shoulder to see where the ball was and noticed it was rolling toward second base. I took off and scored easily. Eddie later told me he was shouting, *'Run! Go! Go! Go!'* Thankfully, I noticed the ball getting away and scored the winning run."

Despite the dramatic ending to the game, which put us one win away from the unlikeliest of world championships, everybody was still abuzz about Rocky's unforgettable catch in right field.

"I remember leaving the ballpark that day with Bob Scheffing," Joan Hodges once told me. "I turned to him and said, 'Bob, I've got to tell you. My husband had four outfielders today. And one was up there in the sky!' That catch was not to be believed. You've seen some catches in your lifetime. You've seen some *great* catches in your life-time. But just the way things worked out . . ."

Mrs. Hodges paused for a moment and then finished her thought: "Gil was supposed to have that glory before he left us."

CHAPTER 20

A DATE WITH DESTINY

– October 16, 1969 –

THE FEELING IN NEW YORK ON THAT CLEAR, CHILLY DAY WAS electric. From the time I got up in the morning, whether turning on the television or picking up the paper, the Mets were all over the news. It was more than just New York or the country that was captivated by us, it was the entire sports world. But while we, as players, were still somewhat rational about our chances of wrapping up the World Series in game five—our last game at Shea that season—the fans were anything but. As the gates opened to let them enter the ballpark, we could sense an incredible buzz that was impossible to describe. The fans were all so deeply caught up in what was happening, they were downright cocky that their onetime lovable losers—a team that had lost 120 games just seven years earlier—would complete the miracle that afternoon at Shea. And much of the responsibility for making that happen rested on Kooz, who was nervous as hell. For all of his grit and intestinal fortitude, he knew what was on the line. He understood the circumstances and appreciated the gravity of pitching in a potential Series-clinching game.

"When I got out to the bullpen," Koosman recalled, "I was so nervous, just pacing around. I couldn't wait for my time to warm up."

But then a calming influence tried to help settle him down.

"Pearl Bailey was out there because she was going to sing the national anthem," Koosman said. "So as I'm walking around, she goes,

'Kooz, settle down, settle down. Just relax. I see the number eight, and you're going to win.' I said, 'Oh really.' I didn't put much credence in that. So I went ahead and started warming up while she went in to sing the national anthem."

Later we would all learn what the *Hello, Dolly!* Broadway star's "vision" of the number eight would come to represent.

Despite the butterflies, Kooz breezed through the first two innings but faced trouble in the third. After giving up a leadoff single to shortstop Mark Belanger, Orioles pitcher Dave McNally, in an obvious sacrifice bunt situation, instead swung away, taking Koosman deep to put Baltimore in front 2–0.

"He should have been bunting! He should have been bunting!" Kooz recently reminisced to me, still obviously agitated over it. "I throw him the high fastball, and he's swinging away. We were ready for the trap play, but he swung away and shocked the heck out of all of us!"

Two batters later, Frank Robinson made it 3–0 by blasting a tremendous home run to left center field into the bus parking lot area. "When I came back into the dugout, I was so pissed off!" Kooz said. "I told the guys, 'We'll hold 'em right there. Let's score some runs. They're *not* getting any more!' And I know Gil and Rube heard me say that. I think that's one reason they left me in there longer."

For as fired up as Kooz was, there really was no panic on our bench. There was confidence that we were going to come back because we had done it so many times. It wasn't like it was 10–0—we were down only by three runs. We were just waiting for something to happen. Plus, the fact we were up three games to one made it a little less worrisome a situation. Not that we wanted to lose this game and go back to Baltimore up three games to two, but it wasn't a must-win game for us, and that helped us stay relaxed and focused.

Kooz would settle down and pitch perfect fourth and fifth

innings. Then in the sixth, after retiring leadoff hitter Blair, he plunked Frank Robinson. However, instead of Robinson being awarded first base, home plate umpire Lou DiMuro ruled it a foul ball. Frank was incredulous and argued vehemently with him. Weaver came out to join the argument, while trying to keep his heated star right fielder from getting ejected from the game.

"I threw a slider and hit him right in the upper right thigh," Kooz told me. "It came off his leg, hit his bat, and DiMuro called it a foul ball. But I *know* I drilled him. I was *trying* to drill him. So I was kind of puzzled by the call from the very beginning. In fact, I don't even think it hit the bat, but evidently DiMuro thought so."

While Earl continued to seethe at the umpire, Robinson went back into the clubhouse for several minutes to receive treatment from their trainer. Most of the crowd stood, booed, and shouted continuously while the whole charade continued.

"I'm out on the mound, and I can look into their tunnel," Kooz said. "I see Frank pulling up his pants after they iced his thigh. They had an ice bag up there, so I know I hit him. And Earl's out there just raising holy hell!"

When Robinson finally emerged from the dugout, the boos grew even louder. But then Kooz struck him out looking with a slow, arcing, breaking pitch, and the crowd erupted in cheers. You could almost sense that the bizarre sequence could be the beginning of another magical comeback.

Cleon would lead off the bottom of the sixth inning, with our club in desperate need of a baserunner. McNally appeared to oblige, hitting Jones with a pitch off his foot. But for the second time in the same inning, DiMuro didn't see the ball hit the batter and called it a ball. But this time, after the ball made contact, it ricocheted into our dugout, setting off a chain of events that would alter the course of the ball game.

"McNally threw a slider down and in," Cleon recalled. "The ball hit my foot—I *knew* that. But when the umpire didn't say anything, I wasn't going to, either, because I wanted to *hit* off this guy. I didn't want the free base. I was hitting the ball as hard as I wanted to during that stretch, so I wanted to swing away."

While I loved Cleon's confidence and determination to get a hit, what we needed, first and foremost, was to get guys on base by any means possible.

"I was standing back and watching as Donn started yelling at the umpire, 'The ball hit him! I saw it hit him!'" Cleon told me. "I mean, that shows the confidence he had in himself. Clendenon wants me to get hit by a pitch so he can get up there and hit. Then he raised a ruckus that somebody should pick up the ball. Well, we all know what happened after that."

What happened was that the ball was in our dugout for exactly twenty-three seconds. I was sitting with Boz all the way at the end of the bench, nowhere near where the ball ended up. However, I did notice a little commotion going on over there. That's when Boz and I kind of looked at each other like, *Did it hit him?* A few seconds later, Gil walked out with the ball to show the umpire a smudge of black shoe polish on it—proof that the ball hit Jones's spiked shoe.

"I put shoe polish on the ball just in case," Kooz confessed to me. "It could have been on there already—I don't know. I didn't look at the ball. Gil just said, 'Swipe it on your spike.' I did and handed him the ball right away. That's the kind of manager he was. He was always three steps ahead of the opposing manager."

After DiMuro examined the ball carefully and listened to Hodges calmly explain his position, he awarded Cleon first base. But perhaps caught up in the moment and feeling as good as he did at the plate, Jones was slow to move to first.

"Cleon still wanted to hit!" Clink exclaimed. "I told him, 'Get your ass to first base!' Then McNally started arguing, and I told him, 'Get your ass back out there and throw that shit up here!' He was pissed and tried to throw one by me, but I hit it out."

Clendenon's blast over the auxiliary scoreboard in left field on a 2–2 hanging curveball got us right back in the ball game, cutting Baltimore's lead to 3–2. It was Clink's third home run of the series, just one shy of the World Series record at that time. I couldn't help but think how wonderful this was for him when considering the state of flux his career was in just a few months earlier.

"That home run gave us a boost of confidence," Kooz said. "I thought to myself, *Hold 'em right there. Our club's going to come back.* We knew how to manufacture runs. Just get 'em on base. We begged the Baltimore pitchers to hit one of our guys so we could get a runner on first and bunt him over. We could always get them around to score somehow. But Clink's home run, of course, was so much better."

We would tie the game in the bottom of the seventh courtesy of a home run by the unlikeliest of sources: light-hitting Al Weis. His first-ever home run at Shea Stadium—and just the eighth of Mighty Mite's lengthy career—cleared the 371-foot sign in left field by a good twenty feet.

"When I hit it, I had no idea that it was going to leave the ball-park," Al told me. "I certainly didn't break into a home run trot around the bases. Actually, I think Buford came in on the ball at first. But the ball carried and landed in some seats that were reserved for veterans. And actually, I still have that ball—Pignatano went out there and gave whoever got it an autographed one in exchange. I have all the games on tape and every once in a while break it out. Hitting that home run in the fifth game still pumps me up a little bit. Actually, I have a little tidbit about that game as well.

"My family was there, and it was October 16: my son's sixth birthday. So my wife was driving to the ballpark that day with Grote's wife, Sharon, and, out of the blue, my son told her, 'My dad's going to hit a home run for my birthday!' Now, the odds of that happening were probably a million to one, but he actually said it. And then to actually be able to *do* it in front of my family—which also included my mom and dad, my sisters, and my aunt, who was a nun, was amazing. In fact, my aunt brought six other nuns to the game. So we had a little bit of 'extra help' that day!"

I guess Al's son turned out to be just another prophetic Mets fan. But with the unorthodox way we were winning games, his home run probably didn't really shock anyone. Another day, another hero. And if you're into superstitions, Weis wore the number six, the same age his son turned that day. In a funny way, I really wish Tug would have come up with that "Ya gotta believe!" rallying cry in '69 rather than in '73 because it would have been more apropos. But maybe Al just had McNally's number a little bit, too—at least, relatively speaking. McNally was the only pitcher that Weis had homered off of twice in his career.

In any event, Al's clout put a dagger into the Orioles' hearts.

"When Weis hit the home run," Clink said, "you could see Brooks and Frank Robinson on videotape put their heads down. When those guys dropped their heads, that's when you knew it was over. There was nothing they could do to stop us."

Weis, who had a .455 batting average in 11 trips to the plate against some great Baltimore pitching, will be forever linked with the '69 World Series. "Everybody wants to play in the big game," Al told me. "I tell people I played ten years in the major leagues and had really one good week of baseball. But that one week came in the World Series."

I was reminded that the light-hitting Weis used a bat made solely for the purpose of obtaining autographs. But then, to have all the success a guy could dream of—winning the Babe Ruth Award for the outstanding player in the World Series—is remarkable. But again, it was just so typical of our season. And I can't blame Al one bit for using a souvenir bat if it felt good to him. Hitting is all about balance, a comfortable stance, concentration, and having a bat that you like. If I had a good game at the plate, I wouldn't care if it was a Little League bat or a tennis racket—I would use it as long as I could. And I would never let it out of my sight. When I was on a hot streak, I might even bring it home and place the bat right next to my bed. That's how protective I was of a bat that was bringing me success. So I certainly understood where Weis was coming from. And it couldn't have happened to a nicer guy.

Al's game-tying home run also allowed Kooz to stay in the game. Tug had been warming up in the bullpen, and, with Kooz on deck, Gil almost certainly would have pinch-hit for him down a run late in the game.

Now with a 3–3 tie, Kooz was really locked in, setting down the Orioles in order in the top of the eighth. We then went back to work offensively in the bottom half of the inning, this time against Baltimore's right-handed relief specialist Eddie Watt, who sported a terrific ERA of just 1.65. After Cleon doubled halfway up the left center field wall at the 396 sign—just missing a home run—to start the frame, Clink grounded to Brooks Robinson, failing to advance Jones to third. With Watt still on the mound and the right-handed-hitting Swoboda coming to bat, Hodges played his hunches and left Rocky in there instead of going to his left-handed-hitting bench. And, yet again, this hunch worked out just fine. Rocky swung at an outside pitch and hooked a fly ball down the left field line that dropped in for a double to score Jones and give us a 4–3 lead.

"Watt was a right-hander, and I wasn't sure if I was going to get to hit against him, honestly," Rocky recalled. "It wouldn't have been unusual for Gil to send Shamsky up to hit in that situation. Art had a really solid year and playoffs. He had such good hands, great bat-head speed, and, boy, he could turn a fastball around. So I couldn't have said anything if Gil used Sham there because we're trying to win this freaking game. But I had been swinging the bat good, and Hodges would go with you if you were hot—and maybe save Sham for later. Anyway, Watt was sort of a three-quarter-arm sinker-slider guy, and I went up there trying to hang in against a pretty tough pitcher. On the double, I just reached out for the pitch with one hand and kind of slapped it down the left field line. I hit it off the end of the bat, and it's a good thing I didn't hit it too hard because that had everything to do with Buford not getting to it. I still think it was a catchable ball. But Buford was not a very good outfielder, and his poor jump had something to do with the fact the ball fell in for two bases."

After the Glider flew out to left field for the second out, Grote rocketed a ground ball to first base that Powell bobbled and then lobbed to Watt, who was late covering first. The ball glanced off Watt's glove and allowed Rocky to score all the way from second, making it 5–3. The crowd was now as loud as I've ever heard it at Shea in anticipation of the improbable becoming a reality.

"When the Mets took the lead in the eighth inning," ground crew member Pete Flynn once told me, "you couldn't see any space in the field-level seats. The aisles were full of people. Everyone was coming down from everywhere ready to charge the field. The excitement was unbelievable!"

•　•　•

It was now the top of the ninth inning and only three Baltimore outs were all that stood between our craziest fantasy just six months earlier and reality. We were on the verge of making history, not only because the Mets had never had a winner but also because the organization had never finished higher than ninth. All of us—the guys on the field, those of us on the bench and in the pen, and our fans—were pretty anxious at this point. If anyone wasn't, he or she wasn't alive! And if Kooz was nervous prior to the game, he was now downright petrified as he took the mound.

"I go out there for the ninth inning, and the crowd is just going crazy," Kooz recalled. "I mean, they're standing up and hollering, and the guards were already coming down to the front gates along the box seats. It was so noisy, so loud, you couldn't hear yourself think. I was so nervous from the excitement of the moment that when I threw some curveballs during my warm-up pitches, I wasn't even close to getting them over. I kept thinking, *I don't want to blow this game.* I was just so scared of losing. So I decided that I was going to throw only fastballs. But I didn't even have good control over that pitch, either. I was too nervous and excited to be able to control anything, so the only thing I could rely on was velocity. I was just trying to throw my best fastball *someplace* over the plate. I was like, *Shut your eyes and throw the hell out of it!*"

Not surprisingly, Kooz walked his only batter of the game, Frank Robinson, to open the frame. But then, after falling behind Powell, 2–1, he induced the big man to hit into a force play for the first out. Kooz then got quickly ahead of Brooks, 0–2, before getting him to fly out to Swoboda in shallow right field for out number two.

"I stayed with my strategy of just throwing fastballs," Kooz said. "I would describe my pitches that inning as being 'wild in the strike zone.' In other words, a pitch I meant to throw up and in might be down and away. But I was throwing hard; I would guess mid-nineties."

That brought up the Orioles' final hope in Davey Johnson, who would later become the '86 Mets World Series champion skipper. Working quickly, with the crowd roaring on every pitch, Kooz starting him off with two fastballs and a 1-1 count, Koosman then threw his first curveball of the inning, but, predictably, missed way outside to give Johnson a hitter's count at 2-1. Kooz went back to the fastball, and Davey belted what, off the bat, looked like it might go a long way.

"Normally, you can tell by the sound of the ball how deep it's going to go or how well it's hit," recalled Kooz, who watched the ball wing its way to left field. "Well, hell, when Johnson hit that ball, I didn't know if he hit it good enough to go out of the park or not. It was so noisy in the park that you couldn't hear the bat hit the ball, so it was hard for me to judge how hard it was hit. But it was a fastball up in the strike zone, approximately in the middle of the plate. With Davey being a hitter that would go on to hit forty-three home runs in a season, I'll bet his eyes lit up upon seeing that pitch. But, again, because of the noise, my judgment was foiled. I didn't relax until I saw Cleon stop running backward right before he set foot on the warning track. Then I said to myself, *Cleon, don't drop the ball! Squeeze that ball!*"

Said Cleon, "When Davey and I worked as coaches in the Mets organization, we were roommates, and he maintained that it was the hardest ball he'd ever hit in his life. But to me, I thought it was just a fly ball when it came off the bat. Davey and I once sat up all night talking about it. I told him, 'It was a weak fly ball. When it came off your bat, I knew the game was over.' While I was waiting to catch the ball, I was saying to myself, *Come on down, baby. Come on down.*"

And then, in what has become as iconic a symbol of triumph as ever seen in sports history, Jones caught the ball and went down on one knee—a beautiful exclamation point on a glorious season. "I didn't plan to do that," Cleon explained. "I just saw the ball coming down and, after I caught it, just went down on one knee."

The World Series championship was ours, and the wild celebration began on the field. Grote sprinted toward the mound, and Kooz leaped into his arms as the Glider ran over to join them—arms spread wide—with a smile that could have lit up the city. It remains one of the quintessential images in New York sports history.

"You know what I was thinking about?" Charles said to me once. "Prior to Jackie Robinson breaking the color barrier, we used to get the Dodgers games on the radio in Daytona Beach. I used to listen, and it was really exciting. I often said to myself, *Gee, I wish I could play in the World Series.* Everybody was into baseball back in those days. But Jim Crow was saying blacks couldn't do it. So I used to say my little prayers when I went to bed at night that something would happen to change this. I'd pray, 'God, please make it possible.' And that's what I was thinking about as we celebrated and came off that field. It happened! The prayers I sent up before Jackie made it, praying that somehow I could play major-league baseball, play in the World Series, and win it—all of that stuff happened! And I'm like, *I don't believe it!* But it happened. I was just so happy. Now I could say, 'Gee whiz, I prayed for this as a young kid.' That's why I had that big smile."

As most of us joined the celebration on the mound, all hell broke loose around us, as thousands of fans stormed the field. "I was in the Mets' dugout and rushed out to get second base," Pete Flynn recalled. "The ground crew wanted to save the bases. But I didn't get within fifty feet of second before people were all over me. So that base wasn't gotten. But it was the greatest thing I've ever seen in sports."

Said Kooz, "The oceans opened up there. Boy, that was crazy. The fans came over from the sides—I mean, there was nobody stopping them. I grabbed my cap and my glove and squeezed those suckers as I'm trying to get off the field. When I went down the steps, fans were already piled three or four feet high—lying on top of each other—as they fell from on top of the dugout. I walked over the tops of bodies with my spikes. Others were jumping down from over by the bullpen. One guy broke his leg. It was nuts!"

Cleon had to scrap his original escape plan.

"The outfielders planned to go through the right field bullpen," Jones said. "They were supposed to have the gate open. When I caught the ball, Tommie and Swoboda took off, and by the time I got halfway over there, I saw the gate was closed. Those two were getting into the clubhouse to celebrate, and I'm still out there! So I made a U-turn and ran to the other bullpen, jumping the fence. It was easier to jump the fence than to go through the crowd. The three of us had a big laugh over it afterward."

By the time our delirious fans were done with the field, it was practically unrecognizable. There were literally thousands of divots left behind from where grass was dug up. Streams of paper and the remnants of smoke bombs littered the field. But this was hardly an act of destruction. Quite the opposite. It was a display of exuberance the fans had for our team. When Cleon caught that final out, I don't think any of the fans who surged onto the field were thinking, *I'm doing this to protest the war in Vietnam!* Or, *I'm angry at Mayor Lindsay and city hall!* I think it was more like, *Hey, I want to be a part of history. I want to grab some sod from the field that the Mets won the 1969 World Series on.* It was a time for them to feel like they were a part of our miracle—a moment to celebrate, not protest.

As for the ground crew, you would think after we won the division and they repaired the damage the fans caused, they could take a deep breath. But then we win the pennant, and the same thing happened. And now, we win the World Series, and they have more work to do than in the first two celebrations combined. They truly did a marvelous job for us. In fact, so appreciative were we over their efforts that we voted them a full World Series share of money to divide among themselves.

The clubhouse celebration was a display of unbridled joy. A big part of that, I've always believed, was because *everyone* contributed to the club's success—not just five or six stars like on a lot of other championship teams. There were chants of *"We're number one!"*; the spraying and lathering of shaving cream on one another; and the requisite dousing and imbibing of champagne. Back then, players weren't putting on protective goggles and covering their lockers with plastic. So it was champagne at its purest!

One of my fondest memories was bringing my dad into the locker room to take it all in. He was such a big baseball fan and was the one that got me involved in the game. He got so caught up in all the hoopla, and I was so happy to share that experience with him.

Some of my teammates had the same idea.

"My dad truly loved baseball and, even though we lived in Iowa, always loved the Yankees," McAndrew told me. "I remember my dad and father-in-law walking around the clubhouse with a bottle of champagne in their hands. It was the most emotional moment for me to sit there in Gil's office, watching my father talking to Hodges, Yogi Berra, and Whitey Ford, who was brought in by Yogi. It was almost like being a parent with a ten-year-old, except the roles were reversed. I think about how special that moment was to see my dad so happy and to have the opportunity to meet and have a bottle of champagne with his idols. That was the most moving moment of the year for me. It made me feel special to see him having such a good time."

Kooz had a different kind of special memory.

"We're in the clubhouse after winning, 5–3—which, if you add them together, equals eight," he said. "So Pearl Bailey, who told me to relax before the game because we were going to win, and she saw the number eight, comes in. Well, I went right over to her and gave her a big kiss—hit her right on the nose!"

A "big kiss" may have actually been an understatement. As I recall, it was a kiss that lasted about thirty seconds. Maybe Pearl should have gotten at least a half World Series share for trying to help Kooz stay calm that day.

Back in Gil's office, Joan Hodges paid her husband a visit. "After it was over, I went to kiss him to congratulate him," Mrs. Hodges told me. "The first words out of his mouth were 'I was able to bring the championship back to the greatest fans in the world!' He was such a special man. I was so privileged to have been his wife. I don't want that feeling to ever die if I possibly can."

Even Gil, never one to show much emotion, was caught up in the moment like the rest of us.

After the clubhouse celebration, the party moved to the Diamond Club, Shea Stadium's exclusive restaurant of the day. That night, it was like Times Square on New Year's Eve. It was festive, with lots of adulation, back-slapping, and words of gratitude. It was just a continuation of the locker room, although we were no longer dousing one another with champagne. But Scotch—well, that was another story.

"We go up to the Diamond Club afterward," Kooz recalled. "We've got our sports coats and ties on and whatever. So Cardwell and his wife and a bunch of players and their wives are sitting at this one table. Cardy was a Scotch drinker. So I went over to the bar, grabbed a brand-new bottle of Dewar's, uncorked her, went over to their table, stood behind Cardy, and just dumped the whole damn thing on his head. He stunk like a pig with all that Scotch on him. But he wasn't really shocked—he and I always played a little bit rough. I always owed him for something. But that was our own fun and games. We never hurt each other."

On the other side of the room, things were a bit more subdued.

"I was a nobody," Whitey Herzog told me with great humility. "I played in the big leagues eight and a half years. Well, I shouldn't say 'played,' but rather I should say that I was *in* the big leagues eight and a half years. But the night of the celebration, I went up to the Diamond Club to see Gil. I went over to him with the purpose of congratulating him and Joan, and he jumped out of his chair and said to me, 'I want to congratulate *you*!' Now, coming from someone like Gil to a guy like me, that might have been the greatest compliment I ever received in my life.

"Then Gil said, 'Every time I've asked you for help from the minor leagues, you sent me the right guy. And how did you know that those starting pitchers should be in the bullpen—like McGraw?' And I said to him, 'I always thought the guys that were hyper couldn't be starters because if you told them they were going to start the next day, they wouldn't be worth shit—they'd worry themselves to a frazzle. Those guys are better off when they're down in the bullpen and don't know whether they're going to get in the game or not. McGraw turned out to be a pretty damn good relief pitcher, didn't he?' Gil nodded and smiled. But I'll never forget Hodges congratulating me the way he did. It was pretty damn nice."

After the Diamond Club, a number of us went over to an Upper East Side nightclub called Mr. Laffs. Dubbed as one of the earliest sports bars, it was owned by former Yankee and '68 Mets teammate Phil Linz, who would become a future business partner of mine in three restaurants. Prior to heading over there, Boz had done an interview with sportscaster Sal Marchiano of WCBS-TV, in which Marchiano asked him, "What are you going to do tonight?" And Boz answered, "I'm going over to Mr. Laffs." So when we got there, they had closed off First Avenue because so many people were waiting for him and other Mets to arrive. It was crazy. We were living in a world you dreamed about if you wanted that kind of adulation. You couldn't buy it. We were larger than life—like rock stars, if you will. And the meaning of what that period in our lives meant to us hasn't been lost.

"It was a great time to be in New York and an even greater time to be a Met," said Ryan, who, despite a magnificent twenty-seven-year career, enjoyed his only World Series appearance with the '69 Mets. "When I look back at personal accomplishments, I feel really fortunate and blessed about them, but when you experience something like we did in '69, you understand those things just don't come along very often. There are a lot of people I run into that were children in those days that lived in New York or New Jersey and were Mets fans. That world championship was a big event in their lives, and they'll comment to me things like, 'Boy, I was a fan in those days, and I was really excited about what you all did.' They want to talk about it. I think it's neat to think about how what we did impacted so many people. I think you even appreciate it more and more with time, realizing how unique and special it was."

Said Rocky, "I was part of the first Mets team *not* to lose a hundred games in a season," in 1966, the franchise's fifth season. "And then I was a part of the first Mets team to win a World Series. And, of course, the World Series, that's the *ultimate*. That's what every kid dreams about when you're hitting rocks into a field mimicking the hitters you grew up watching. Or when you're playing step ball by yourself and inventing games. You're thinking about the World Series, man! The World Series is the mountaintop! I can't imagine anything in the game sweeter than what we experienced in '69. We weren't supposed to do anything, and we did it all. It ain't ever going to be sweeter, because you can only win the first one once."

Cleon, who like Rocky goes back to the Casey Stengel era, has remained a close friend of mine through the years. And whenever the subject of '69 comes up, he shares in my view of how our season impacted so many folks.

"I still get letters all the time from people saying what a difference we made in their lives," Jones remarked to me not long ago. "They write how their brother might have pretended to be Tommie Agee, and he was Cleon Jones or Ron Swoboda. So many things were happening in the world then, and a lot of it was negative. And here comes this young ball club in New York City—benefiting from all of the media there—getting written about and talked about all over the world. Even guys who were in the service at the time in Vietnam were following us. We helped a lot of people."

True to Cleon's words, the fact that our miracle happened in New York, the baseball-hungry city that a decade before had lost *both* of its National League clubs, only added to the mystique in so many ways. And Eddie Charles, who played for so many years in so many different cities, can certainly attest to this reality.

"Never in my wildest dreams would I think people would still be talking about us almost fifty years later," the Glider told me the last time I saw him before he passed away. "But it's amazing. We can thank God it happened in New York because this whole town, they love their baseball. Even now, on the streets, people might say, 'There goes Shamsky' or 'There goes the Glider.' It's great that it happened in New York as opposed to, say, Kansas City."

While all of us covet our title, perhaps none of us can verbalize the pride we felt about being members of the '69 Mets more than my old roommate, Kenny Boswell.

"There aren't very many people, no matter what they do, that can say they reached the pinnacle of their sport," Boz said. "Now, we didn't do it individually. Most all of us didn't make an All-Star team.

Most all of us didn't make the Hall of Fame. But our team was the best in the world in 1969. The Cubs weren't better than us. The Orioles weren't better than us. I don't think our team gets enough credit for being as good as we were that year. I watched Frank Robinson on a television show talking about the '69 Series. He gave us credit for winning, but really didn't give us credit for being that good a ball club. I'm going to tell you one thing: from August through October of '69, we were unbeatable. You weren't going to outpitch us, you weren't going to outrun us, and you weren't going to outscore us because of our pitching staff and defense. It wasn't a fluke—we just had good young players that knew how to play the game.

"I think about winning the '69 World Series every day," Boz continued. "And I wear my ring every day. And because of it, there isn't a day that goes by without someone asking, 'Hey, what kind of ring is that?' When I tell them it's a Mets World Series ring, they'll often ask, 'You mean, the Amazin' Mets?' They don't say the '86 Mets. It's always the Amazin' Mets!"

Pfeil wears his ring every day as well.

"It's incredible how many people tell me that the '69 Mets were their favorite team—and I live on the West Coast!" he said. "The ring brings excitement to me. It brings some perseverance. I look at it and think that, after eight years in the minor leagues, I was fortunate enough to stick with it. I thought about quitting several times before '69 because I thought I should have been in the big leagues. The ring always reminds me in difficult times personally and in business that, boy, if you just try to be consistent and honest and keep plugging away, things will go your way."

"People still want to talk about the Miracle Mets—that's the *real* miracle," said Krane, a Met from the very beginning in 1962 and still the longest-tenured Met in team history. "We went from last place to first, and there will never be another World Series like that one. There'll never be another ball club like that one. The fans love us and still respect us after all these years. When I walk down the streets of Manhattan, doormen will still talk to me about '69 as if it were yesterday. Of course, they *all* say they were there at the ballpark during the World Series. People I don't even know will call out, 'Hey Ed, I was there! Remember me? I was there!' But you know, back then, baseball was still the workingman's sport, still cheap enough for people to go. They could relate to guys like me, and Art and all the guys that filled in, like Al Weis. Those fans fought for their team every day. And you know what? That's why New York is such a great town. The Miracle Mets were a great thing for New York. We'll never forget it. They'll never forget it."

Our players and fans are still captivated by our miracle season. It all goes back to where we were as a team early that year and how far we had come. It didn't take me long to realize just how important everybody was on that '69 team. Just thinking about all those bizarre regular-season games and then the World Series and how so many different players contributed to our success was awe-inspiring. We were truly a collage of guys who were thrown together by really strong leadership and accomplished something that was very special.

CHAPTER 21

TO THE VICTORS GO THE SPOILS

– October 17–December 31, 1969 –

THE PARTY RAGED ON IN THE WEEKS AND MONTHS AFTER the final out of the World Series settled softly into the waiting glove of Cleon Jones. We were, without question, at the pinnacle of our respective baseball careers. You simply couldn't be more on top of the world after winning a World Series than we were at that time and place in history. During a period of so much pain and suffering throughout society, we gave millions of people a reason to celebrate. And to hope.

Under the category of "perfect timing," I had just opened up a nightclub with Phil Linz in New City, New York, called the Marshmellow. The night after the World Series ended, I had Tug McGraw and Wayne Garrett, who was barely old enough to drink, work as guest bartenders. Tug was his usual funny self, and nobody was better with customers. There is no doubt in my mind he would have been a great bartender had he done it professionally. He was witty and comical like Kooz, but somehow different in the way he lit up a room. And Tug might say outrageous things in an outspoken manner like Swoboda, but when Tug said them, they just came out even funnier. I have a feeling he had a few drinks while working on the job. If there was Irish whiskey around, Tug was always going to enjoy drinking some.

As for Garrett, it was just a continuation of the World Series celebration.

"I didn't mix drinks too well," Wayne told me recently. "So I just poured drafts and champagne—but a lot of them! I was bartending for a couple of hours and really enjoyed it. You know, I think I'm still waiting to get paid. But it didn't matter. I had a great time, and I'm sure you made it up to me in some way."

Two days later, we all appeared on the weekly Sunday night broadcast of *The Ed Sullivan Show* to sing "You've Gotta Have Heart," the inspiring song from the Broadway play *Damn Yankees*. It was an appropriate choice, considering the lyrics are all about overcoming great odds. But there was just one problem. Following rehearsals, most of us went next door to a Chinese restaurant and drank mai tais. "We were all hammered," Rocky recalled. "Sullivan came out and said, 'Oh my God! These guys can't go on—they're all drunk!' We still went on, but they had to bring a choir to sing behind us—out of sight."

We were set up onstage in three rows, all attired in jackets and ties. As we "sang"—if that's what you want to call it—the camera spanned and stopped at most of us, eliciting cheers from the audience. But the reality was, we all kind of ad-libbed the words. "I didn't know the words to that song," J. C. Martin admitted. "But it was fun to be on that show. You watched it your whole life on television and then, to get on Ed Sullivan's program and to know you're on live TV, it was quite a treat."

Said Kooz, "We were out there singing, and it was the last thing we were good at. It was a good experience, but I know it was certainly out of our realm."

Yet a few weeks earlier, on the day after we clinched the NL East, we actually cut a vinyl LP for Buddha Records entitled *The Amazing Mets*, singing songs like "Green Grass of Shea," "God Bless America," and "We've Got the Whole World Watching Us." The back of the album cover had all of our pictures on it with our full names—no nicknames, like Buddy or Tug. I still get people today bringing copies of it for me to sign. But despite its being a best-selling hit record, some of us were pretty hammered recording that one, too. Thankfully, they brought in some professional singers to help us out there as well.

"Except for Rocky," the Glider told me. "He could *really* sing! Oh man, we had a wonderful group of guys!"

As memorable as *The Ed Sullivan Show* appearance was, nothing could top what we experienced the next day. The Canyon of Heroes ticker-tape parade along Lower Broadway was nothing short of epic. An all-time New York City record number of people came out to cheer us on as more than 1,254 tons of ticker tape, paper, and other forms of debris came raining down on our motorcade from the buildings above. That was even more tonnage than they had for numerous parades after World War II in 1945 or for the Apollo 11 astronauts following the moon landing just two months earlier. What really hit me the most during our parade was how these millions of people knew who we were and what we had accomplished. It felt like we were under a microscope with all of those countless people looking down at us. The adulation and love from these fans for the joy we brought them in 1969 was truly incredible.

"Tom and Nancy Seaver rode in the same car as my wife, La-Vonne, and I," recalled Kooz. "The wives were sitting down below, and Tom and I were sitting on top of the back of a convertible. The paper was up to the wives' knees from the floor of the car. I mean, they threw everything from those windows. It was so dark out from all the paper coming down."

There were literally twenty or more rows of people along the narrow, cavernous parade route, with approximately a hundred rows on the side streets. The jubilant fans chanted, "We're number one!" and many came armed with some rather original signs and banners. As we passed the front of the historic Trinity Church, a young man hoisted on the shoulders of two of his buddies held a sign that read, "God isn't dead, he's playing for the Mets."

"Only in New York," Garrett said. "If it's any other city, you don't go through that experience. You probably meet the mayor, but there's no *Ed Sullivan Show* and nothing like the ticker-tape parade we had. But it comes with the territory when you play in New York. It was just so exciting. When I returned home to Sarasota, they had a day for me and were happy for me, but nobody got too excited about it. After that, it was over with."

Our day was hardly over after the completion of the parade. At city hall, there was a grand reception engineered by the mayor himself, John Lindsay. His visible association with our club throughout the postseason benefited his reelection efforts tremendously. After all, this was a man who lost in the primaries that June as a Republican and was now running on the ballot of the relatively small Liberal Party. Many pundits were saying he was done politically. But there he was, at our clubhouse celebrations when we won the division, when we won the pennant, and then when we won the World Series. And the day after winning the National League pennant, we'd enjoyed cocktails and hors d'oeuvres at his Gracie Mansion residence. Lindsay didn't know very much about sports, but he was riding our coattails to his own personal political victory.

"There's no doubt we got him elected," said Gaspar, whose iconic photo of him pouring champagne over Lindsay's head in the clubhouse after the World Series would become etched in the minds of millions of New York City voters. "He wanted Swoboda and me to make an 'experience' for him which, I think, we did. Politicians—they know what they're doing. I got a number of pictures of us dousing each other with champagne."

Lindsay wasn't the only New York politician who was swooped up by our success. After the earlier fete at Gracie Mansion, we loaded into a bus and were taken to Governor Nelson Rockefeller's spacious apartment at 812 Fifth Avenue, across from Central Park. His residence, which featured a wraparound terrace with incredible westward views of the park, was positively stunning. Inside, the duplex was impeccably decorated with antique furniture and Picassos hanging on the walls. The governor would entertain us again soon after we won the World Series—this time at his town house on Fifty-Fourth Street. That place remains especially vivid in my mind because it's where Rockefeller famously died of a heart attack late one evening in 1979 while in the company of his twenty-seven-year-old assistant.

The surreal had become the norm.

"I kind of expected it all after a while," Gaspar told me. "It became a part of the deal. With the ticker-tape parade—I didn't really think about how historical that was, that Charles Lindbergh and the astronauts were celebrated the same way we were. And then the parties at Gracie Mansion and Rockefeller's apartments—how can you beat that? It was like, *Okay, here's the next thing. We're going to see the governor now. Next, we're going to see the mayor. All right.* It's something that I didn't give a lot of thought to then. It didn't surprise me."

Said McAndrew, "We got caught up in it. I look back at that whirlwind year, and I've gotta shake my head. We did all kinds of stuff. We were so young and naïve, we were thinking, *Gee, this is what everybody does.* But, I mean, at the time, you're living your life, and you're just a kid doing things as they came."

Next up, for seven of us—Agee, Seaver, Clink, Krane, Kooz,

Cleon, and me—was a seventeen-day Las Vegas singing act put together by comedian Phil Foster at Caesars Palace. You can't get much higher than to have your name in lights on Caesars's large marquee along Las Vegas Boulevard. But there we were, the middle act between Jerry Van Dyke and the headliner, singer Jimmie Rodgers. And best of all, we were each getting paid $10,000 for the gig, which was only slightly less than what most of us were making in a whole season of playing baseball. The show was financed by a gambler who'd won $1 million on the Mets, picking us to win the World Series at 100-to-1 odds before the '69 season started. He made sure we all had suites with a wet bar, and all we had to do was sign for our meals. And for all of this, our ensemble basically made fools of ourselves two shows a night.

"We found out quickly we weren't entertainers," Krane said. "We were baseball players."

Foster would open up our act with a few jokes and then say something funny about each of us as he introduced us individually. The dinner show was a little bit uptight, much different than the late show, which tended to be wild because the audience was kind of tipsy and more free spending at that hour. Also, at the dinner show, we wore tuxedos, while at the midnight act, we dressed more casually. Again, we were so bad that they had to put three professional singers behind the curtain. I generally sang between Agee and Seaver, and none of us knew the words to songs like "The Impossible Dream," nor did we really care.

"We couldn't sing!" Cleon said. "That was the whole issue. We had no one that could sing. I actually did learn the words eventually, but nobody else did."

When it was over, we would go and see even later shows and performances, some starting as late as two in the morning, like comedian Redd Foxx and singer Tom Jones. And they usually made it a point to introduce us to the crowd and, in Foxx's case, make us a part of the act. We had become a symbol of pop culture.

One of my most vivid memories of the trip involved Clendenon. Every day, Clink would get paged at Caesars over the loudspeaker. So one time I said to him, "How many times did *you* page yourself today just to hear your name?" Of course, he denied it, saying, "No, people are looking for me."

"Bullshit people are looking for you. You're paging *yourself!*"

"It was a lot of fun and a tremendous experience," Krane said. "There was a lot of drinking, a lot of gambling, and most of us came home broke. Every night, I'd play with these chips, which was how I got paid, and say, 'I'm going to play until I lose them—and then go to bed.' I wasn't smart enough to bring them to the cashier and get money for them. I wasn't thinking about turning them into 'green.'"

Not all of us went home empty-handed. But while some of us managed to hold on to the money we earned for our act, the big winner in Vegas was Kooz—who made a fortune in the casino.

"I couldn't stay the whole while because LaVonne was going to give birth to my son Shawn," Kooz recalled. "So I had to hurry up and catch a plane and go home. But the night before I left, I met Tom Redmond, the owner of the Las Vegas Cowboys of the old Continental Football League. So Redmond says, 'You ever play roulette before?' I said, 'No.' So he goes, 'I'll teach you. And look, whatever we make, you keep half.' So one of the things we did was bet on my uniform number, '36,' every time. He had a little notebook with him to keep track. He said, 'Every ten times you lose, you double up.' So every ten spins I didn't win, I doubled down. When I finally won, I had something like $4,000 on that number, hitting it on the 127th try, but we only broke damn near even on it. But while we played '36' each time, we were also putting black $100 chips on other numbers and were up about $150,000 at one point.

Big dollars! So we started betting $4,000 on different numbers, had a big crowd around us cheering us on, and when we'd order drinks, the cheapest chip we had was $25, so that was our tip money. The cocktail waitresses absolutely loved bringing us drinks! Anyway, we watched that roulette wheel spin, and we lost everything except for $1,500.

"After around three hours, we quit. We had to rest. Your eyes are just watching that ball go around and around. So we went to the bar, sat down, and just started going over how stupid we were to have kept playing like we did. But Redmond owned a big insurance company, and he made many millions, so losing money really was no big thing to him. After finishing my drink, I said, 'Well, I'm going home in the morning, so I should go back to my room.' That's when Redmond said, 'Well, listen, we're going to play some craps, and I need a left-handed roller.' I said, 'What time? I've got an eight o'clock flight.' He said, 'Be down here at six.'

"So we meet, and there's only one craps table open, and it's full. We wait, and finally a guy craps out and leaves. I jump into his spot. Redmond does all the betting. I'm rolling the dice for forty-five minutes, and he's betting big—and winning big. Every $5,000 we win, he gives the chips to a 'coach' to go cash in. That way, in case I have to leave to catch my plane, I'll have my money ready to go. Meanwhile, the coach called me a cab and loaded all my luggage into it. But we keep winning, so I kept the cab waiting at the front door for forty-five minutes. By the time we were done, we were up $70,000! So I took $35,000—my share—plus what I made for the Vegas act, got a check from Caesars, went home, and bought one of the best houses I could find for $38,500. And, remember, we had quite a run on that roulette table the night before. If I was smarter, I could have taken home another $75,000 out of that deal, too. Dumb."

Still, it was an incredible time for us all whether we scored big or not. "They actually wanted us to stay an extra two weeks," Krane re-called, "but we took a vote, and the guys wanted to go home."

Boz, Garrett, and Gaspar. I always thought the three of them to-gether didn't have one personality! So late that December, when they went on the popular TV show *The Dating Game*, and the female contestant picked Gaspar as her date, I got the feeling she wanted to turn right around and go back the other way! I joke with Boz and Garrett all the time, saying, "You lost to *Gaspar*?! You guys should be ashamed! How do you live that down?" And then, of course, they make all kinds of excuses. I just love having fun with them over it. I still have a video of their appearance and seeing those guys—all good friends of mine—on *The Dating Game* make it one of the classic shows of all time to me.

"I actually came in third place!" said Boz. "What does that tell you?! I've got that tape, and to look at that—*ugh*—it's just so embar-rassing. I don't let very many people watch it. All three of us were just rubes. We didn't have any idea of what was going on. But LA was always a good place to be. I remember there wasn't a person on that staff of *The Dating Game* that was older than twenty-five. But the three of us all had girls with us. They had a party the night before, and we all had dates to go to that deal."

Said Garrett, who came in second, "When that show first came on television, I felt sorry for the participants that were on it. Gosh, they were asked the most ridiculous questions. And sometimes they had to make up songs to sing about something, and I thought, *This is the stupidest show!* So after the season, someone from California called and said, 'Hey, would you like to be on *The Dating Game*?' I said, 'I don't like your show. I don't watch your show.' And the per-son said, 'Well, two of your teammates are going to be on it.' And I asked, 'Who?' And they said, 'Ken Boswell and Rod Gaspar.' I'm like 'Really?' And they asked, 'Now do you want to join them?' I thought, Well, what can you say? You can't say no. So I said, 'Yeah, I'll do it. But, my God, whatever you do, don't ask me to sing a song.'

"So I get on the show, and what does this stupid girl do? She asks me to make up and sing some damn song. And I thought, You've got to be kidding me! So, of course, I go blank and just sang something— I don't even know what it was. But then Rod ends up winning this thing, and I'm thinking, What?! His fiancée is out in the audience! The guy was engaged to get married, and he's the winner! But, hey, I didn't really care. I didn't want to win. Nobody wanted to win!

"But the funniest part of it," Garrett continued, "was how Kenny and I arrived late to the show. The makeup people were so pissed at us. One of them said anxiously, 'God! We've got to get you out there! But we've got to do your makeup and everything first!' So I look over at Gaspar, who arrived on time and already had his makeup on, and said, 'Rod, are you okay?' He says, 'Yeah, why?' And I go, 'God, you're white as a sheet! You look really bad, Rod.' So I turned to the lady who was about to put that makeup on me and said, 'If I have to look like that, I don't want it.' And Kenny said the same thing to her. So Rod gets up, goes to the bathroom, and washed all of his makeup off, and we went on there just as we were. That was the funniest part of the show!"

"The three of us drank champagne before we went out on the program," the reigning champion Gaspar recalled. "None of us wanted to win and go on the trip. But we were the only three single guys on the team that year. Why she picked me, I've got no idea. Anyway, the girl, myself, and a chaperone, flew to Zurich, Switzerland, and stayed at the Hotel Regency. It was supposed to be a ski trip for five days. I think we were on the slopes for maybe an hour the whole time. I didn't even know how to ski! And then the chaperone moved into the girl's room because she was under twenty-one. I guess the chaperone didn't trust me—which makes sense. Obviously, the chaperone and I didn't get along very well. So this was basically a trip where I was there by myself over there in Switzerland."

Poor Gaspar. He simply couldn't win for losing!

There were just so many perks that came our way following our miracle season. Winning a championship in New York was one thing, but winning it on a team known as the lovable losers was something else altogether. Everything was for the asking. We couldn't have a meal in a fancy restaurant or a drink at a bar without the check being picked up by some well-wisher. The level of gratitude was almost hard to believe. And while it was never taken for granted, at times I was torn. In one respect, there were moments in public when you wanted a little privacy, but on the other hand, you didn't want the adulation to ever end.

"We became a team of individuals that people idolized," Gentry observed. "In '69, everybody on the Mets was considered a star—it didn't matter whether you started in the World Series or not."

Said Gaspar, "It's incredible what happens when you're a winner. We got all kinds of things: free gasoline, certificates to restaurants, and some even got cars. Just about anywhere you went, you didn't have to pay for anything. Even places where I used to go and pay normally before the World Series, now I didn't."

While Eddie Charles was a part of many of our glamorous postchampionship experiences and enjoyed the perks of our success, he would also travel to a far less glitzy place when he visited servicemen badly injured in the war.

"I was at a hospital base in Manila on a USO tour with some other major-league players," Charles told me. "And there was one experience I had that really dug deep in me. These guys were laid up there with shrapnel all over their bodies, limbs cut off, and terrible things like that. I thought to myself, *What the heck can I possibly say to these guys to raise their spirits?* Well, one of the kids answered that question for me. I went over to his bedside, and all he wanted to talk about was the '69 World Series. But the thing that really touched me the most was the fact that, here's a kid that looks like he's about sixteen years old, both legs off, shot all over his body, and all he was worried about was that he would eventually be transported to a naval hospital in Jamaica, Queens. He said to me, 'I don't know how I'm going to get to Shea Stadium to see you guys.' I just looked at him and went, 'I'll tell you what. When you get home, you give me a call, and I'll make *damn* sure you get to Shea Stadium.' That's all he was worried about. I can still picture that kid in my mind."

It was just another incredible story that we, as '69 Mets, heard variations of over and over again from those affected by the Vietnam War. So many lives were devastated during that dark time in our history, but somehow what we accomplished gave heroes like this young man something to root for and feel a part of. We did more than just win a championship. In our own way, we made the lives of people in dire circumstances a little better. And is there anything more important than that?

Beyond the miracle, that is perhaps our greatest legacy.

CHAPTER 22

THE JOURNEY

— May 12, 2017 —

"GOD IS LIVING IN NEW YORK, AND HE'S A METS FAN," SEAVER said back in '69.

Well, maybe Tom was on to something, because on the morning of our flights to see him, the country was experiencing magnificent weather, and we all arrived into San Francisco International Airport on schedule. Shortly after Buddy, Erik, and I landed, we met Koosman over at his Delta gate and then took the short walk down to the United Airlines terminal to meet Rocky about twenty minutes later. We really lucked out with how everything fell into place.

Kooz, now a large man, wore a striped button-down shirt and had his gray hair parted to one side. In his typical high spirits, he engulfed Buddy and me with warm embraces. Rocky, dressed in a light polo shirt more appropriate for the hot New Orleans weather he had left earlier that day, was happy to see us all again, though he was far more subdued than Kooz as he gave us a medical update on his wife, Cecilia, which was cautiously optimistic.

We picked up the large van we had rented from Hertz to make our way out to the Country Inn in Santa Rosa, about a thirty-minute drive from Tom's house. We had wanted to get a house for all of us in Calistoga, where Tom lives, but nothing was available for less than $8,000 for the weekend. The Napa Valley is home to some of the most expensive real estate in the world.

Kooz, easily the most talkative of our group, sat up front in the passenger seat, holding court, with Erik Sherman behind the wheel, while Rocky, Buddy, and I sat in the second row. We talked about baseball, politics, and the requisite clubhouse humor—just as if no time had passed since we all played together a half century ago. As we drove along the freeway and passed Bayview Hill, which once loomed over Candlestick Park, the former home of the San Francisco Giants, the flashbacks to our playing days began to set in.

"The fog would roll in during the early evening after the game started," Kooz reminisced out loud. "But the wind started much earlier—usually just after one in the afternoon. I always did well in Frisco because it was always cool, and I liked that kind of weather. You know, I never had much trouble with the Giants' big home run hitters Willie Mays and Willie McCovey. In fact, I didn't have much trouble with most of the other big home run hitters, either—guys like Willie Stargell, Johnny Bench, and Hank Aaron. I think Mays and Aaron only homered once each off of me. And the *Daily News* writer Jack Lang told me that Bench had a batting average of, like, .123 against me. It was the little guys I had the most trouble with: the Punch-and-Judys."

"So who was the toughest hitter you ever faced?" Erik asked.

"Probably Lee May," Kooz said after a pregnant pause to ponder the question. "You had to throw him changeups, and a lot of times I couldn't get that pitch over, so I had to go to my fastball—and he *loved* fastballs."

Jerry then turned to Buddy, who hadn't said much since we left the airport, and asked, "What's wrong, *Cheech*?" Kooz had long ago given Harrelson this nickname after the golfer Chi-Chi Rodriguez.

"You know I can't drive anymore," Buddy told him. "I've got Alzheimer's. I have trouble remembering things that happened just two days ago."

"Well, so do I, Cheech," he said reassuringly. "But do you have trouble remembering '69?"

"*Shit no!*" Buddy answered enthusiastically. "I'm so happy to be here with you guys. You can't put a price on this trip. The '86 team was one thing, but no one expected what we did in '69 to happen—coming back against the Cubs and then winning the World Series."

"Speaking of the Cubs," I interjected, "I recently saw Fergie Jenkins at a golf tournament. It was a few days after Bill Hands died. He told me that sixteen of the '69 Cubs are now gone. They were a more veteran team than ours, but it's still kind of shocking."

"That game we had against the Cubs in July when Hundley was catching and Agee slid into home safely," Kooz reminisced aloud. "Hundley went nuts, thinking he had him. That was the beginning of everything for us."

"Agee just beat the throw and got the call," Rocky chimed in. "All those series with Chicago seemed to be gripping that year. They were all pretty tight. We didn't catch them until September. It was ten days in September when we went from, like, five down to five up and never looked back."

"Seaver and I won eighteen of our last nineteen starts at that time," Kooz added. "Once that cool air came around . . ."

"That was ridiculous!" Swoboda exclaimed, speaking over Kooz. "And I remember you talked to me about that problem you had under your arm which caused you great discomfort."

"Yep, a muscle knotted up. I missed a month that year," Kooz explained.

"You guys remember the trainer we had the following year, Tommy McKenna?" I asked everyone. "We nicknamed him 'Fifty-fifty.' Tug came up with Fifty-fifty because Tommy couldn't hurt you, and he couldn't help you."

Laughter filled the car, as we remembered the sometimes

"prehistoric" medical assistance we received from the training staff—as well as McGraw's priceless wit.

"Oh, Tug!" exclaimed Kooz. "I came into the clubhouse on a night I was pitching, and he asked, 'Hey, Kooz, you pitching tonight?' I said, 'Yep.' And he said, 'Me too!'" The car again erupted in laughter. "I tried so hard to never let him—or any of those relievers—get into a game."

Now the memories of the beloved McGraw were coming out.

"I always read the stat sheet of the opposing hitters before every game," Kooz said. "I wanted to try to find one extra little thing to do besides win. So one night in LA, Willie Davis is on a thirty-six-game hitting streak, and I thought, *I'm going to stop that SOB's hitting streak!* Anyway, in the ninth inning, I'm leading, like, 1–0—all of our games with the Dodgers seemed like they were 1–0 or 2–1. I think I had two outs, and Davis is coming to the plate. Gil comes out, takes me out, and brings in Tug. I was not going to go to the dugout until Tug arrived at the mound. When he did, I said to him, 'Listen, I got him out four times. I want to break up his hitting streak. So bear down on his ass.' But no sooner had I gotten to the bench and sat down—*boom!* Single!"

"Tug couldn't pitch unless he had someone on base," Rocky interjected as Kooz broke us up again.

"We played what seemed like an extra-inning game every other day out there in LA," he said.

"Well, in '69 you had that fifteen-inning game against them," Erik added. "The game that Jack DiLauro pitched."

"Fifteen innings was nothing for us," Kooz said smirking, shaking his head.

"Hey, I've got one for you," Swoboda said. "Who picked up the first save for us in '69?"

After a long pause, with everybody trying to think of less obvious choices, Kooz offered one of the more likely ones: Ron Taylor.

"Nope. How about *Nolan Ryan*?" Swoboda answered. "Two-inning save. I think he only had two or three saves his whole career."

"Well, I've got saves for both Seaver and Jon Matlack," Kooz said to everyone's surprise. "Usually Gil would put starters in the pen right before the All-Star break. So that's how some of the starters ended up with saves."

"Gil didn't let players screw around," Buddy said. "He was *the man* and didn't take any shit, no matter who you were. If you're not doing your job, then somebody else was going to have a chance to take it."

"Who was it that messed up and Gil sent to the minor leagues?" asked Kooz.

"Hodges sent Krane down for a few days in '70," I reminded him.

"That's right," Kooz said. "Gil did send him down. I forgot about that. He did it to straighten Krane out on something."

But Krane was hardly alone when it came to raising Gil's ire.

"I opened my big mouth, too," Rocky chimed in. "It was in Pittsburgh where I opened my big trap. It was our first road trip of '69, and Gil said, 'Okay, we're going to set curfew. You guys decide what it's going to be because you're going to have to live with it.' Someone suggested it be three hours after games. Gil said, 'That's too long.' So I go, 'Why don't you just *tell us* what you want?' He just sort of glared at me. Jesus Christ, why didn't I just shut up?"

I then offered my own Gil story.

"Hodges once caught me in Houston coming back late to the Shamrock Hotel. I lost a bet to Kenny Boswell, my roommate, and had to go get us something to eat because there was no room service. I had to walk right through the lobby at one o'clock in the morning, and there's Gil—just sitting there, not looking at all happy with me."

"Oh, I did that in Philadelphia," Rocky adds. "I was coming down the elevator with no shoes on. The doors open, and it's my dumb ass standing there in front of Gil and his coaches. I'm like, *Oh, geez!*

Kooz has always enjoyed talking about occurrences on the field, but he seems to relish telling stories about what occurs off of it even more so. He was one of the greatest practical jokers we had on the ball club, and he took a special kind of pride in it. And what he would tell us next, appropriately involving Seaver in honor of our visit to see him, was one of his all-time greatest pranks, albeit later in his career with the Mets. A great storyteller, he kept us glued to his every word for the next few minutes.

"Hey, did I ever tell you guys about the time I bugged Seaver's radio?" Kooz asked rhetorically. "This was around '75. I was reading a magazine one day from my locker, and in the back, they've got an ad for a bugging device. I was into gadgets then, so I sent for it. It wasn't too big and had a rubber antenna on it with a little microphone inside. The directions said to tune a nearby radio to FM-1270, and, when speaking into this gadget, your voice would come over that radio. So I took it into the clubhouse during a game and got Nick Torman, our clubhouse guy, to test it. 'Let's see how far this thing works,' I said to him.

"Seaver had an FM radio above his locker, so I had Nick take the bugging device into Yogi's office and told him to hold it under his desk and talk." Berra was the Mets' skipper by this time. "Well, I could hear him just as plain as day over Seaver's radio. So I came up with this idea. Jack Simon, our TV director, could do a perfect impression of Howard Cosell. *Perfect!* I mean, you couldn't tell them apart. We had just had a brawl with Houston, which involved the Astros' Doug Rader. They also had a pitcher named Doug Konieczny, whom we just pounded whenever he came into a game. So I thought up a trade and told Simon, "You're going to be Howard Cosell and announce a deal over Tom's radio." I went over and over with him what I wanted him to say for probably a week until he had it down right.

"So the time came to put my plan into action—right after batting practice, when all the guys were in the clubhouse. I told Jack, 'You go into the trainer's room, where everything is set up. Then count down from ten so I can get over to Seaver's locker, get up on his footstool, adjust his radio, and turn the volume up.'

"When I get out there, Tom's talking in front of his locker with M. Donald Grant, the team chairman. Still, I thought, *Oh, what the hell?* At first, I turned it on very low so only I could hear it. I had instructed Simon after he counted down to zero to give me five more seconds to get the heck out of there. So on zero, I turned the volume way up and went to the training room door to listen to Simon.

" 'Well, hello everybody, this is Howard Cosell with a sports bulletin,' Jack began. 'The New York Mets have just announced a major trade sending right-handed pitcher Tom Seaver and left-handed-hitting first baseman Ed Kranepool to the Houston Astros for third baseman Doug Rader and right-handed pitcher Doug Konieczny.'"

We were all in stitches as Kooz continued his story.

"The clubhouse was in *shock*!" Kooz continued. "You could have heard a pin drop in there. Right, Buddy? You were there. Anyway, nobody could understand the reason behind that trade. Why would we want Rader, who we all wanted to beat up, or Konieczny, who had, like, a 25.00 ERA against us? But it sounded legitimate. After all, coming over the radio and out of Cosell's mouth, everyone thought it's gotta be true!

"What followed was chaos. Don Grant goes, '*Who* was that?! *What* station was that?' before storming through the TV room.

Kranepool is over by his locker, *furious*, taking his bat and beating his locker with it. Just pissed off! Nobody knew what was going on—pure panic. So I come out from the trainer's room and go over to Tom, and he's simply dumbfounded. I put my hand out to shake his and tell him, 'I can't believe this.' He didn't want to shake it but just held his hand there, mesmerized by this news. I went back to the trainer's room, to where Simon was still sitting.

" 'Jack, get out of here now and don't say a word about this to anybody. They'll cut our heads off if they find out about what we did. Don't tell *anybody*!'

"And we didn't. We kept the practical joke to ourselves until two years later, in '77, after Seaver gets traded to Cincinnati. The Reds come to New York, and by God, we're pitching against each other. He beats me 4–3. Jack Simon has us come on *Kiner's Korner* afterward. I'm sitting there next to Kiner, and Seaver is to my right. Ralph goes, 'You two guys, you were teammates for ten-plus years—you must have some good stories. Kooz, you got any good ones?' I said, 'Yeah, I do,' and I told this one. Seaver was hearing it for the first time. Well, we all knew where the monitors were, and you could see when you were on TV. So when they had a close-up of me telling the story, Seaver gets right up close, so he's just barely out of the monitor's picture, and whispers in my ear, 'You mother-effer. *You mother-effer.*'"

After our laughter subsided—and it took a while—Rocky told another hilarious Seaver-related tale that revolved around Tom's trade to the Reds and the light-hitting second baseman Doug Flynn, whom the Mets acquired along with Pat Zachry, Steve Henderson, and Dan Norman.

"Apparently, Flynn was in the Reds dugout in Cincinnati when Pete Rose came over and said, 'Flynner, you just got traded.'

"He said, 'Really? Where?'

" 'The New York Mets.'

" 'For who?'

" 'Tom Seaver.'

"So Flynn asks, 'Straight up?' "

As the guys broke into uproarious laughter once more, I wondered when I'd last had as much fun as I was having at that very moment. So far, this trip was all that I had I imagined it could be and more.

Nancy Seaver forewarned me that the San Francisco–area traffic would be *horrible*. But Erik is doing his best with the GPS to avoid as much of it as possible. Still, after an hour, we're just now driving over the Bay Bridge. As the Oakland Coliseum is off in the distance, it brings back memories for all of us. For me, it was the final stop in my baseball career. For Kooz, it represented the bitter defeat of the '73 World Series.

"We should have won that Series," Kooz says in a rare serious tone. "Up three-to-two, and we blew it."

"I talked to Kranepool about it at an event I saw him at last year, and he's still *really* upset with Yogi about it," Erik chimes in. "He said he got into it with him for not going with George Stone in game six, so that, if needed, a *fully rested* Seaver would have been ready to go in game seven. Instead, Berra, of course, went with Seaver in the sixth game on short rest and paid the price."

"Yeah, and Yogi should have pulled Matlack early in game seven," Kooz adds. "You know, a bunch of us had tickets that night to go see Johnny Mathis in San Francisco after losing the Series. We went but weren't very excited about it. A bad time to go out, really."

By the grace of God, we eventually get on Highway 101 heading north toward Santa Rosa. But by the looks of the crowded road on this Friday afternoon, and what the GPS is telling us, we still have a long haul ahead of us. I decide to give Nancy Seaver a call to let her know our whereabouts.

"She's God-sent," Buddy says appreciatively. "She's so good for Tom. Tough to find someone as good as her."

Everyone agrees in quiet contemplation.

"Winding road here," I observe. "How are you doing, Erik? I hope you don't go to sleep."

"Oh, I'm fine," Sherman reassures us. "I have some pretty valuable cargo in here."

"I can't believe this traffic," Kooz says, glancing at the GPS on the dashboard. "Thank God I don't live out here! We still have another forty-two miles to go? Once we get over this bridge, let's find a place to stop. We could stop at a bar, have a couple, and let the traffic disappear. I've got to have a smoke."

"Okay, the first decent exit I see, I'll get off," Erik says.

"Cheech, you drink?" asks Kooz.

"Nope," Buddy says. "Not for eleven years."

"I'll be darned," Kooz replies. "Why did you do that, Cheech? I know guys that lose their memory for doing something like that."

"Yeah, like me," Buddy replies self-deprecatingly, as the guys laugh at his response.

"I kept feeling like shit, so I stopped, too," offered Rocky, perhaps with a touch of solidarity for Buddy. "It's been three years now."

"Really?" Kooz asked, clearly surprised. "About a month ago, I said the hell with it. I'm not going to drink vodka tonight; I'm gonna have Scotch. I hadn't drunk Scotch in thirty years. I quit it because it was *so good*, and I knew it was gonna get me. So I ordered a Scotch and water, and that first one was just superb. I mean, I never had the first Scotch and water taste so good. It was *absolutely* delicious. I got half loaded that night just drinking Scotch. I haven't had any since because I like it too well."

The guys broke out into laughter. Few people can be as entertaining as Kooz when telling a story. And throughout this long car ride, he was on top of his game. Quite simply, Kooz was pitching another masterpiece.

As we near Petaluma, about thirty miles north of San Francisco, Kooz's cell phone rings. From the sound of the conversation, it's clear the caller is a former big leaguer. As it turns out, it's hardly just *any* former player, but one of the all-time greats.

"Well, you'll never guess who that was," Kooz says after finishing the quick call. "That was your boy, Rocky: Steve Carlton."

It was a playful dig at the liberal-minded Swoboda, as Carlton is a staunch conservative who has gone off the grid by living in the mountains north of Durango, Colorado.

"We talk about every day," Kooz continues. "Lefty's in great shape. He's got his greenhouse, his garden, plants about five hundred trees a year. He's really happy."

As I'd told Erik beforehand, there would likely be some interesting exchanges between Kooz and Rocky. And sure enough, the two of them begin debating the origin of the country's political divisiveness. Kooz naturally pins the blame squarely on eight years of President Barack Obama, while Swoboda counters that at least the former president didn't embarrass the country like "your guy." The releasing of Donald Trump's tax returns—or lack thereof—and Obama's birth certificate come next, with the back-and-forth between the two ending with how Rocky called the political satirist and comedian Bill Maher one of his heroes.

"He may go overboard sometimes, but he holds politicians accountable," Swoboda asserts.

"Oh, yeah," Kooz says with a husky laugh. "I'd kick him in the nuts."

But even as different as their views are, it never gets nasty or uncomfortable. They have the utmost respect and admiration for each other. If anything, it is fun to watch, and the two of them, while strong in their respective convictions, sort of play it up for our little group.

We exit in Petaluma looking for a bar. It's now almost five o'clock. We drive around town for fifteen minutes and all we see are vegan and gluten-free cafes, an Old Chicago Pizza, three French bistros, and a dining theater. It's clearly not Kooz's kind of town.

"In Wisconsin, we wouldn't have to drive this far before seeing a bar already," he grumbles. "Maybe we shouldn't have gotten off here. Don't listen to me all the time, Erik—just when I'm right!"

"Geez, looks like a swinging area," Rocky adds sarcastically. "Really jumping."

"You know, California is one of those snowflake states," Kooz remarks with a grin. "You can't do anything here."

"I think it's a cute town," I say.

"*Why?*" asks Kooz rhetorically. "It's *not* cute here. There's no bar around. They're all on salads out here!"

We finally see what looks like a sports-themed bar but, without any signs of parking in sight, decide to get back on the freeway. Traffic has picked up a little bit, so I give the Country Inn a call to let them know about when we will arrive and to not give away our rooms. It was me again probably acting a little paranoid.

The car is quiet, except for Rocky softly singing a few lines of a sweet, mellow, rhythm-and-blues song: "Won't you please, come to me . . ." I find that Swoboda actually has a pretty melodious voice. He once told me how, living in New Orleans, he developed a great respect for traditional jazz and rhythm-and-blues music and hangs out with musicians whenever he can. The conversation and stories have been great, but everybody by this point just wants to get to the motel.

"How long have we been on the road, Erik?" asks Rocky.

"I'd say close to three hours."

"Geez, time flies when you're having fun," Swoboda notes.

About thirty minutes later, at long last, we arrive in Santa Rosa.

"There it is: the *Country Inn*! That place is hopping!" Kooz says sarcastically, while at the same time sounding relieved that we finally arrived. "And look, there's a liquor store right across the street. And here's KFC right next to the Country Inn. I guess we're having chicken tonight, boys and girls!"

We pile out of our van and Rocky and Kooz share a glance, smile, and give each other a big embrace in the hotel parking lot.

"Hey, I still love ya," Swoboda says to Kooz, fully accepting their differing point of views.

"I still love you, too, Rock," replies Kooz with a big grin before saying to the group, "Hey, who wants to join me in my room in ten minutes for a drink?"

All of us are in, except for Buddy, who retreats to his room for an early night. It was a long day for Harrelson, and I was thrilled that he enjoyed it as much as he did. Rocky, Erik, and I convene to join Kooz following his quick trip to the liquor store, where he's picked up a bottle of Ketel One vodka to mix with soda. Who knew there was such a concoction?

The room was downright cold, as Kooz, at last able to smoke cigarettes, sat at a table by an open window, which created a cross breeze through the open front door. Rocky sat on the edge of the bed sipping water, while Erik and I were in chairs across from Kooz enjoying this newfound cocktail of his. Sherman took a gift out of his black backpack for Kooz: a *Life* magazine from September '69 with Kooz on the cover. He was thankful for the copy, as the one he had at home, he said, had faded badly.

"I'm glad you got some of the publicity you deserved," Erik told Kooz. "I know that Tom was a very serious, ultracompetitive pitcher and, partially as a result, got much of the praise for that '69 season."

"You know, Erik, I never was jealous of Tom," Kooz said earnestly. "He liked that number one spot, was good at handling it—much better than me. I didn't need to be representing the club the way he did as a so-called leader, captain, or whatever you want to call it. I was fine being second and just doing my own thing, having fun, and having less of a load to carry on my shoulders. Tom was good at it; was good with the press. And he was certainly our best pitcher."

"Well, that's commendable of you to say, because as Art will tell you, a lot of your teammates would say in a big game there was nobody better than you," Erik remarked, clearly recalling how Kooz won two games—including the clincher—in the '69 World Series.

"Well, it just worked out that way," Kooz said humbly. "You're as good as your team is that day, and so when I pitched, maybe the team was better. Tom and I had a lot of competition throughout our careers, but they were *fun* competitions. Tom always went for strikeouts. If he got to, say, 1-2 on a guy, he would probably throw a nitpick on a corner or something like that. And if he missed, he might nitpick again or throw a breaking ball and maybe go 3-2—and then strike him out on the full count or something. Well, I didn't believe in that. I figured there's only so many throws in your arm, so I wanted to make the batter hit that first pitch because I'm better off; to *hell* with the strikeout. But Tom went the other way; he *wanted* strikeouts. We had a bet one time on who could get the side out on three pitches—and I won. You've got to be lucky; make them hit the first pitch. But you've got to throw it right down the middle—it's a really hard thing to do."

"Well, they were just so lucky to have you both," Erik said. "What's really interesting is how you both came around to signing with the Mets. With Tom, he was originally signed illegally by the Braves, which allowed the Mets to sign him via a lucky draw of the hat. And with you, the son of a Shea Stadium usher discovered you at army camp."

Kooz smiled, took a drag off his cigarette, and then gave us the real deal.

"The Mets like that story," Kooz said, "but it isn't really what happened. I mean, it wasn't the reason I signed there. My catcher in the service, John Lucchese, had a dad who was an usher at Shea. And, of course, John knew I threw good. In fact, I tore his thumb off with a fastball that I could make tail away on the outside corner. A hitter nicked one of those pitches off the end of his bat, and the ball hit John's thumb badly—it was just hanging. He was going to sign with the Boston Red Sox for thirty thousand dollars after our championship game at Fort Sam Houston, but his career was over because of that injury. Anyway, I was actually scouted by Red Murff, a Mets scout who signed Ken Boswell, Jerry Grote, and Nolan Ryan. But the Mets loved the usher story because it played so well. The reality was they had been scouting me a year before the usher knew who I was."

"All I know," Rocky interjected, "is that if we didn't have either you or Tom, I ain't in the World Series. I don't have 1969 to look back on. And that thought's never very far away from me, especially when I'm around you both."

Kooz smile and thanked Rocky for the kind words, while I nodded in agreement.

"How about the offense on that '69 Mets team," Erik asked.

"There wasn't as much of it as you see on championships teams today. Did that put added pressure on you and the other pitchers?"

"Well, it did, but it wasn't like we could bitch about it," Kooz told us. "Yeah, we wanted more runs, but in '69 we had over a thousand strikeouts and a 2.43 ERA. That's pretty good for a staff. You look out there today, and some staffs are five-something. We won a hundred ball games—but certainly a run here or there, and we could have won a lot more. But we were built around pitching and defense until we got Donn Clendenon. He could hit the long ball; Holy God, that made our pitchers feel good! We knew we were going to get more home runs, you know. That guy could just crack the game open."

Kooz then glanced over at Rocky and me and amended his last comment.

"I take that back. Shamsky was also one of our home run hitters—and Swoboda, of course."

"You're just talking like that because we're here," Rocky said, giving Kooz a hard time.

Kooz turned to Erik and said, "He's a little jealous of me talking that way about Clendenon. Got to piss him off a little bit, but, you know . . ."

"Well, those two did combine for twenty-three home runs," Sherman told him.

"Who did?" Kooz asked, playing along.

"*These two guys,*" Erik said, nodding toward Rocky and me.

"Twenty-three? There are guys today—*shortstops*—that hit that many," Kooz replied, continuing with his good-natured ribbing. "Of course, the ball's wider, too, ain't it, Sham?"

"Yeah, a lot wider," I said, going along. "Smaller ballparks, too."

But then Kooz got serious about the role Rocky and I played on the club.

"These two didn't get enough credit," he said. "When they came into a certain situation, they did their job. *Boom*, it happened! And they were players, not like today. These guys didn't wear hitting gloves. They'd pick up some dirt by home plate, rub it in their hands, and *let's go*! These snowflakes today, they've got shin guards, elbow guards, two gloves on, and helmets that come around to protect their jaw."

"You're right," Rocky said. "I didn't wear an ear-flapped helmet until '71 or '72 when I was with the Yankees."

"You were grandfathered in like I was," Kooz replied. "Only the new players had to wear the ear-flap helmets. But seriously," he went on, "there was never just one hero on our club. We had heroes at different times that entire season."

"You know, living in New York, I get reminded daily about the impact we had on people's lives during that tumultuous period in our nation's history," I said. "We were like a tonic for the times."

"Even living in Wisconsin, I get fan letters at least once or twice a week saying just what you said, Art." Kooz turned to me and added, "And I save them all—a big stack of them. Some are well written, and then others you can hardly read. But there's something in them all that I thought were worth saving. I have a scrapbook just of fan letters, with a lot of them saying how we took their minds off of the bad things that were happening in '69."

"That would be an interesting book," our author-friend Sherman noted. "Just that angle alone would be terrific."

"Yeah, I need somebody to put it together," Kooz said.

"And that team you had: what a well-diversified group," Erik noted. "Some wore love beads while others were more conservative."

Kooz chuckled and looked over at Rocky.

"I'll tell you a story about love beads," Kooz said. "We're on a flight from the West Coast, and Don Cardwell sees our love child over here wearing a set of beads. We're about halfway across the

United States coming back from a trip to LA, everybody's drinking, and, finally, Cardy grabbed those beads and gave them a twist—yanking them off of Rocky's neck. The beads went all over the place. Remember that, Rock?"

"Yeah, they were plastic beads," Swoboda said. "A kid had given them to me leaving Dodger Stadium. So I had a couple of strands around my neck, and Cardy goes, 'What are you doing with that shit on?' He wasn't having any of it. A few minutes later, I went down to Cardy, and it's a good thing he was loaded, because I really gave it to him. The next thing I knew, Cardy went *boom*! and hit me in the jaw. But it was with a soft hand. If he hit you with a hard hand, he could hit you upside the head. He once popped Doug Rader so hard it looked like Cardy's knuckles were still in his face the next day. Cardy joked how he had to call a surgeon to get them removed.

"Cardy was a tough guy—just like Cleon Jones and Tommy Agee were. I will tell you this," Swoboda added, "when the shit hit the fan and there was an incident where teams go on the field trying to be macho after a hard slide or somebody getting knocked down, those three guys were the shock troops. They were on the front line and went out there to take somebody on. And if you didn't have guys like that, you were less of a team. The '86 Mets had that in Ray Knight and Kevin Mitchell; we had it with Cardy, Jones, and Agee. You get them pissed at you, you've got trouble. They didn't go out on the field to find a slow-dance partner, *okay*?"

"I used to go to Cardy's room and wrestle him all the time," Kooz told us. "One time we're staying at the Hilton in Pittsburgh. He's rooming with Cal Koonce, so Cal lets me in the door. Remember those big picture windows in the rooms? I don't know if I pitched that night or not, but I go run and made a big swan dive on Cardy. But when I land on him, he's kinda ready for me. I grabbed him, and we come off the bed and hit that picture window at the same time—*hard*. Now, we're both well over two hundred pounds. We hit that picture window together and just froze. We stopped our wrestling right then and there. We were seventeen floors up—could have gone through that window! Scared the crap out of us! It was my fault, but *geez*!"

"I did some silly things in hotels, too," Rocky added. "Tug McGraw and I were rookies together, and Kranepool was my roommate, and the three of us would throw water balloons out a window in Philadelphia to amuse ourselves. When you've got too much time on your hands, you do stupid things, and we thought that was funny. It was usually after a few pops following a game. That seemed to be the theory back then: win or lose, you would drink."

Fueled by couple of rounds of vodka and soda, the stories of our playing days continued to flow. It was both fascinating and wonderful at the same time. We were so comfortable reminiscing in Kooz's room that we decided to stay just where we were in lieu of going to a restaurant. I left briefly to bring us back a bucket of fried chicken from KFC. We ate off of paper napkins, drank out of plastic cups, and felt like kids again—just like we were back in the minor leagues. We continued talking about the old times well into the night, while looking ahead to the morning when it would continue with our dear friend, the Franchise.

CHAPTER 23

VINEYARD OF DREAMS

– May 13, 2017 –

THE DAY HAD FINALLY ARRIVED. AFTER FIVE MONTHS OF planning, anticipation, and my own personal anxiety, we were now just two hours away from our early golden jubilee reunion with Seaver. We all arose early on that pristine morning, congregating at seven o'clock outside of Sherman's door, with the fresh, crisp Sonoma Valley spring air invigorating us all.

Before the final twenty-mile leg of our journey out to Tom's house and vineyard atop Diamond Mountain in Calistoga, we stopped at a Denny's down the road from our motel for breakfast. As we walked toward the front door, I couldn't resist the urge to playfully try to rile up Koosman as we passed a newspaper vending machine for the *Santa Rosa Press Democrat*.

"Hey, Kooz, *look*! How could they do this to you?"

"Yeah, Swoboda should subscribe to it," Koosman said, only minimally taking the bait as he led the way into the restaurant.

We sat at a long table in the middle of Denny's and, admittedly, stuck out among the other diners. It was Northern California, after all, and both Buddy and Rocky were wearing Mets jackets, I had on my large World Series diamond ring, and Kooz was intently reading the front page of a remarkably well-preserved October 17, 1969, edition of the *New York Times* that Erik had brought him with the headline "Mets Win 5–3, Take the Series, and a Grateful City Goes Wild." A fit, bespectacled, middle-aged waitress with short black hair and a tattoo covering her entire right forearm—who was from upstate New York, it turned out—couldn't help but notice it all.

"Are you guys famous or something?" she asked in a direct but friendly tone.

"These gentlemen played for the world champion '69 Mets," Erik answered. "I'm just along for the ride."

The woman, a self-professed "huge" sports fan, had an appreciation for who we were, and, after putting in our breakfast order, had a fellow waitress take cell phone photos of her with us while she asked questions about the '69 Series. One thing was for sure: the service we received that morning was as good as it gets. Our coffee never got cold with all the refills.

We then got back to what we did most that weekend: reminisce about the old days. The recall from a half century ago was more than impressive. The guys wouldn't just simply remember some midseason game but would provide precise details such as what type of pitch was thrown on a given count to a specific hitter; a conversation they had in the dugout; or, even more mind-blowing, what the weather conditions were like on that particular day. The banter was practically nonstop, and it wasn't lost on me that, during our long car ride the previous day, not once did we turn on the car radio.

As we finished up breakfast, we talked about Tom and the toll Lyme disease has taken on him. For some of us, like myself, it had been a number of years since I last saw him, so I didn't know fully what to expect. Perhaps the most prepared of the group was Buddy, who has visited Seaver almost annually as a part of his trips to see his daughter and brother, both of whom live within a couple of hours from Tom in California.

"He can forget things that happened just a few minutes before," Harrelson forewarned us. "And he repeats himself a lot. But when he gets his rest, he still has a lot of energy."

We got back on the road and, according to the GPS, would arrive at Tom's a few minutes before nine o'clock. But then about five minutes into our ride, the maintenance light on the dashboard came on. Erik, who maintained a rock-solid, optimistic demeanor over the five months of planning leading up to this moment, turned a bit pale.

"Umm, okay, I'm not sure what's going on here," he said. "We may have a slight problem."

The van was still driving well, but a slight sense of panic quickly set in. After all of my concerns about whether Tom would be all right for our visit, a quick stream of thoughts entered my head. *Will our van, of all things, keep us from getting there? If we're late to Tom's, will he still be okay to see us?*

We forged ahead, not knowing what the issue with the van was, simply hoping it would get us at least a little farther to the Seavers' home. Thankfully, it did. As we approached Tom's exit off the highway, the maintenance light went off. I gave a sigh of relief.

Before long, we were driving up a dark, steep, winding hill, the bright morning sun blocked by big redwoods on both sides of the road. With me being me, I still had my concerns. Would Tom be having a bad day and would we only be able to stay for five minutes? And then this seemingly endless climb up this road where we couldn't find the entrance. Were we lost? Again, I admit it: I'm a worrier. But with our early-afternoon flights out the next day, this was our only chance of the weekend to all be together again—and maybe our last chance, period.

At the very top of the hill, we at last found Seaver's house number and drove along a short path to his gate. Erik pressed the intercom button to let them know we'd arrived.

"Hi, is that you guys?" Nancy asked in her typically warm and welcoming voice.

"Yes, we're all here, Nancy," Sherman responded.

The gate opened, and we drove down around a bend, parking in front of their large, modern light-gray house with picture windows. Nancy, still a stylish woman with her short, silvery-white hair and a perfect smile, greeted us warmly at the front door and invited us in. She wore an oversized yellow button-down shirt, perhaps one of Tom's, with the sleeves rolled up slightly. The inside of the house has high ceilings and incredible natural lighting. Nancy apologized for it being "a little messy," despite the kitchen and living room appearing immaculate.

A moment later, Tom, wearing a "Seaver Vineyards" baseball cap covering his full head of salt-and-pepper hair, made his entrance from a side room into a hallway, where we all greeted him. Fresh from a power nap, he still had the same facial characteristics, thousand-watt pearly-white smile, and strong build he had when he dominated hitters during his baseball career. He remains a larger-than-life figure—even to his teammates—and on this day, he was as gregarious as ever, with a booming voice that filled the house. It was clear to me immediately that he was enjoying one of his "good days," and I felt happy not just for him but for all of us who were hoping we could spend some quality time with him.

Just moments into our visit, before forgetting, I presented Tom with the 2017 Gil Hodges Unforgettable Fire Award from the QBC (Queens Baseball Convention), a Mets fans' winter event, which I had accepted several months earlier on his behalf. Gil always held a special place in Seaver's heart, and I knew the honor would mean a lot to him.

"Well, I've got a bunch of other stuff here that's gonna be interesting to you," he told us enthusiastically as we admired the three Cy

Young Awards and dozens of momentous baseballs that adorned a wall in his office. But by interesting stuff, he wasn't talking about the memorabilia he had amassed over his Hall of Fame career. That part of his life, while cherished, was now over. Instead, he couldn't wait another moment to share with us the passion he had for his property. While we stood toward the back of his living room near the entrance to the terrace, he told us how he and Nancy had come upon this palatial estate.

"Toward the end of my broadcasting career, my brother-in-law asks me very poignantly, 'What are you going to do when you're done?'" Seaver said. "I told him, 'I'm gonna go to California and raise grapes.' Now, I didn't know exactly where, but it was what I wanted to do. I had just gotten to the point that I was done with all the fanatical stuff that was going on—the just always *going, going, and going* with the travel, the hotels, et cetera. Of course, at that time, we had this beautiful home, an all-renovated barn in Greenwich, Connecticut. Nancy loved renovating that house. So when I said to her, 'Honey, we're going to California, and I'm going to raise grapes,' she probably thought, *Okay, well, he'll get over it. Either that, or I'll kill him!*

"So when we got out here, she placated me. She knew the idea of the Napa Valley fascinated me, though she still had some doubts. But then we found this piece of property: one hundred sixteen acres to build a house! And then Nancy said, 'What if you don't find anyplace for a vineyard?' And I said, 'Well, something will work out.'"

"Did you use a broker to find this place?" I asked him.

"No, I just came up here!" Tom said incredulously, his energy level astonishing me. "I got a sense from a real estate sheet about it—you know, a hundred sixteen acres. But there was no house on it. Not a single tree down. There was nothing . . . *nothing*! Just undeveloped land. So I went down from where we are now and walked and walked and climbed a tree near the top of a hill, looked down, and saw Sterling Winery, which is the big white winery down there. I saw the vista of the valley floor and said to myself, *My God! This is it!* Hey, have you been out on the terrace yet or not?"

We stepped out onto the terrace with Tom to take in the breath-taking spectacle of his mountain range view. Out in the distance to the right were thousands of tall Douglas firs surrounding a valley, with another mountain ridge behind it; to the left, rows and rows of perfectly symmetrical grapevines lined the slope of Seaver's vine-yard. The splendor of it all was almost indescribable.

"I don't think there's anything more beautiful in the world than this right here," I tell the group. "You could be on the French Riviera, and it wouldn't be as pretty as this."

"If you have to be *stuck* somewhere," Nancy joked, "*this* is the place to be *stuck!*"

"What year did you buy it?" Erik asked.

"I've got that Lyme disease stuff, so I'm not sure," Seaver said. "The Lyme disease came from Connecticut—it's in the East. A lot of people have it, you know? Hey, man, once you've got it, you've got it forever. I've had a couple of good weeks lately, though. When we started our wine business, I said to Nancy, 'Honey, get this business going,' because I was pretty foggy with Lyme disease for quite a while."

We started taking photos of the view and then with one another. And when Erik went to take a picture of Tom and Kooz, that's when the fun banter really began.

"Between us, we've got over five hundred wins right here," Seaver announced. "But you don't want to hear how many home runs we had."

"But wait, can you name the three players that combined to hit 1,417 home runs?" Kooz interjected with a poker face before giving pause for effect. "Willie Mays, Hank Aaron, and *me*! They couldn't have done it without me!"

Everyone burst out laughing. But Kooz was right: of the 1,417 home runs those three hit, he contributed exactly *2* of them! Now on a roll, he began busting Rocky's chops.

"You know, for all the wins Tom and I had, we may have had some more if Rock wasn't always running over Cheech on short fly balls," Kooz said.

"Yeah, he was *always* running over me!" Buddy exclaimed.

"Well, you know what I tell people," Swoboda said. "If you let Harrelson, he would play left field, too. You knew any of those balls to short left—he's coming to get them."

"Hey, Rock, what were you doing in left field anyway?" Kooz asked. "Shouldn't you have been in right?"

"Well, because Sham or someone else was playing over there. But Buddy would come so hard on those in-between balls, I ran his ass down a few times. But understand this: Shea Stadium was hard on pop-ups because it was a very high stadium, so a lot of fly balls and line drives never came out of the seats. It was hard to read those balls because the background was constantly changing with the lights, people's shirts, and fans moving around. You really had to adjust and get used to it, and sometimes I had trouble doing that."

But Buddy wouldn't let him off the hook, displaying to us how Ron would flail his arms to show he was under the ball to make a catch and yet *still* shout, "I got it!"

"I remember on one in-between," Swoboda went on, "I see Buddy, and he ain't stopping. But I didn't even have time to make the call to say I had it."

"I remember that, too," Tom said. "I was pitching!"

"Yeah," Kooz said. "Cheech caught the ball, and about three seconds later, you ran over him!"

"I know I did," Swoboda said. "But you didn't want the ball to fall in, did you? I didn't know what to do."

"Did anybody bother to use the English language out there?" Seaver quipped, drawing more laughs.

The talk turns to the pitching of our era—arguably the greatest the game has ever seen. And one of the very best and most intimidating of all time, Bob Gibson, comes up.

"Wes Westrum takes over for Casey Stengel as manager in '65," Rocky starts out. "And Gibson's on the mound one night. He couldn't wait to face us. The last time he faced us, it took him just two hours to shut us out. So Wes gives us a pregame strategy session. 'We're gonna call time-out, go back, get pine tar, keep stepping out. Really mess with his rhythm.' The result? It took Gibson *two and a half* hours to shut us out!"

Everyone laughs before Buddy chimes in with his own Gibson story.

"He was always walking me," he said. "So one day he yells out at me, 'Goddammit, you have to swing at that!' And I yelled back, 'I would if I could see your fastball! But I can't hit what I can't see!'"

"Is that what Yogi told you to do?" Seaver asked Harrelson. "Yogi's hitting instruction was always, 'If you can't hit it, don't swing at it!' So one time I asked him, 'What about two strikes, Yogi?' And he said, 'Well, then you might have to swing at it.' So I just said, 'Thanks for clearing that up.'"

Tom's recollection kicked off a barrage of other Yogi anecdotes.

"Once I said to him, 'Yogi, I'm struggling,'" Kooz said. "And he goes, 'Well, see it, hit it.' And then another time, one of our guys hits into a double play, and he came back to the dugout, and Yogi goes, 'Rather than hit into a double play in that situation, strike out next time. That way, there's only one out.'"

"Bozzie once went over to Yogi by the batting cage," I added, "and he goes, 'Yogi, I just don't know what I'm doing wrong. It feels like I'm swinging up on everything.' And Yogi simply says, 'Well, swing down.'"

Even though I must admit that I never talked hitting with Berra during my years with the Mets—*and he was the hitting instructor!*—the Berra stories were all in good fun and Swoboda did invoke some praise for one of the true giants of the game.

"I remember before the rest of you got to the Mets, they activated Yogi, and I hit behind him one game," Rocky says. "And Yogi goes to me afterward, 'I couldn't see the pitch that guy was throwing me.' Still, despite the pitcher throwing a fastball up near his face, Yogi went *boom*!—a base hit up the middle! I thought to myself then, *Boy, he can hit everything*. He was a good bad-ball hitter and a better good-ball hitter. Man, I'll tell you what, we wouldn't have stories like this if we worked in a bank or drove a bus."

"And use them for all these years," Kooz adds.

"But, you know, they get better with time," Rocky concludes.

Erik wants to take a group photo and asks Nancy if she could join her husband and his teammates, but at first, she declines politely.

"Oh, no pictures of me—thank you," she tells him. "I wasn't a player. I can't be in this beauty."

But Erik convinces her to be in the first shot.

"Hey, Buddy," calls Seaver, "get your ass over here!"

"I don't have an ass!" remarks Harrelson as he joins the photo opportunity.

"I'll give you some of mine," Nancy jokes, now like one of the boys.

The memories that will last a lifetime are recorded in priceless photos, and the very loud banter, joking around, and laughter start up again. Everything is perfect.

•　　•　　•

Nancy decided to stay in the house and pay some bills—a likely excuse to enable our locker room talk—while the guys and I followed Tom up and down the steep hills of his three-and-a-half-acre vineyard. As we walked and talked, Seaver, clippers in hand, pruned the grapevines that would be used for his GTS (George Thomas Seaver) wine at harvest time come September. He relished in educating us about things like drip irrigation systems, watering emitters, the growth process of grape bunches, when they flower, and how it takes six years from the time you put in the first vine before you make a dime off of it.

"I really wanted to check this out," Rocky told Tom. "I'm so glad you had the time to show us your vineyard like you did."

"I had the time, my friend Ronnie, because I don't go anywhere," Seaver explained to him. "I don't go out of the valley. I'm the designated gofer for the Queen (Nancy)."

We made our way to the top of the hill where Tom first envisioned the great potential the land had to become a first-rate vineyard. Excitedly, he told of his epiphany. "I came in here, and I was just walking all over the place until I got to the area we're standing in now," he said.

"You had a vision," Rocky said.

"It was a vision, but it was also wanting to find it," Seaver said. "So I'm standing around this place, and I'm looking out at the topography and had an idea of what it could be. I thought, *Holy shit! This could be it!* I got Jim Barbour, one of the most respected winemakers in the Napa Valley, who manages big vineyards, to come up and take a look. I told him I wanted to do Zinfandel, and he exclaimed, 'No you're not! You don't do Zinfandel here! This is Diamond Mountain! You're going to put *Cabernet* here!' And then he said something I'll never forget. Remember, Jim Barbour is the best in the business, and he goes: 'How the hell did I miss this?' Honest to God, 'How the hell did I miss this?' You know, it's the same thing in baseball. You hang a slider, and the guy pops it up. It's *exactly* the same with what happened to me here. It gives me chills just thinking about it. This is perfect—*absolutely* perfect."

"We accept good luck!" Rocky told him. "Luck is the residue of good design."

"Well, I would rather be lucky, then!" Tom said. "I would rather be lucky!"

"Hey, you did have a vision, and you achieved it," Buddy added, giving his pal some credit.

"Well, I wanted to do it because it fascinated me, and I ended up with a 'Rolls-Royce'!" Seaver said excitedly. "And the best part of it is, I can't wait to get to work! I'm seventy-two years old, and I can't wait to take my dogs, learn a new learning curve, and work outside. And do I ever work! I work my *ass* off! And if I don't, I have a chair underneath those big trees right there. And if I want to do a goddamn crossword puzzle, I'll sit down and do the goddamn puzzle with my three Labrador retrievers!"

"Are they any help?" joked Rocky to everyone's amusement. "But seriously, this is all so wonderful for you. It's just so, 'wow!' It's really a 'wow vision' because none of this was here. None of it!"

"Ronnie, Ronnie, it is a *wow*! It is a *wow*!" Seaver agreed, the pitch of his voice elevated. "Can I just say that I've had a lot of people come up here, and that's the word they use: 'wow.'"

"So was there any kind of local problem in taking trees off of their natural land?" Rocky asked. "I mean, no issues doing that?"

"No, none at all," Tom told him. "You know what the valley does? The valley does wine. They wanted it done."

"It sounds like you've had the best of everything," I told Seaver. "You've got the peace of what you're doing now and the incredible life that we all had in New York."

"Absolutely true, Art," he said. "I got to the point where I was not going to do the baseball life any longer. Because for a while, I was going to manage. I was going to do all that other stuff, but by the time I did the broadcasting for a while, I was done. When it's over, it's over."

We continued our walk, which had easily exceeded an hour by this point, when Tom brought up another great story. "Does anyone remember a clubhouse kid we had named Jimmy?" he asked.

"Assistant clubhouse guy?" Rocky said aloud. "Jimmy? Yeah, I remember him."

"Well, I was pitching one of those games where I felt great; so good that I was like, *Just give me a run, and we're out of here in two hours*," Seaver recalled. "So Jimmy used to bust my chops all the time. This one game, I come into the clubhouse to get a Coke, and he said, 'What the hell are you doing here?' I said, 'Getting myself a goddamn Coke. What's it to you?' He goes, 'You get your ass out to the dugout!' And I said, 'Well, what are *you* doing?' 'I'm not doing nothing. You want to play gin rummy?' he asked. True story! True story! So I said, 'Great, okay.' We had the game on the radio, so I knew when I would have to go back out to pitch. In walks Buddy, and he goes to me, 'Roomie, what the hell are you doing?' I said, 'I'm playing gin rummy. What does it look like?' And Buddy goes, 'You're crazy!' You remember that, Buddy?"

"Yeah, I do," Harrelson said.

"Geez, was Gil managing then?" I asked.

"No, it would have been Yogi," Tom said. "I may have been dumb in a couple of spots, but there are a couple of things you don't do, right? So anyway, we're in the middle of a game, and I hear Bob Murphy say, 'And a fly ball will end the inning.' So I said to Jimmy, 'Don't look at my hand, or I'll kick your ass!'"

"You should have put your cards in your back pocket," Kooz said.

"I just put them down, went outside, and *boom, boom, boom*, three outs, came back to the clubhouse, sat down, and asked Jimmy, 'Okay, where were we?' Swear to God. But that's how good I felt that day: 'Just give me a run, boys, come on!'"

After we completely circled the grapevines, Rocky, Buddy, and Kooz, as fate would have it, walked ahead along a gravelly path toward Tom's barn—perhaps to take a bathroom break—enabling Tom, Erik, and me the opportunity to talk. I thought how fortunate it was that we would have some time alone to speak with him. How the heck did this just happen?

Now away from the more gregarious members of our group, Seaver took on a more pensive mood in telling us another reason— besides his dream of owning a vineyard—on why he left broadcasting.

"I was in Pittsburgh one day before a game, just talking with my mom on the phone," he said. "And she asked me what city I was in. And you know what? I didn't remember! I couldn't tell her. It was the Lyme disease, you know. That was another reason why I knew it was time to move on."

While Seaver once again communicated the pride he took in his second act as the self-professed "worker bee" of his vineyard, adding that no other former player had ever done anything like it before, he shared with us other cognitive symptoms of the disease that keep him close to home, such as anxiety and panic attacks.

"Nancy and I were going to visit a friend, the announcer Gary Thorne," Seaver began. "Nancy's driving, and when we got to the bottom of the valley, I froze up. I put my hand on hers, pressed my feet against the floorboard as hard as I possibly could, and said, 'I can't go.' I was so frightened. Man, it just made me breathe heavy like this. We turned around and went home. I mean, this Lyme disease ain't fun. It can be absolutely frightening. The more cardiovascular I do, the better off I am. And drinking wine helps. I drink about a half bottle of wine per night. I haven't had a beer in about eight years. But the traveling, no, I just can't anymore. I try to go to Cooperstown, but it's been a few years."

"Well, it's a tough trip because you can't fly right in there," I said, noting how there are no direct flights.

"No, no, no," Seaver said, alluding again to the effects of Lyme disease. "It isn't the flight. It isn't tough to get there. You just go to Chicago and connect to Syracuse, and they pick you up from there. It's not a big deal at all. But it's like when I was in the car with Nancy at the bottom of the valley that time and pressing my feet as hard as I could. It's always there—just always there."

"But I hope it's nice for you, on a beautiful day like this, to see some of your teammates come back to see you," I said. "We were such a special team in history with our cast of characters, the way we won, the teams we beat, and how everyone contributed."

"You're like *brothers*," Erik added.

"Of course! Yeah! Yeah!" Seaver exclaimed. "It's absolutely perfect. I love it. I love seeing your faces. I love seeing your emotions. It's a special moment when I get to see you and Buddy and the rest of the guys. Or when I would go to Cooperstown and see the Hall of Famers. And I understand the magnitude of what we accomplished—believe me, I do. It all has its place, but I've left it. I had to let it go and take my focus and put it all here, on the vineyard.

"This is where I have to think and be disciplined. This is where I have to be all the things that I was over there. And it's not easy. But I have to pay attention to this role I have now. And, God, I want to share it with you. You can see the energy that I have here. I'm lucky to be doing this. But I told you about going down the valley and Nancy turning around and coming back. I'm gone."

"I understand, Tom," I said. "It's special being here with you, and playing together was a special time for us all. Can you believe it's been almost fifty years since we won the World Series? A lot of people still talk about it."

Seaver gave pause to reflect and then said in a lower, calmer tone, "How the hell did I get to be seventy-two years old? How did that happen to us, Art?"

I shook my head, also wondering where all the years had gone.

"But at least we share the incredible legacy of being a part of the '69 Mets, a team that still has a love affair with New York City," I said. "I always say, 'It wasn't the greatest team ever to win the World Series, but it's the most memorable.'"

"But you know what?" Tom said earnestly. "It was a goddamn good team! And we could pitch. And we could defend."

"And especially good up-the-middle defense," I added.

"You bet your ass!" Seaver said. "Agee in center, Buddy at short, and Weis, and Boswell, and *Jerry Grote*! How great was Grote?!"

Seaver reflected on his longtime catcher for a moment, grinned, and said, "Grote was an ornery SOB. I would tell him, 'You're not calling this game.' I think it was Don Cardwell who came to me and said, 'Don't let that catcher tell you what to do.' That's because I knew what I was doing out there. In fact, no catcher ever called my signs, my pitches, unless I went to them and said, 'Hey, John [Bench], hey, Carlton [Fisk], I'm having trouble with my stuff. Whatever you put down, that's it.'"

"God, you had some great catchers," Erik noted.

"I know!" Seaver exclaimed. "Think about it! People don't think about that."

"And you had Rube Walker as your pitching coach," I said. "He was like the liaison between the guys and Gil. Hodges, of course, was a tough, tough guy."

"I don't know if I've ever told you this story, Art," Seaver began. "As you know, Gil could scare the shit out of you. And *I'm a marine!* But he was a marine, too. So one day, I'm doing a crossword puzzle, and Nick Torman, the clubhouse guy, says that Gil wants to see me. I said, 'What the hell did I do? I was like 9-3 at the time. What did I mess up?' Gil wasn't known as a warm and fuzzy guy, so when I go into his office, he says in his typical serious tone, 'Sit down.' I thought to myself, *Okay, I'll just commit suicide right now to save time.* Then he goes, 'Do you ever look at your wife in the stands when you're playing?' I said, 'Yeah, she's a great visualization.' So what do you think he meant by asking me that question?"

Tom paused, perhaps for effect, before Erik took a couple of stabs at answering the question. "Concentration? Staying focused?"

"Hold on, hold on," Seaver said, letting out a big sigh and becoming a little emotional. "I'm not done with the story. I know, I know, now you're dying for the tagline. After asking me that question about my wife, he gets up out of his chair and hands me an old newspaper with a photo of him crossing the plate for the Dodgers. In the picture, his hand is pressed to his lips—he's blowing a kiss to his wife, Joan. He had been in a terrible slump—0-for-18—and Gil had just hit a home run after she asked him to hit one for her. The connection Gil made was the love we shared for our wives. He wanted to show me his kiss to Joan. He just wanted to share that with me, like a father would with a son. I was speechless. Then he simply says, 'That's all.' He didn't say another word—none was needed. And I put the photo down in front of me and walked out of his office. It still gets to me, you know? It still gives me chills just thinking about it, because my wife and I have been married for over fifty years."

"You know, Tom, Joan's ninety-two now and still going strong," I said.

"Oh, God love her," he said.

After composing himself, Tom wasn't done talking about Hodges.

"One of the things that I used to do during the last nine outs of a game was to get rid of my WCS." By that, Tom meant his worst-case scenario. "In this one particular case, ahead by a run with two outs in the ninth, my WCS would have been to give up a walk to put the tying run on base. But that's what I did: I walked a guy. So Gil comes out to the mound and says, 'You pitched to him like you *wanted* to walk him.' I'm dying as he's saying this to me—like he's going to rip my heart out. But I answered him by saying, 'Just about.' I didn't agree or disagree with him, didn't say anything affirmative or not, and he turned around and left. In my brain, my computer's going, *Let's strike out the next guy for the twenty-seventh out.* And that's exactly what I did to end the game. Afterward, I stuck my head in Gil's office, and one of the most poetic things happened between us. I said, 'Gil, you didn't agree with me walking that guy in that situation because I put the tying run on.' And you know what he said? He goes, 'If I had known you were going to strike out the next hitter, I wouldn't have *wasted* my time coming out to the mound.' How *beautiful* was that? God, I loved that guy."

I related to Tom's tales of Gil's toughness with my own feelings about playing under him.

"You know, when he used to come to the mound when I was playing first base," I began, "unless he called me to the mound and wanted to talk about a certain thing like positioning, I just went halfway there. I didn't need to know what he was going to say to the pitcher. I just got this kind of apprehension every time I saw him—as did most of us. He wasn't a guy that showed a lot of emotion one way or another."

"We *knew* who the boss was, didn't we?" Seaver asked rhetorically.

"Yeah, we sure did," I said. "I don't know if he could manage today with the way players are, because he was such a disciplinarian."

We started walking toward the barn, where the other guys were waiting for us.

"Hey, Tommy, did I mention that Gil Jr.'s youngest sister just passed away?" I asked. "She was living in Iowa. I talked to Mrs. Hodges about it two weeks ago. You know, she still lives by herself in Brooklyn. She's such a strong woman, but, you know, is so disappointed Gil didn't make the Hall of Fame. She's been through the trials and tribulations in her efforts to help his cause, but she's pretty burnt out now with all that stuff. You know, there was a year when he had seventy-four-and-something percent—missed getting in by less than one percent. Guys that were behind him eventually made it over him. That's the shame of the whole thing."

"It's a crapshoot in that depending on the year and the field of candidates, it can make or break someone's chances of getting enshrined," Sherman said.

"You know what," Seaver confided with a look of disbelief, "I think about it, too, and I don't think so much about his family—I think about *Gil*. And if I had one question to ask Gil if he were around today, what would I ask him? I would ask *him* if he felt he belonged in the Hall of Fame. I'm sure he would say, 'I *don't* deserve it.' But I would tell him, 'I didn't ask you if you deserved it.' Because here's the thing: he should be in for two reasons—all his World Series and . . .'" Tom had to pause to compose himself. Then, with his voice cracking, he finished his sentence. "And for covering Jackie Robinson's back."

"That's a great point about Jackie," Erik said.

"You bet your ass!" Tom exclaimed.

After taking a deep breath, his booming voice back, Seaver continued by saying, "Okay, Gil hit only .260." (Actually, .273.) "He couldn't run. But he sat in the middle of that Dodgers lineup all of those pennant-winning years, beat the freaking Yankees in '55, hit

370 home runs, managed the '69 Mets, and, just as importantly, he was a great teammate and friend to Jackie—the *first* black guy that ever played in the majors and was a damn good player. That last one pushes him over. Get him in there! Get him on a plaque! You can't overlook how much his support of Jackie Robinson meant. The breaking of the color barrier was one of, if not the *biggest*, changes in baseball history."

"Sure," Erik agreed. "It's been said the three biggest names that revolutionized the game of baseball were Babe Ruth, Jackie Robinson, and Marvin Miller," the last of the three being the executive director of the Major League Baseball Players Association who created one of the strongest unions in America and ushered in, among other things, the free-agent era. "Would you agree?"

"Oh, yeah," Seaver said. "It would be tough not to agree."

Kooz was admiring some photos Tom had up on his barn office walls and couldn't help himself; he had to ask Seaver *the question*.

"Hey, Tom, when you heard on the radio that you were traded to Houston . . ." Koosman asked with a straight face before Seaver cut off the end of his inquiry.

"I know, I know," Tom said slowly and dismissively, as everybody laughed as much at his quick reaction as we did at the practical joke itself.

"Did you buy that when you heard it?" Rocky asked Tom. "Did you believe it?"

"No, hell no!" exclaimed Seaver.

"We were talking in the car yesterday about it, and we were going to ask you about it, and—" Rocky continued before Tom cut him off, too.

"I wish I had been smart enough and quick enough to have put tears in my eyes," Seaver said as everyone howled. "I saw Koosman walking in and I figured . . ."

"Do you remember who the announcer was?" asked Koosman, talking over Tom.

"No," Seaver answered. "Hell, no!"

"Jack Simon was doing Howard Cosell," Kooz said.

"Hey, Koosy, come here, come on over here," Tom said in an obvious attempt to change the uncomfortable subject. "Here he is: *the Boss.*"

The black-and-white photo Seaver is pointing to is a matted and framed one of him with Hodges—both men smiling—and appears to have been taken prior to a postseason game, by the red-white-and-blue bunting displayed in the background. The picture has been signed by most of the '69 Mets team. Of all the photos in the room, it's obvious this is his favorite.

"I've got a picture of Gil and me, too," Kooz said. "He's squeezing my cheek so freakin' hard, I thought he was gonna pinch it right off!"

Then Kooz switched gears and reminisced about the day Hodges passed away. April 2, 1972.

"*Jesus* . . . just forty-seven years old," he said, shaking his head. "The players went on strike, and I was the only Met staying in a hotel down there in West Palm Beach when he died. Everybody else had gone home. I had decided to stay there and that I'd just go up to New York with Gil. So while he's playing golf with Piggy, Yostie, and Rube, I got a bag of balls out of the team truck and went to throw in the back of the hotel with Jack Sanford, the former pitcher with the Giants. After finishing up, I go up to my room, and, just as I started taking a shower, I hear a siren."

"Oh Je-sus," Tom said slowly.

"Hol-y shit," Rocky added incredulously.

"So I get dressed," Kooz continued. "And I go downstairs and run into the *Daily News* writer Red Foley, who says, 'Did you hear about Gil?' I said, 'No, what about him?' He says, 'The ambulance just came and picked him up—took him to the hospital.' I said, 'Which hospital? I'm going.' He said, 'Well, I wanna go, too.' So we got a cab to Good Samaritan Hospital, and somebody at the door asks me, 'Are you one of the players with the Mets?' I said, 'Yeah,' so she led me into this room where Rube, Yostie, Yogi—all the coaches—and the statistician Art Friedman were. I said, 'Artie, What happened?' But he wouldn't turn around to talk to me. Then I go over to Walker and go, 'Rube, what happened to Gil? How is he?' And all Rube said was, 'He's dead.' After golfing, Piggy had asked Gil when to meet for supper and after he gave a time, Hodges started turning around, went backward, and cut his head on the ground. He'd had a massive heart attack. They said he was dead before he hit the ground."

"They put him on the Yankees plane," Swoboda added solemnly. "I was playing for the Yankees by then, and they just loaded him on our plane. Gil had played twenty-seven holes of golf that day with his coaches—I heard he felt great."

Swoboda then let out a sigh. "I wish I could have just shut the hell up when I played for him," Rocky said with obvious regret over his occasionally butting heads with Hodges. I should have said, 'Yes sir, how high do you want me to jump? I'll *jump* it, I'll *do* it! You want me to do *that*—I'll do it!' If I'd have just done that . . ." Rocky's voice faded off.

"And Rube," Seaver said with a grin, "what a good guy."

"We gave him so much crap—but we *loved* him," added Kooz, letting out a husky laugh. "Rube was like my father. You could sit down and bitch to him and tell him what was going on—he was like a punching bag. In those days, we didn't get so mushy-mushy like they probably do today. There's so many snowflakes out there now that you can't crush their feelings. But with Rube, I'd call him even during the winter. He had a way of putting up with our BS and still have a smile on his face—just always glad to see you the next day.

"Oh God, we had so much fun back then."

We left the barn and started to make our way up the driveway toward the cars we would drive into town for lunch. As we did, talk turned to the one player on the '69 Mets who may have had the most fun of all: the late, great Tug McGraw.

"He had some great lines," Swoboda said, then in rapid-fire succession, proceeded to give us a few. "He once told a writer, 'First time I had sex was pretty scary.' And the writer went, 'Scary? Why?' And Tug goes, 'Well, it was dark, and I was alone.' Another time, another writer asked him, 'What did you do with your World Series money?' So Tug goes, 'I spent most of it on whiskey and women—the rest of it I just pissed away.' Then yet another writer once asked him, 'What do you prefer: real grass or AstroTurf?' And McGraw says, 'I don't know. I've never smoked any AstroTurf.' He was one hundred percent authentic!"

"I'll tell you one thing," Seaver said of McGraw, "I want him right *here* in my *foxhole*; I'll tell you that! He could get us out of trouble coming out of the bullpen. He'd throw that little roller and get guys to hit it on the ground."

"He called it his 'Peggy Lee' fastball," Rocky explained. "You know, when he threw that little batting practice fastball where he would take a little something off of it. The hitter rolled it over on the ground without realizing what happened and thinks, *Is that all there is?* Well, he named it his Peggy Lee fastball after her famous song 'Is That All There Is?'"

"Yes, his Peggy Lee fastball!" Seaver exclaimed. "I forgot about that! He called it that all the time!"

"And he figured out a few other things," Swoboda added. "He figured out that screwball, and then when hitters got really hot on that, he'd throw that little slider, and he was like a different pitcher. He was *really* good. With the uniform off, he was a whacko, but when he had his uniform on, he was *real*, man. He could get us out of trouble."

While Erik took Kooz and Buddy in the van, I joined Rocky in Tom's car to make the ten-minute drive to downtown Calistoga. I was in the front seat while Tom drove, and I must admit I was a little apprehensive about it after all he'd told us about the effects of his Lyme disease. After all, maneuvering down the steep, winding road wouldn't be an easy drive for anyone, let alone someone in Tom's condition. I also wondered if he would forget the way. Remember, Tom wasn't traveling any longer in part due to his short-term memory loss. But to my relief and happiness, he got us into town without incident.

We parked in a hardware store lot ("Don't worry, guys, they know me," Tom assured us), walked through the back of the Calistoga Wine Stop, where we were introduced to proprietors Tom, Tammy, and Tara Pelter, and into the Palisades Deli Cafe, where, by the greetings Seaver received from the staff, it was clear he was a regular. The cafe was an old-fashioned, modest-looking place, with sandy-beige and mint-green wood-paneled walls and a few full-window doors along the perimeter. A round Corona beer mirror hung on one side, with a full-size American flag on another, while a large-screen TV had CNN turned on with the sound off. We took a long table in the middle of the dining area, and, while looking over the menus, Tom promptly ordered a couple of bottles of red Zinfandel wines from the Brown Estate Vineyards of Napa Valley. Even Rocky and Buddy, who had both stopped drinking alcohol long ago, took small samples of the wine to take in the momentousness of the occasion.

"This is spectacular high quality—great fruit," Seaver announced enthusiastically.

"How much does a bottle go for?" Swoboda asked.

"Retail is forty-five dollars," Tom answered. "And you know what I wanted to put in my vineyard? *Zinfandel!* But the farmer came in and said, 'You can *buy* all the Zinfandel you want, but up here on Diamond Mountain, you're going to produce *Cabernet.*'" It was a story that Seaver had told earlier, though out of respect, no one interrupted him.

"He probably said, 'You lay out a good Zinfandel, here's what it's worth. But you lay out a good Cabernet . . . ' Swoboda said before Tom interjected "Yeah! A *hundred-thirty-five* bucks a bottle! *Duh, Tom, let's not be a dunce here.*"

"You can't coach stupid," Rocky said to laughs. "Of course, I had a couple of managers figure that out with *me!*"

"Here you go, Grandpa," a very young waitress familiar with Tom said to him as she served us three club sandwiches, two chicken Caesar salads, and a Cobb salad for Buddy—which drew a glance from Tom.

"I've got to watch my weight," Harrelson said preemptively.

"Watch your *weight?*" Seaver asked incredulously of his still 160-pound former roommate. "You've been doing that for sixty years!"

"Actually, for *seventy*," Buddy replied.

"Hey, Tom," Kooz called over to Seaver between bites of sandwich. "Take a guess which one of the games you pitched in '69 impressed me the most."

"It's gotta be the Imperfect Game," Tom said after a pregnant pause.

"Nope."

"Okay, but I'm going to tell you why that one jumps out at me," Seaver said. "You go into the ninth, you get one out with two outs to go. And then I gave up the base hit to Jimmy Qualls after he hit the ball hard a couple of times. The point being, Kooz, is that I said to myself, *Get the last two outs.* To have the discipline to focus on the last two outs and to get them both, that was as important to me at that moment as anything else."

"To not let it get away from you," Kooz concluded.

"To keep your composure," Sherman added.

"You bet your ass, Erik!" Seaver said. "The *composure* where I said to myself, *Okay, Tom, you've lost the perfect game. You've sent the message to the Cubs—okay, that's wonderful. If you had pitched a perfect game? That would have been an even bigger deal. But dammit, get these two goddamn outs!* After the game, Nancy's crying, sobbing. I went to hug her and said, 'Jesus Christ, I just pitched a one-hit shutout, struck out ten, and then closed the door on them. What the hell are you crying about?'"

"That game has taken on a life of its own," I told him. "It's gotten as much publicity as if it *were* a perfect game."

"An entire book was written about just this one game," Erik added.

"Oh yeah, I know it," Seaver said.

"Okay," Kooz said, "but actually the game I'm talking about that impressed me the most was when you pitched against San Diego at Shea Stadium and struck out the last ten guys you faced with a fastball—*just a great fastball.*"

"That was the kind of game where you go to yourself, *The Padres are not a real good-hitting ball club,*" Seaver responded. "They looked like frightened children when they came to the plate. And I was throwing the living crap out of the ball the last three or four innings."

"Yeah, I could have sat down at shortstop," Buddy remarked.

"Or we could have called the outfielders in," Rocky said. "Didn't Satchel Paige do that once: call his outfielders in?"

"Legend has it that he did," Sherman said. "Satch pitched well into his fifties on barnstorming tours after his major-league career was over. Hey, Jerry, weren't the Mets interested in bringing you back at age fifty?"

"Yeah, Frank Cashen wanted to bring me back as a left-handed reliever," Kooz confirmed. "I was still throwing ninety. It must have been around the spring of '91."

"What happened, Kooz?" asked Tom. "Didn't want to give up your hunting days? You know Nolan Ryan pitched until around then, right?"

"Well, I was in Port Saint Lucie at the minor-league complex as a pitching coach for their Columbia, South Carolina, team when Buddy, who was managing the Mets then, asked me to come over to the major-league field to throw batting practice," Kooz began. "My arm was in good shape, as I had been throwing BP all spring. So I go over there, and Buddy told me to heat it up and see what the hitters could do. I did, and, going through the lineup one time, ninety-five percent of them never got the ball out of the batting cage. After I was done, Buddy called me over to the area behind second base and said, 'You are really throwing well. How would you like to come back and be a left-handed reliever for us?' I said, 'Are you serious?' And Buddy goes, 'Yes, I am. We badly need a left-handed reliever, and you throw harder than three-quarters of our staff.' I said, 'Buddy, if I have a bad game, the press will bury you, me, and the Mets.' But he said, 'Don't worry about that. You can pitch with our Triple-A team for a month, get in shape, and then we'll call you up.'

"Buddy talked to Frank Cashen about it, and he was in complete agreement. And remember, I was going to turn fifty that year! The next day, I called Buddy and told him I didn't think it was a good idea but that I appreciated his confidence in me. My reasoning for that decision was coming back at that age and getting buried by the press if I had a bad game. Not that I didn't think I could be an asset for one, two, or three innings. And I felt privileged that they thought enough of me to ask me back. But I thought it best to remain a pitching coach working with the young players. It was simply time to move on."

"You guys," Swoboda remarked, shaking his head incredulously while looking over at Koosman and Seaver, "were like horses. Nolan, too. What were the most pitches you guys ever threw in a game?"

"One-forty, maybe one-forty five," Seaver replied.

"One forty-seven," Kooz answered, his recall for such numbers as sharp as ever.

"Well, I remember a night when Ryan threw over one-fifty," Seaver remembered. "And he was still going strong."

"You guys didn't walk many hitters," I remarked. "Why were your pitch counts so high?"

"I have no idea," Tom said.

"It was all the strikeouts," Erik concluded.

"But rarely did they ever go 3-2 on many batters," I argued.

"Well, Rubie Walker liked to always say, 'Ah, fellas, we like strike one, please,'" Seaver told us. "But you know, sometimes I would tell him that I liked getting behind some guys because they might have a longer swing."

"How about the '69 Series—which game do you guys feel was the most pivotal?" I asked the group before interjecting my own theory. "I always felt it was game two because, had we lost, we would have gone back home down two games."

"I agree with you, Art. I would also say the second game," Tom said. "That game made a statement. Kooz, our so-called *number two* pitcher, didn't give up a hit through six innings. We won, and, oh, by the way, it was a two-hitter and yada yada yada. We were not going to get more than a couple of runs."

"Some say the third game was more pivotal because Gentry surprised Baltimore," I added. "And then Ryan came in to get the save with two-plus innings of relief."

"And don't forget the two catches Agee made," Swoboda noted.

"Right," Erik agreed. "But while the Orioles knew about Tom, and they knew about Jerry, they completely underestimated Gary."

"He had great stuff," Swoboda said of Gentry. "I used to warm him up in the bullpen when I wouldn't play, and his fastball jumped all over. Hey, does anyone remember Hodges saying to us after game one, 'You guys don't have to be anything but what got you here'?"

"Well, what I *do* remember," Buddy interjected, "was Don Buford jogging by me after his first-inning home run in game one and saying, 'You guys ain't seen nothing yet!' I thought, *Yes!* So after the inning ended, I told the guys in the dugout what he said. What a mistake on his part."

"It was a little eerie how we won four straight after that," Rocky noted.

"But I was thinking that between Tom and Kooz, we had the best pitchers in the Series," I added.

"They didn't have the power pitchers we had," Seaver noted. "Was Jim Palmer a hard thrower?"

"He was tall and threw straight down with a pretty good breaking ball," Rocky answered, sounding like a scout.

"But I think if we lose the second game"—I began before Tom jumped in. "Oh, yeah!" he said. "We're in trouble. Absolutely! But the Orioles had a bunch of guys who were 'chirpers,' too."

"Well, sure," Erik said. "Like when Frank Robinson told the press after the first game that the Mets looked lifeless in the dugout."

"It was the first time we'd been there," Seaver noted. "Think about that. We weren't old pros like they were. We were still trying to get our feet on the ground. We were still trying to find out what this was all about. We didn't have all the success the Orioles had—you know what I mean? That's the point."

"Your *first* time in the *big show*," Erik said.

"Yeah!" Tom exclaimed. "You've got to push that emotion away. You can't go to a psychiatrist and have him tell you what the World Series is like. He'd go, '*What?* What are you talking about?' You've got to go through it on your own. It's the World Series! It's a dream! How can you deal with that? And I couldn't focus my energy in the first game, but Kooz could in the next one. Just give Kooz the ball—to a degree, it didn't bother him at all. Not a bit! Part of the excellence here [as Tom gestured to himself] was the fear of failure. I remember one place I was at in Triple-A, I got my clock kicked. I cried like a baby, and I'm a *marine*! But this is the love that you have. A manager put his arm around me and said, 'You'll be all right. Keep going.' And then he patted me on the back. He didn't say, 'Don't cry.' Because the emotion that you have, you want it so bad. You want it more than your life. I learned how to control that and took everything out on the garbage pail—I'd kick it just right. But we've all gone through that. We all *have* to go through it. It ain't fun, but you can use it."

And Tom certainly did use it the next time he pitched in that Series: going ten innings in our game four victory. For that matter, I could probably count on one hand the number of times when we were teammates that I saw him get hit hard. He was a special kind of pitcher on a lot of Mets teams that didn't have a whole lot of offense.

"Here was our thinking," Kooz said, speaking on behalf of his Mets pitching brethren. "If we got one run, we had a pretty good chance to win. If we got two runs, we should win. And if we got three runs, it should be a laugher. That's how we looked at our support."

"Yeah, pretty much," Seaver agreed.

"We didn't lavish you guys with runs," Swoboda admitted.

"Hey, remember the Caesars Palace act we had after the Series?" I asked everyone. "Donn Clendenon would have himself paged every five minutes just to hear his name."

"That's a good one!" Kooz said as everyone laughed. "I must have missed that."

"You know, Kooz, you did the *same thing*," I added. "Did you forget? And what about when Cleon and Tommy would get into some sort of argument and spoke a language nobody could understand. Do you guys remember that? It was like some kind of Mobile-ese. It was a language none of us understood. When they started talking fast, you might catch a word out of an entire sentence."

"Oh, yeah," Tom agreed, "it absolutely sounded like a foreign language."

"Funny stuff!" I said. "I miss those guys together: Tommie and Cleon. We really had fun. I'll give Cleon a call when I get back and send everyone's best."

Now the old stories were really flowing through my head. For some reason, I thought of the plight of our traveling secretary, a former sportswriter for the *Brooklyn Eagle* named Lou Niss.

"What about Niss, our old traveling secretary?" I said. "Remember how Grote used to get on him all the time? If our bus was ten seconds late, Jerry would be screaming stuff like *'What time does this bus leave!?'* Ugh. Grote was just . . . I don't know how to describe him."

"He was foul," Seaver said. Then he turned to Sherman and asked if he knew him.

"I know the story Davey Johnson told me about how they were both from San Antonio," Erik began. "They were roommates during a Hearst tournament for high school all-stars at Yankee Stadium. But despite their history together, once when Davey was playing first base for the Atlanta Braves, he had to stretch to catch a throw and Grote spiked Johnson on the back of his leg so badly that Davey had to be put on the disabled list for a significant amount of time. And remember, they grew up together. He was kind of a mean guy, wasn't he?"

No one actually would go that far—Kooz even saying how he and Seaver liked him—though they all had their Grote experiences.

"I used to drive to the ballpark with him," Kooz said. "He'd be as nice as could be until the ballpark came into sight. Then he really changed personalities. He'd get the *red ass*. But we used that as a plus on the field."

"My wife and his wife were very good friends," Rocky recalled. "But he just wasn't that nice to my kids; he just didn't have that openness about him. I was like, *Hey man, cut them a break!* But the pitching staff—they couldn't have disliked throwing to him. Give him half a chance and nobody steals against him. He had some battles with Lou Brock that were amazing—just amazing. There were so few truly great catchers like Johnny Bench and him."

"Art played with them both," Sherman noted, relaying a story I told him, "and Bench said that if he was on the same team as Grote, Johnny would have been playing third."

"I don't know about *that*," Seaver said. "Johnny *would* say that. It's a very polite thing to say. But Bench could throw like a cannon."

"Bench's throws weren't just thrown, they were *thrown!*" Buddy said for emphasis.

"I thought Bench was the best catcher in baseball the very first day I saw him," Swoboda added.

"The story goes that when Bench was a kid," Sherman told us, "his father would take him to the field, and Johnny wouldn't just throw the ball from behind the plate to second base, but rather to where his dad was positioned in center field. This taught Bench to throw through second base on a line to short center field. This technique was engrained in him, giving him a rifle-like arm."

"And he could swing the bat," Swoboda said. "The combination of hitting and defense was incredible."

Not to be outdone with the Bench stories, Kooz, who was never fleet of foot, told how he once swiped a base off the Hall of Fame catcher—yet still caught some flak from Berra over it.

"One night I did a delayed steal of second on Bench," Kooz began. "Joe Morgan was out of position and not covering the base. Bench threw the ball into center field, and I went to third and later scored. We would win the game 2–1, and Yogi goes"—Koo gives a dead-on impression of Berra— "'I didn't give you the steal sign. The next time, it'll cost ya a hundred dollars.'"

Everyone had a good laugh—so familiar with Yogi and his infamous "Next time, it's gonna cost ya" threats. Tom then glanced over at Buddy, gave him a warm smile, and patted his hand. Buddy smiled back—telling these stories was so good for the both of them—and simply said to Seaver, "Good memories."

Harrelson then turned to the rest of us. "Nine years with this guy," he said. "Nine years Tom and I were roommates. We were in Florida at spring training just before going north with the club for the first time as rookies—both of us married and from California—and he goes to me, 'Nancy wants you to come eat with us.' So I go to the house they were staying in, and they served me something that I'd never eaten before. I didn't like the way it smelled. Then, listen to this: I started to not feel good, so I left. Of course, Tom is kind of a character—he just frowned at me. But as rookies, we had to bunk with somebody, so when the club asked him who he wanted to room with, he told them, 'I don't know anybody but *Buddy*.' So for the next nine years, we were roomies on the road. And we've been like brothers ever since."

"Was Tom the first person to call you 'Buddy'?" Erik asked.

"Yeah, he did a good job of that," Harrelson told him. "I went by 'Bud,' but Tom kept calling me Buddy. Then a lot of other people started calling me Buddy. Isn't that nice to be called Buddy? I was in New York once when a bum came up to me and says, 'Hey, Buddy, can you spare some change?' I thought, *Shit, even these guys know who I am!* So I gave him some money because he said 'Buddy' and didn't say, 'Hey, asshole!'"

We all laughed and then shared other stories with one another while Harrelson turned to Sherman seated next to him—again sharing the limitations of his memory due to Alzheimer's.

"You know, I had to ask Kim when I was coming out to California with you guys," he told him. "That was about three days before the trip."

"You're doing great," Erik assured him. "I'm so glad you were able to join your friends."

"I have to write things down," Buddy admitted before adding, "Kim is a wonderful girl."

"Not just that," Erik replied. "She may be the *best ex-wife* I've ever heard of."

"She's still a part of my life—watches out for me," Buddy said, his blue eyes sparkling. "She'll call me and go, 'You know you have to go to the doctor. Our son T.J. can bring you.' Married, we just didn't gel after a while. But I still love her and give her hugs. Kim doesn't have to do what she does, but I appreciate it."

After we had polished off the two bottles of wine with lunch, and after roughly six hours of nonstop talk at Tom's house, out on his vineyard, and at the restaurant, we were all a little worn out and ready to leave. It had been a perfect visit with Seaver—beyond any of our expectations.

"This has been fun," said Rocky, who had been going through such a trying time during his wife's extended illness. "It's been as much fun as I've had in a while."

But as a sobering reminder of our dear friend Tom's condition, he turned to Erik and asked proudly, 'Did you come and see the vineyard and stuff?'

"I did, I did," Sherman assured him. "I was with the whole group all day."

Without a hint of frustration, the ever-courageous and self-assured Seaver shrugged and told him once more, "You know, I've got a little bit of the Lyme disease going on." He then graciously picked up the check, gave his regards to all the people he knew at the cafe like he was the mayor of Calistoga, and walked with us back out to the parking lot—where the conversations continued on and on. We knew we would never all be together like this again. We were in our seventies, scattered about the country, and Tom could no longer travel.

It was the lengthiest of good-byes. Nobody wanted to leave.

Our ride back to the hotel was relatively subdued. The fact was we were all a little drained from the day's events. There was some chatter, though for much of the trip we were consumed in our thoughts about our time together with Seaver—clearly the best and most significant player from the '69 team—and what it all meant. There was so much going through my mind. First and foremost, I was grateful he was in good spirits and was pretty excited to see us. And I couldn't help but be impressed by how open Buddy and Tom were about their health situations. I thought back to my experience playing first base and witnessing their special relationship by their conversations on the mound. What bitter irony that they now share in the struggle of memory loss. But I also reveled in hearing Seaver tell us how he left the East Coast, the craziness of being a New York baseball icon, and a lucrative broadcasting career to reinvent himself and begin a new life working on his own beautiful vineyard. To hear him talking about it with the passion that he did was deeply gratifying to me. Tom has clearly found some peace and tranquility—a personal paradise—in the Napa Valley, and has been able to translate it into a growing wine business. I was thrilled to witness it with my own eyes.

There was some talk about possibly meeting Tom and Nancy later that evening. In fact, a very tired Tom left me a groggy-sounding voice mail after he arrived back home, asking what time to make dinner reservations if we were up to it. But the day had been so perfect, and the thinking was it would be better for everyone—Seaver included—to just get some rest. So instead, we ended up driving over to a local restaurant in Santa Rosa, where the discussion took a more serious and introspective tone than the razzing of one another through most of the weekend. We talked a lot about our visit with Tom and what it meant to be a part of the Miracle Mets.

"That was just an incredible day," Rocky remarked, sitting across the table from me and next to Kooz. "What he's put together, it's just so *Tom Seaver*, you know what I mean? Years ago, I bought some of his GTS wine and thought it was spectacular and very complex—just like Seaver himself. He's doing all the right things with the right people, aiming high like he always did as a pitcher. But to walk with him like we did today, and to see the joy he had with every step he took, showed just how much he loved to show it all off to us. It's just so impressive that he went out there with a concept to put the whole thing together from nothing—from the beautiful house to the acres of southern exposure that turned out to be perfect for the vineyard. And, of course, it always makes me happy to be with you guys again. We shared the ultimate in 1969."

"It changed all our lives," I added. "We were part of that incredible period and that unbelievable team that nobody thought could win. The reality of it is it's one of those rare teams where, when you look back at baseball history, everyone contributed. Of course, we had the stars like Kooz and Tommy and Cleon, but we also had the other key, if lesser-known, guys like Boswell, Weis, and Gaspar, who, among others like them, all contributed to our success. And I think that was really the true beauty and legacy of our team."

"Absolutely," Rocky agreed. "I felt like *everybody* was involved. Of course, we could see Seaver going to superstardom. If there was a number one player on that team, it was him. But you know damn well Koosy wasn't far behind, and with Jones and Agee and Clendenon, we couldn't have done it without those five guys. If just any one of them wasn't there, it would have been a lot harder to win. But you felt everybody had a piece in our winning the World Series. And after it was over, and we were divvying up World Series shares, players that played smaller roles still got quite a bit more money than a lot of other teams would have voted them. I'm really proud of that. We knew there were key players, but so much of the load was shared, and that was because of Hodges. Gil knew what he had his hands on and knew how to push those buttons. You couldn't argue with a whole lot of things that he did. They seemed to work."

Kooz concurred and added some historical perspective.

"I go back and look at the Brooklyn Dodgers, and the following they had," he began. "And I look at the New York Giants, and the following they had there. And all the newspapers around New York in the fifties—probably at least eight major ones. And the kids back then, they all read the papers. That's why the New York fans are the best, because as kids they grew up studying the box scores in the newspapers. So they were on top of things—you couldn't BS them. Well, then the Dodgers and Giants leave, and there's a sadness in town because they didn't have a National League club. Then the Mets come along, and a lot of them were so glad to see the National League back in town. The Mets got a lot of fans that way. Then we come on and win it all as an expansion team—the first time in history—in our eighth year. It was unforgettable for them. It's like when Kennedy got killed: you remember where you were. Well, Mets fans certainly remember where they were when we won the Series. Of course, a lot of them claim they were at game five but they weren't. I get letters from people telling me how our team helped them with their life—just great fan mail. But what we all did, with everybody playing a part, is why I think our team was so popular. There were no heroes. We were *all* heroes. Every day there was a different one."

Swoboda had a similar, if more personal, take, as he is around baseball all the time as a broadcaster and is more actively involved in golf and signing events.

"We may get some attention for our fiftieth anniversary of the championship," Rocky noted. "And I realize that there are fewer and fewer people who grew up during that time. But what I'm driving at here is how many times I'm sitting at some event, signing autographs, and some guy who was a kid in '69 brings his son up in front of me and tries to explain to him how I changed his life. And I'm like, *Geez, I was just trying to be a player. I was just trying to hang on.* And the son is clueless, looking at me and probably thinking, *Him? That old guy? That old fat guy sitting there? Changed your life? Because he did something in baseball?* But you know that we were able to carve a little niche in people's world, the ones who lived through it as kids. They're getting older but have never forgotten. It shines in their minds like gold. As I've gotten older, I've realized what a privilege it was to have had an occupation that people took such joy from when you succeeded. I think, *How cool is that?!*"

It *is* very cool, indeed. And something I never take for granted.

We left the restaurant with a sense of fulfillment in so many respects. We had reminisced about the wonderful moments and experiences we shared from the past and, on this weekend, the treasured new ones we had created.

• • •

Kooz had the earliest flight back the next day, so we all took the airport tram to his terminal to see him off.

"So, Jerry," Sherman said to Kooz as he shook his hand good-bye. "Was meeting up with your buddies and seeing Tom's vineyard as special as you thought it would be?"

"Yeah, it taught me to go home and start straightening up my life and not follow the precedent set by these guys!" he said, staying in character and not taking the bait to be sentimental. "It's good to see that they're alive and ticking and seem to be taking good care of themselves—especially Harrelson and Sham. I don't know about Swoboda!"

Kooz looked over at Rocky—unable to resist that one final good-natured jab at him—smiled, and gave his old teammates one last hug before making his way to his gate. As he walked off into the distance, and we got back on the tram to reach our own gates, Swoboda said, "You know, I love that crazy SOB. I *really* do. We couldn't be more diametrically opposed politically and otherwise, but I know he doesn't say the things he does to piss me off. He says those things because that's what makes sense in his brain—so he's welcome to them. Besides, he's a fascinating guy and was a warrior for us when we needed players to stand up for us on the field."

Rocky's sentiments stuck in my mind during the plane ride home because, in a nutshell, what he said encapsulated everything that made us a great team. No matter what our backgrounds, where we came from, or what we believed, none of that mattered. We were the closest of teammates during the best of times. We were then and remain today—forever brothers.

ACKNOWLEDGMENTS

The authors would like to give special recognition and thanks, first and foremost, to our editor, the venerable Bob Bender, who always gave sage advice and direction throughout this entire project. It was truly an honor and privilege to work with him. Special thanks also goes out to associate editor Johanna Li for all of her support, and our remarkably thorough copy editor, Philip Bashe.

We would also like to show our gratitude to our agent and friend, Robert Wilson. His expertise in the sports publishing business was, as usual, an added bonus. And we are forever thankful that Robert had the vision to bring us together to write a book of this nature.

At the Baseball Hall of Fame, credit should be given to Bruce Markusen and his staff for all of their assistance in our research of the 1969 Mets.

Writing a book often takes over an author's life during the months and years it can take to produce it. As such, we would like to acknowledge the special people in our lives for their encouragement, patience, and support during the process. Great appreciation in this regard goes out to Art's love, Teresa Taylor, and Erik's bride, Habiba Boumlik, and their children Alex and Sabrina.

Art would also like to give special recognition to Cabot Marks and Fred Cambria for their everlasting encouragement and friendship.

But most of all, our eternal gratitude goes out to the Miracle Mets and all of those associated with the team, who not only have maintained a lifelong brotherhood with Art, but whose memories of 1969 helped make the book you have in your hands a reality.

—Art Shamsky and Erik Sherman

Name	G	AB	R	H	2B	3B	HR	RBI	BB	IBB	SO	AVG	OBP	SLG
20 Tommie Agee	149	565	97	153	23	4	26	76	59	2	137	.271	.342	.464
12 Ken "Boz" Boswell	102	362	48	101	14	7	3	32	36	3	47	.279	.347	.381
27 Don "Big Guy" Cardwell	30	47	3	8	0	0	1	5	0	0	26	.170	.184	.234
5 Ed "The Glider" Charles	61	169	21	35	8	1	3	18	18	3	31	.207	.286	.320
22 Donn "Clink" Clendenon	72	202	31	51	5	0	12	37	19	4	62	.252	.321	.455
1 Kevin Collins	16	40	1	6	3	0	1	2	3	1	10	.150	.209	.300
31 Jack DiLauro	23	12	0	0	0	0	0	0	0	0	9	.000	.000	.000
10 Duffy Dyer	29	74	5	19	3	1	3	12	4	0	22	.257	.295	.446
29 Danny Frisella	3	1	0	0	0	0	0	0	0	0	0	.000	.000	.000
11 Wayne "Red" Garrett	124	400	38	87	11	3	1	39	40	3	75	.218	.290	.268
17 Rod "PP" Gaspar	118	215	26	49	6	1	1	14	25	2	19	.228	.313	.279
39 Gary "Gent" Gentry	35	74	2	6	1	0	0	1	1	0	52	.081	.104	.095
18 Jim Gosger	10	15	0	2	2	0	0	1	1	1	6	.133	.188	.267
15 Jerry Grote	113	365	38	92	12	3	6	40	32	5	59	.252	.313	.351
3 Bud "Cheech" Harrelson	123	395	42	98	11	6	0	24	54	7	54	.248	.341	.306
28 Bob Heise	4	10	1	3	1	0	0	0	3	1	2	.300	.462	.400
38 Jesse Hudson	1	0	0	0	0	0	0	0	0	0	0	.000	.000	.000
38 Al "Jack" Jackson	9	1	0	0	0	0	0	0	0	0	0	.000	.000	.000

#	Name													
29	Bob Johnson	2	0	0	0	0	0	0	0	0	0	0	.000	.000	.000
21	Cleon "Cli" Jones	137	483	92	164	25	4	12	75	64	10	60	.340	.422	.482
V34	Cal Koonce	40	17	1	4	0	0	0	1	0	0	7	.235	.235	.235
36	Jerry "Koo" "Kooz" Koosman	32	84	1	4	0	0	0	1	1	0	46	.048	.059	.048
7	Ed "Krane" Kranepool	112	353	36	84	9	2	11	49	37	7	32	.238	.307	.368
9	J.C. Martin	66	177	12	37	5	1	4	21	12	1	32	.209	.257	.316
43	Jim McAndrew	27	37	0	5	0	0	0	3	3	0	18	.135	.200	.162
45	Tug McGraw	43	24	1	4	1	0	0	3	1	0	6	.167	.200	.208
25	Amos Otis	48	93	6	14	3	1	0	4	6	1	27	.151	.202	.204
1	Bobby Pfeil	62	211	20	49	9	0	0	10	7	0	27	.232	.260	.275
33	Les Rohr	1	0	0	0	0	0	0	0	0	0	0	.000	.000	.000
30	Nolan Ryan	25	29	3	3	0	0	0	2	0	0	14	.103	.103	.103
41	Tom "The Franchise" Seaver	39	91	7	11	3	3	0	6	7	0	34	.121	.200	.154
24	Art "Sham" Shamsky	100	303	42	91	9	3	14	47	36	2	32	.300	.375	.488
4	Ron "Rocky" Swoboda	109	327	38	77	10	2	9	52	43	4	90	.235	.326	.361
42	Ron "Duke" Taylor	59	4	0	1	0	0	0	0	0	0	2	.250	.250	.250
6	Al "Weiso" "Mighty Mite" Weis	103	247	20	53	9	2	2	23	15	1	51	.215	.259	.291

	Name	G	GS	W	L	PCT	ERA	SV	IP	H	ER	R	HR	BB	SO
27	Don Cardwell	30	21	8	10	.444	3.01	0	152.1	145	51	63	15	47	60
31	Jack DiLauro	23	4	1	4	.200	2.40	1	63.2	50	17	19	4	18	27
29	Danny Frisella	3	0	0	0	.000	7.71	0	4.2	8	4	4	1	3	5
39	Gary Gentry	35	35	13	12	.520	3.43	0	233.2	192	89	94	24	81	154
38	Jesse Hudson	1	0	0	0	.000	4.50	0	2.0	2	1	1	0	2	3
38	Al Jackson	9	0	0	0	.000	10.64	0	11.0	18	13	13	1	4	10
29	Bob Johnson	2	0	0	0	.000	0.00	1	1.2	1	0	0	0	1	1
34	Cal Koonce	40	0	6	3	.667	4.99	7	83.0	85	46	53	8	42	48
36	Jerry Koosman	32	32	17	9	.654	2.28	0	241.0	187	61	66	14	68	180
43	Jim McAndrew	27	21	6	7	.462	3.47	0	135.0	112	52	57	12	44	90
45	Tug McGraw	42	4	9	3	.750	2.24	12	100.1	89	25	31	6	47	92
33	Les Rohr	1	0	0	0	.000	20.26	0	1.1	5	3	4	0	1	0
30	Nolan Ryan	25	10	6	3	.667	3.53	1	89.1	60	35	38	3	53	92
41	Tom Seaver	36	35	25	7	.781	2.21	0	273.1	202	67	75	24	82	208
42	Ron Taylor	59	0	9	4	.692	2.72	13	76.0	61	23	23	7	24	42

PHOTO CREDITS

1. New York *Daily News*/Getty Images
2. Getty Images
3. Associated Press
4. Focus on Sport/Getty Images
5. Bettmann/Getty Images
6. New York *Daily News*/Getty Images
7. Neil Leifer Collection/Getty Images
8. Bettmann/Getty Images
9. Associated Press
10. Erik Sherman Collection
11. Courtesy of Al Weis
12. Erik Sherman Collection
13. Erik Sherman Collection
14. Erik Sherman Collection
15. Erik Sherman Collection
16. Erik Sherman Collection

INDEX